THE BARNA REPORT

WHAT AMERICANS BELIEVE

THE BARNA REPORT

WHAT AMERICANS BELIEVE

"Barna succeeds admirably
in giving us a clear picture
of spiritual life in America."
GEORGE GALLUP, JR.

AN ANNUAL SURVEY OF
VALUES AND RELIGIOUS VIEWS
IN THE UNITED STATES

GEORGE BARNA

DID YOU KNOW:

*MORE MEN THAN WOMEN
FEEL THAT THE PURPOSE OF
LIFE IS ENJOYMENT AND PER-
SONAL FULFILLMENT*
PAGE 93

*NEARLY HALF OF ALL CHRIS-
TIANS THINK SATAN
IS JUST A SYMBOL OF EVIL
AND NOT A LIVING BEING*
PAGE 205

*ONLY 28% FEEL THE
CHURCH IS RELEVANT TO
THE WAY THEY LIVE TODAY*
PAGE 186

Regal Books
A Division of Gospel Light
Ventura, California, U.S.A.

Published by Regal Books
A Division of Gospel Light
Ventura, California 93006
Printed in U.S.A.

Library of Congress Cataloging-in-Publication Data
Barna, George.
     What Americans believe / George Barna.
     p.   cm.
     ISBN 0-8307-1505-3
     1. United States—Religious life and customs—Statistics.   2. Christianity—
United States—Statistics.   I. Title.
BR526.B38   1991
277.3'0829—dc20
                                                                    91-19104
                                                                        CIP

2 3 4 5 6 7 8 9 10 / KP / PM4 / 95 94 93 92 91

Rights for publishing this book in other languages are contracted by Gospel Literature
International (GLINT). GLINT also provides technical help for the adaptation, translation,
and publishing of Bible study resources and books in scores of languages worldwide. For
further information, contact GLINT, Post Office Box 488, Rosemead, California, 91770,
U.S.A., or the publisher.

ACKNOWLEDGMENTS

THIS BOOK IS TRULY THE RESULT OF TWO TEAMS WORKING IN CLOSE cooperation.

The first team goes by the name of the Barna Research Group. Cindy Coats, Vibeke Klocke, Ron Sellers, Nancy Barna, and Paul Rottler worked with me to develop, field, tabulate, and prepare for presentation the research underlying this book. In addition, our team of telephone interviewers, all 50 or so of them, deserves thanks for their role in collecting this information.

A special word of appreciation must go to Paul Rottler. Besides serving as our field director, Paul also used his special talents in computer applications and graphic design to take the raw manuscript and translate it into the final, print-ready product. His efforts were monumental in turning this project around quickly and superbly.

My wife, Nancy Barna, has again proven to be a stellar colleague in research and a tireless source of emotional strength for me personally. As always, I am privileged to have such a loving and supportive partner in life and ministry.

The other team is best known as Regal Books. They, too, have earned my gratitude for their belief in the potential of this project, their ideas regarding its development, and their commitment to producing resources that will build the kingdom of God through the efforts of the local church. Many people at Regal contributed their talents to this book. In particular, I am grateful to Bill Greig Jr., Bill Greig III, Mark Maddox, Kyle Duncan, Ron Durham,

84571

Tim Howard, Nola Grunden, Gloria Moss, Barbara Fisher, Sharon Hamilton, Dennis Somers, Kim Pitman, and Bill Denzel for their help. The rest of their team, while unnamed here, is also appreciated.

Sometimes I think those of us in the research industry take for granted the time and effort expended by the people whom we interview in our studies. In this case, I'd like to thank the anonymous 1,005 people we interviewed for sharing their hearts with us. May the information they have provided for this book enable our leaders to create a better society—thanks, in part, to the insights our respondents offered.

CONTENTS

SECTION II
MEDIA AND ELECTRONICS
113

SECTION III
WHAT AMERICANS VALUE
147

10. What We Value: Family, Health, and Time . . . 152

Who and what do we value? (Elements tested: family; health; our time; having close friends; religion; the Bible; our careers; living comfortably; money.)

11. Our Confidence Level: Institutions and Organizations . . . 159

How much confidence do Americans have in social institutions and organizations? (Institutions tested: public schools; Christian churches; Congress; the Supreme Court; the military; hospitals and health care organizations; the media; private business; charities and non-profit organizations.)

12. Our Hope for the Future: Friends, Faith, and Fame . . . 165

What do Americans desire for the future? (Conditions tested: friendships; a close relationship with God; personal integrity; a high-paying job; church involvement; influence; a large home; to live close to family; fame; to live comfortably; to not have to work for a living; good health; old age.)

SECTION IV
PERSPECTIVES ON RELIGION
171

13. How We View Our Religious Identity . . . 176

How many Americans call themselves "religious"?
How many Americans call themselves "born again"?

14. The Relevance of Christianity in Our Lives . . . 182

Is the Christian faith relevant?
Are Christian churches relevant?
Are Christian churches tolerant of different ideas?

15. How We View Christ and Life After Death . . .191

How many Americans have made a personal commitment to Christ?
What do Americans believe about life after death?

SECTION V
CHURCH INVOLVEMENT AND SATISFACTION
229

INTRODUCTION

WHAT DIFFERENTIATES A SUCCESSFUL COMPANY FROM A struggling company? Sometimes it is the capabilities of the personnel involved. In some situations the difference relates to the nature of the products they sell. Occasionally it relates to the levels of capitalization of the firms. Often, it has to do with who has the most complete and accurate information on which to base important decisions.

Warriors Without a Battle Plan

In my work with churches, denominations, and parachurch ministries across the nation, one reality constantly arises: the Church attempts to operate effectively without having the necessary information on which to base key decisions. I'm not dismissing the importance of prayer or the leading of the Holy Spirit. But God can use information to lead us into a better set of circumstances. Simply put, I have consistently observed that much like secular, for-profit organizations, when ministries make informed decisions, they make better decisions. The basis of being informed is having current, comprehensive, and reliable data.

The major reason for producing this book is to assist you in making better decisions for the building up of the Church. Part of my goal in life is to enable people who are involved in Christian ministry to have access to pertinent information that could help provide perspective, insight, creative ideas, or confirmation in the process of making decisions about ministry.

Not a Panacea

I am under no illusions that this book is a panacea for the myriad of challenges facing the Church today. But I do believe that the information contained in this volume may be one small step toward enabling you, whether you are engaged in the practice or study of Christian ministry, to have a better understanding of the market-place in which that ministry takes place.

By being better informed you will hopefully make better decisions and therefore experience a greater positive impact in ministry.

An Overview

The information in this book is drawn from an annual nationwide telephone survey conducted by the Barna Research Group, Ltd. The survey covers a broad range of topics (some of which were excluded from this book) encompassing people's values, attitudes, beliefs, and experiences.

The overall thrust of the book is to give you an overview of the America of 1991—an examination of aspects of the mindset, life-style, and heart of the nation at the close of this century. As described at length in *The Frog in the Kettle*, I believe that the Nineties will be seen as a make-it-or-break-it era for the Christian Church in America. The information in the chapters that follow is meant to provide you with some of the pieces to the emerging puzzle that we must solve if we hope to penetrate this culture with the message of Jesus Christ.

Armed with these insights, it is my hope that you will be able to reflect on our culture, our people, and your mission with a keener sense of reality. These data should enable you to begin to identify some of the perceptual myths that plague ministries seeking to penetrate a resistant culture. The information described will enable you to identify some of the assumptions that we hold about the population, but which are not as accurate as you might have believed.

Analysis

Throughout this book, I have tried to offer the information with some context, but a minimum of subjective interpretation. It is my hope that this approach will enable you to arrive at your own conclusions, using the information as intelligently and carefully as possible.

This collection represents the first in a series of such volumes. Regal Books has agreed to publish a similar volume each year, based on the tracking survey (OmniPoll™) we conduct each January. This regular updating of the data will provide you with further ammunition in making sophisticated, data-based decisions. By observing the trends as they occur from year to year you will gain a heightened sensitivity to the changes that are most important and those that are of little consequence. Such tracking will simplify the task of determining how the Church is progressing. Rather than basing our statements on vague assumptions, we will have a body of information from which we can draw such conclusions.

Source of the Information

From mid-January to early February of each year, the Barna Research Group, Ltd. conducts a nationwide telephone survey among adults (people 18 or older). The number of people interviewed ranges from 1,000 to 1,500 people, depending upon the design of the study.

The telephone interviews are conducted by the professional interviewers hired by our company for the numerous surveys we conduct every year. Our clients range from major Christian ministries to churches that have not yet been planted; from Fortune 500 companies to one-man retail operations.

All of the interviews take place from our centralized data collection facility in Glendale, California, under strict supervision and in accordance with the accepted standards for the marketing research industry. A variety of quality control procedures are employed to verify the reliability and accuracy of the information collected.

The Reliability of the Information

The 1991 survey included the opinions of 1,005 adults randomly chosen from across the nation. The geodemographic profile of the people interviewed very closely reflects that of the population at large. Further, based on statistical tests, we can be 95% sure that the figures derived from this survey are accurate to within four percentage points of what would be found among the total adult population had we conducted a census rather than the survey.

People often ask me how respondents are chosen for such research. Like many companies, we employ what is known as a "random digit dial" sample. This means that a computer generates telephone numbers randomly, based upon the working blocks of numbers that have been assigned by the telephone company within any given community.

Every adult living in a household that has a telephone (which is about 96% of all households) is therefore a potential respondent, even if they have an unlisted or unpublished phone number, or if they just had their telephone service installed that afternoon! We do not work from telephone books or other types of lists because of the inherent bias in those lists. We can use this type of listing because we do not ask to speak to people by name, nor do we ask people to tell us their names. These surveys are meant to provide people with anonymity and to hold their answers in total confidence.

Of course, not everyone whom we contact agrees to participate in the survey. On the average, telephone surveys gain about a 60% cooperation rate. This means that of every 10 people we contact, six will answer our questions.

How Can the Opinions of So Few Represent the Opinions of So Many?

When I speak to people about survey results and the projections made on the basis of those results, the most frequently expressed concern is how the opinions of 1,000 people can possibly represent the opinions of the 180,000,000 adults currently living in the United States.

Based on exhaustive statistical research conducted over many years, social scientists and mathematicians have learned that if random sampling techniques are properly used, it is possible to derive a representative understanding of a population by measuring the attitudes or behaviors of a small but carefully chosen slice of that larger group. A certain number of times the sample will be off the mark by more than the estimated rate of error due to sampling inefficiencies. In the vast majority of instances, however, the statistics collected via the random sample survey will be an accurate reflection of the population from which the sample was drawn.

Format of the Book

As you read through the book, you will notice that each of the core sections has the same format.

First, the section will have a brief overview of some of the key findings that will be related in that section (called "Section Highlights").

Next, there will be an expanded description of the findings called "In Brief." These findings will relate to each of the questions addressed from the survey within that section of the book.

Then, within each section, questions will be grouped topically into chapters. Each of the questions in the chapter will be examined individually and will include three elements. The first of these is a brief descriptive analysis telling you what the survey found in response to that question. The second will be a graphic presentation of one or more aspects showing what we learned from the answers to that question. The third area related to the question will offer a table of data in which the statistics related to that survey question are provided.

This three-part approach—question analysis, data table, graphic—will be provided for each of the survey questions addressed in this volume.

Reading the Data Tables

Many people look at a page filled with data—percentages, raw scores, indexes, frequencies, or whatever—and break out in a cold sweat. Let me emphasize that you can get a multitude of insights out of this book without having to look at the pages that contain the data tables. The statistics on which the survey commentary is based are provided for those hearty souls who can make sense out of the data, and who may wish to do some of their own data interpretation.

If you want to examine the data tables, here are a few helps. The sample data table on the accompanying page is coded to help you understand what each of the elements on the page represents.

A   This is the wording of the question that was asked in the survey.

B   Each of these columns represents one of the answers that respondents might have given. Also remember that each of those figures is a percentage, not the raw number of respondents who gave that particular answer. The percentage sign will appear after the column percentages for the first row only. An asterisk (*) in a column indicates a percentage that is less than 0.5%. If an entire row of percentages is comprised of asterisks, then the question was not asked of people in that subgroup.

C   This is the total number (not a percentage) of survey respondents who are described by the label in the far left column of the row, and who answered this question. For the question on the sample page, there were 1,005 adults who were asked the question. The second row, which is the results among people 18-25 years old, shows the responses of the 190 people in that age group who were interviewed for the survey.

D   The "total population" row presents the aggregate survey data. Among all of the people involved in the survey who answered the question, their answers are always shown in the top row.

E   The rest of the population segments listed on the page represent the other people groups who were interviewed, and how they responded. In this case, for instance, the independent variable measured was age. The statistics across from the 18-25 age segment tell us that 50% said they had attended a church worship service in the past seven days; 50% said they did not attend such a service; and less than 0.5% did not know whether or not they had done so. The data under the

How to Read the Data Tables in This Book

See Accompanying Pages for a Complete Description of Items A through E

A

Q: During the past seven days, did you attend a church worship service?

B

D

C

E

		Yes	No	Don't Know	N
Total Population		49%	51%	*	1005
Age:	18 to 25	35	65	*	190
	26-44	50	50	*	464
	45-54	52	48	*	141
	55-64	52	48	*	101
	65 or older	69	30	1	92
Education:	High school or less	47	53	*	453
	Some college	51	49	*	242
	College graduate	50	50	*	306
Ethnicity:	White	48	52	*	744
	Black	53	47	*	119
Household Income:	Under $20,000	41	60	*	184
	$20,000 to $39,999	51	49	*	397
	$40,000 to $59,999	53	47	1	186
	$60,000 or more	50	50	*	142
Gender:	Male	42	57	*	490
	Female	55	45	*	515
Married:	Yes	57	43	*	570
	No	39	61	*	432
Community:	Urban	46	54	*	340
	Suburban	51	49	*	387
	Rural	53	47	*	245
Region:	Northeast	43	57	*	227
	Midwest	55	46	*	228
	South	49	51	*	210
	Mountain	51	49	*	171
	Pacific	47	53	1	169
Born Again:	Yes	66	34	*	355

column labeled "N" tells us that there were 190 people 18-25 who answered this question. The next row of data shows the responses of the 26-44-year-old respondents, commonly referred to as the Baby Boomers. Among them, 52% had attended a church worship service in the past seven days, 48% did not, and less than 0.5% did not know. The "N" size for this question was 464 people who were 26-44 years of age. Notice that for any row of data shown in the table, the three answers will add up to 100%. If the numbers are off by one or two percentage points, it is due to the rounding off of the figures.

Who Responded to Each Question?

For most of the questions addressed in this book, all 1,005 people were asked to respond. However, there are some questions which have a smaller group of respondents. For instance, one series of questions was asked only of the 825 people who described themselves as "Christian."

Keep these things in mind as you evaluate the data, remembering that the smaller the sample size, the greater the potential for sampling error in the resulting data. (In the appendix of this book is a table which provides the degree of error associated with different sample sizes at the 95% confidence level.)

When you describe the data, be careful how you describe differences in the data. For instance, look at the proportions who said "yes" in the accompanying table among those who are 55-64 years old and those 65 or older. You could describe the difference as a 17 percentage point difference. It is not a difference of 17 percent. Those two descriptions offer a radically different perspective on the responses given by people.

How You Can Benefit from This Book

There are probably as many different ways to benefit from the information in this book as there will be people who read the book. In a general way, though, let me offer a handful of ideas concerning how you might gain value from the information on these pages.

- You can identify trends in the thoughts, attitudes, values, expectations, and behaviors of the adult population, and even among the different subgroups of the population.

- You can glean insights into the spiritual beliefs of people and what specific misconceptions they hold about the Christian faith.

- The data provide a base of information that can be used in public speaking, teaching or writing related to Christianity or any of the other aspects of contemporary life-style alluded to in this book.

- The statistics included in this volume represent a benchmark against which you can compare your own situation: your region, your state, your community, your friends, your congregation, etc.

- Careful analysis of the figures can provide you with information about target groups to pursue if you wish to provide a specific ministry, service, product, or communication.

- Understanding the mindset of different people, as defined within these pages, will better prepare you to discuss your faith and its applications with people by being better informed and more sensitive to where they are coming from.

There are, without a doubt, many other uses, including some that might be more pertinent for your own situation. May this information be stimulating, challenging, and informative for you.

AN OVERVIEW OF
WHAT AMERICANS
BELIEVE

SOCIAL ANALYSTS ARE ALWAYS SEARCHING FOR NEW TRENDS, social transformations, and cultural upheavals to dissect. The media pounce on such pronouncements with greater speed than the Concorde. Judging from the books that have made it on to the best-seller lists, the general public has an ever-increasing appetite to understand what its latest interests and preferences may be, and how outsiders pass judgment on those changes in behavior, belief, and expectations.

Signposts of a Changing Nation

Based on the information derived from the survey on which this book is based, we can add the following insights into the mix.

- America's values are shifting in unexpected ways: away from some traditional values, back to some traditional values that were rejected during the past two decades, and toward some new values that have not yet become ingrained in the heartbeat of the nation.

- Despite the decreasing levels of confidence people have in the media, the onslaught of new technologies is increasing the exposure people have to messages communicated through an ever-broadening array of electronic messengers. There is no evidence to suggest that the media are having a lesser impact upon people; an argument could be made that more than ever we rely upon the media to help sort through the crushing volume of information now available due to more sophisticated data-gathering equipment and procedures.

- The Nineties have ushered in an era in which Americans are quite interested in religion—but not as enamored by the Christian faith as in days past. If there is a revival going on— and it seems a real stretch to make that argument—it must be viewed as a religious revival, not a Christian revival.

- Overwhelmed by information, rocked by innumerable opportunities and a limited number of hours, and struggling to remain abreast of the sweeping changes that are impacting life-styles and relationships, a substantial number of adults are adopting non-traditional perspectives on some fundamental realities of life. These realities relate to their spiritual perspectives; their views about people; and even their understanding of the reasons for life.

An Overview

In these next few pages, let's explore some of the macro-view insights provided by our 1991 survey of the American people. In the chapters that follow, you can examine each of these dimensions more closely, gaining the micro-view on the data that have led to these conclusions.

ISSUES OF THE HEART: OUR VALUES

The family is making a comeback. During the Seventies and Eighties, family suffered a tarnished image, and adults were less inclined than in prior decades to devote time and energy to the building of strong, nuclear families. Behaviors that are now accepted as normal—divorce, co-habitation, delaying the bearing of children until older ages, spending less time in family activity—were initiated, causing quite a stir.

Don't get the wrong idea. Adults today are not returning to the pre-Seventies notions of what makes a strong family. Divorce remains high, child care centers are booming, co-habitation is more prolific than ever, women are continuing to have the first child at a later age than previously. The incidence of premarital sex has reached epidemic proportions, as has the number of births of illegitimate children.

A Higher Ranking on a Long List

The key is that adults today are undergoing a psychological transition in which the family is capturing a higher place on their list of priorities. They are more likely to acknowledge that family is important; to spend greater amounts of their time engaged in family activities; and to prioritize family needs above certain personal needs.

This transition has ignited a domino effect, impacting many other aspects of people's lives as well. It has helped to make time a more cherished and more carefully allocated commodity. It has also impacted the premium people place upon the development of personal relationships, and the types of relationships that people are seeking.

Other critical priorities in people's lives these days include an emphasis upon personal health; being known as an individual who has high integrity; and having a personal relationship with God.

This religious concern is not unusual. For decades, Americans have been considered to be among the most highly religious people in the world. What is changing is the nature of their religious focus, as we will discuss shortly.

Defining Success

In America, success means many things to many people. However, we can see that among the definitions declining in acceptance is the possession of things. The acquisition mentality of the late Seventies and early Eighties has largely passed from its position of prominence. Even so, that philosophy is dying a hard death. Rather than turn their backs on the approach, most people are developing variations of that definition, variations which may include a reference to possessions, but which are not based primarily on the quantity of things owned.

Increasingly, success refers to achieving a delicate balance of time spent with the three most important aspects of an adults' waking hours: family, job, and leisure. Among the activities that adults seem less likely to integrate into that balance are time devoted to watching television; time committed to religious activity; and hours volunteered to non-profit organizations or other types of charitable work.

ATTITUDES THAT DETERMINE HOW WE LIVE

In the midst of the changes we see happening related to people's values, we also note a disruption of the optimistic perspective people have traditionally held toward the future. Whether we are witnessing a simple compression of people's perspective—i.e. we are still optimistic about tomorrow, but not so sanguine about next year—or a fundamental change in people's expectation of a bright future is not yet known.

What We Do Know

What *is* known is that people are less likely to expect the years ahead to be a continuation of the golden years represented by the Eighties. In looking back, people recall the Eighties as a time of economic prosperity, personal achievement, satisfaction with self, emphasis upon enjoyment of life, and national as well as personal security.

Things have changed. Instead, adults now look cautiously to the future, expecting a time of slower economic growth, faster change, and personal challenges that will require greater degrees of sacrifice and circumspection than has been true for the last 20 years. There is an increasingly widespread recognition that "the good life" must be redefined.

A Self-oriented Attitude

Basic attitudes about life are also undergoing the constant process of evaluation and redefinition. More than before we are witnessing the entrenchment of what some refer to as "secular humanist" attitudes.

This means that more people now believe that people are responsible only to themselves; that they determine their own destiny on the basis of their decisions and capabilities; and that simple acknowledgment of the existence of a universal spiritual force is sufficient to appease that force.

Americans currently assert that people are, overall, good creatures and are capable of managing their world without assistance from any external force. In fact, there is a prevailing perspective that much of what the Christian faith holds to be so critical toward understanding the world is either false or simply a non-essential part of understanding the fabric of life.

Where We Have Doubts

Among the attitudes and beliefs that people are likely to doubt are the existence of Satan; the existence of absolute truth, rather than pure relativism; and the distinction between the God who created the universe and rules it today and the gods of other non-Christian religions.

In the same manner, Americans presently adopt a series of philosophies which are at odds with biblical thinking related to life-style. For instance, the notion of "quality time" reigns supreme, despite studies which show that there is no viable substitute for spending quantities of time with those whom we seek to impact or to be in relationship with. One could easily predict this condition, though, given the higher priority placed upon self-fulfillment and the importance of allocating time to a variety of activities rather than concentrating that resource upon a limited number of endeavors.

Who's Fooling Whom?

Another example of the ability we have to cajole ourselves to believe that which is convenient or comforting—rather than true or realistic—is that people are basically good. It may be this philosophy that, more than any other, has harmed the Christian Church in the past two decades. Gone are people's memories of the very reason that Christ had to come to earth and suffer—i.e. the weakness of nature, the sinful heart of mankind. The typical adult will focus upon the love of God for His creation, rather than the pain He was caused by the enduring disobedience and selfishness that has characterized that creation throughout history.

Gone, too, is a sense of necessity for accountability for our actions. Over the last 25 years we have consistently built a mindset which allows us to view each person as responsible only to himself. Americans today generally ignore the aspects of confession or the deeper meaning and obligations associated with a vertical relationship with God.

Instead, we tend to concentrate upon the feeling that we deserve the respect and acceptance of others simply because we are human beings. Because God created us, gave us tremendous abilities, and is said to love us, we grasp onto this truth, out of context as it may be, and treat it as if it were the entirety of the issue. Indeed, to portray people as anything less than capable of perfection is, in the current mindset, to commit unwarranted judgment and to unjustifiably limit the potential of other people.

THE ROLE OF RELIGION IN AMERICA

The religious behavior and thinking of Americans continues to develop along lines that demonstrate confusion of purpose and perspective. And the local church cannot be exempted from a considerable part of the blame for why Americans are wandering astray in their spirituality.

Religion Is Important—in a Way...

Religion remains important to most Americans. That is, we tend to believe that religion is an integral part of life and that if life were a puzzle, the puzzle could not be completed unless we had the pieces related to spiritual matters in the right position. The question, though, is whether we view those pieces as being at the heart of the puzzle, or on the outer edges.

The evidence continues to mount which suggests that while religion is important, it is not *central*. People are more likely than ever to state that they do not have a high degree of confidence in religious institutions; to feel that being part of a local church is not a necessity; or to reject the idea that reading the Bible regularly will enhance their lives. Religion—and especially Christianity—is increasingly being viewed as just one of many competing alternatives in life.

Do Americans doubt the importance of religion? No. Do we question the existence of God? For the most part, no. Do we deny that religion can be a very integral and powerful part of a person's life? No.

Enough to Get By

However, we *do* separate religious thought and activity into the necessary and the optional. A massive realignment of thinking is taking place in which people are transferring many elements formerly deemed "necessary" into the realm of the "optional." And, of course, the optional then becomes a personal matter, which many people might choose to define as desirable, but inconsequential. Church attendance, Bible reading, prayer, worship, involvement in a local church body—all of these appear to be in transition, shifting from the necessary to the optional.

Not the Faith of Our Fathers

Traditional Christian beliefs are eroding, too. We increasingly doubt the existence of Satan; we deny the existence of one true God; we question whether there is really a God who hears and responds to our prayers; we devalue the local church body as an instrument of God and a resource for mankind.

The local churches of America face a tenuous future, given the deteriorating image they possess. While half of the population strongly believe that the Christian faith remains relevant to the way we live today, only half as many believe that local Christian churches possess such relevance.

In a related manner, people are increasingly less likely to view manifestations of their faith, such as evangelism and discipleship and church involvement, as personal responsibilities which they bear.

THE MEDIA

Churches are not the only institutions experiencing faltering credibility and loyalty. In fact, most social institutions are feeling the pain of such scrutiny and skepticism. The media are no different.

Among the social institutions evaluated in this study, the media were among those that currently have the lowest levels of credibility in the eyes of the public.

An associated reality is that any one medium is likely to have a diminishing impact upon people due to the constant expansion of electronic equipment introduced into the marketplace.

The growth of most types of household electronic equipment—from VCRs, cable television, and audiocassette players to color televisions, telephone answering machines, and personal computers—has plateaued. While there are a few devices that will likely continue to experience higher penetration (compact disc players, laptop computers), we may have reached a stage at which people are waiting for the equipment they now possess to provide them with greater benefits before they rush out to their local electronics dealer to buy ever-more sophisticated technologies.

The Waning Importance of Christian Media

The Christian media appear to have plateaued in their impact, too. In fact, it seems that they have a more extensive than intensive reach these days. In other words, the Christian media seem to be invading more households than before, but with less influence to show for that penetration.

The Christian media also have a greater ability to gain entry into the "downscale" households of America—the homes of people who have lower levels of education and income, and which generally house older adults. This, of course, does not diminish the importance of the Christian media or question the significance of those people groups or of reaching those groups. Rather, it does raise the issue of whether or not the Christian community can create a media presence that will address the needs, the concerns, the interests, and the standards of other segments of the population.

The encouraging aspect of Christian media is that a large number of people who are not Christian do gain exposure to these media. The danger here is that we not rely upon these media as the primary or sole means of evangelizing these individuals. Credible research has yet to be conducted which shows that the media are an effective means of leading people into a true relationship with Jesus Christ, or even leading them into a local church where that relationship can be fostered.

EXPLORING THE EVIDENCE

In the pages that follow, you will be able to examine people's responses to a multitude of questions about their life-styles, their beliefs, and their expectations. You may come to different conclusions, or emerge with a different series of perspectives than those provided in this section. The critical challenge is to emerge with a better-informed understanding of the American people, and how you can incorporate those insights into your own responsibilities to this world.

AMERICAN LIFE-STYLES AND PERSPECTIVES

SECTION HIGHLIGHTS:

◆ Compared to the past, adults say they are now spending increased amounts of time with the family, on the job, exercising, and reading for pleasure.

◆ Adults claim they are spending less time than in the past watching television, participating in church-related activities, volunteering their time to organizations, and seeking formal education.

◆ Most people felt the quality of life diminished in the past year, but expect next year to be about the same as this year.

◆ People have great confidence in the human race and believe that people should receive all possible good things in life.

◆ Adults tend to believe that there is no absolute truth.

◆ In response to the recession, people's most likely responses would be to reduce the money they spend on entertainment and restaurants. Reductions in giving to churches ranked toward the bottom of the list of potential cutbacks.

IN BRIEF

As THE ECONOMY GOES THROUGH MAJOR CHANGES—THE recession, increasing numbers of people working from their homes, more dual-income households, the shift from a manufacturing-based economy to one dominated by the service sector, impacts in responsibility and position due to new technologies—people are responding by shifting their daily activities and their attitudes about how best to cope with a changing world.

The Future Is Bright...Brighter to Some than to Others

One key change has been the disruption of optimism about the future. Among the trademarks of the American spirit has been our enduring optimism about the future. Currently, however, people are more likely to feel that the quality of life has deteriorated over the past year or so, and is not likely to change much in the coming year.

Overall, while about half of the adult population say that the quality of life today is about the same as it was one year ago, the remaining half overwhelmingly assert that things have gotten worse (39% say it has gotten worse, while 11% say things have gotten better). Looking ahead, 37% say that the quality of life will be about the same next year as it is currently; 32% say that things will be worse; and 27% believe the quality of life will improve. The least hopeful adults are Baby Busters (ages 18-25), those of lower socio-economic backgrounds, and women.

Tightening Belts

Economically, people are most likely to attempt to cope with a tougher economy by reducing or eliminating the luxuries from their budget. For instance, when asked how they are most likely to respond to the recession, the most common solutions are to spend less on entertainment (mentioned by 61% of adults) and to eat less frequently at restaurants (58%).

Strategies appealing to sizable minorities of the population include reducing the amount of driving undertaken (36%); reducing the amount of money that is put away for savings (31%); and cutting back on the amount of money given to charities other than churches (27%). Sixteen percent say they will reduce their giving to churches, while half as many intend to move into less expensive housing (8%) or to buy more items on credit (7%).

Interestingly, the unchurched are less likely than average to indicate an intent to cut back their spending for each of the areas tested.

Catholics were more likely than Protestants to say they will reduce spending on entertainment, eating out, and giving to churches.

Prioritizing Time

People are making other transitions in their life-style as a result of the cultural upheaval that is occurring in their midst. With the well-documented time crunch in full bloom for most adults, there is a significant shifting of priorities in how people are allocating their time.

When asked to describe how they are spending their time compared to one year ago, some important changes are evident. Activities that are experiencing an increased commitment from adults include spending time with family (43% claim they are spending more time with family than was true one year ago); working at their jobs (39%); reading for pleasure (34%); and exercising or working out physically (34%).

Time allocation is a zero sum game, though: whenever one activity gains favor, another must give ground. Among the activities that are receiving less time now than they did a year ago are time devoted to seeking additional formal education (34% say they now spend less time engaged in such endeavors); volunteering their time (32%); participating in activities related to their church or place of religious involvement (33%); and watching television (42%).

The decrease in time committed to the work of the church may not be as serious as it sounds. In examining the segments who are most likely to reduce their involvement, some of those groups commit comparatively little time to the life of the church. That is, although they are important to the ministry of their congregations, they generally are not viewed as the backbone of church activity. These segments include single adults, Baby Busters, non-Christians, and the unchurched.

Overall, people 55 or older are the least likely to exhibit changes in their daily routines. The segment most likely to experience changes in their time priorities are the Baby Busters.

Transitioning Attitudes

Not only are people's ways of life undergoing change, but the attitudes held by adults are also indicative of the nature and direction of American society.

In terms of beliefs, most Americans—particularly older adults—think that the United States is a Christian nation. However, people's perspective on life in this country contradicts a Christian worldview. For instance, two-thirds of all adults (63%) say that the purpose of life is enjoyment and personal fulfillment—hardly a philosophy drawn from the pages of Scripture. Four out of five adults (82%) agree that God helps those who help themselves, another perspective at odds with biblical teaching. Most disheartening of all, though, is the discovery that two-thirds of adults (66%) agree that there is no such thing as absolute truth. This perspective has relatively consistent levels of support across all subgroups. Even a majority of born again Christians (53%) and adults associated with evangelical churches (53%) concur with the sentiment. Unexpectedly, among the people groups most ardently supportive of this viewpoint are mainline Protestants (73%).

A Selfish Nation

Responses to statements reflecting values held by people underscore how far many people have drifted from a truly Christian view of life. A majority of adults (52%) assert that in the end, their first responsibility is to themselves. The vast majority of adults also agree that people are basically good (84%). To their credit, however, relatively few individuals (20%) say that you can tell how successful a person is by examining what they own.

Just Like Real Life?

Statements related to life-style round out the picture. A minority of adults (30%) believe that the life-styles portrayed in television and movies accurately reflect the way that most people live and think. Even fewer (15%) believe that when they have been wronged by someone, it is better to get even than to get mad.

The optimism that has characterized Americans in years past is still evident on a day-to-day basis. More than four out of five adults (84%) indicate that they wake up each morning believing that the new day will be better than the one just ended. This may partly be attributed to the widespread belief that everyone has a right to freedom and prosperity (96% agree with this notion—80% agree strongly). The pursuit of those ends may also have to do with people's support for the concept of "quality time." Nine out of ten adults (90%) say that the quality of time spent together is more important than the amount of time spent together in a relationship.

1 HOW WE VIEW OUR QUALITY OF LIFE

HAS THE QUALITY OF LIFE IN AMERICA CHANGED?

 Question: *Overall, compared to one year ago, do you think the quality of life in America has gotten better, gotten worse, or remained about the same?*

Overall, about half of all adults believe the quality of life in America has remained about the same over the course of the past year. Uncharacteristically, a substantially higher proportion of adults (39%) feel that things have gotten worse than believe that the quality of life has gotten better (11%).

Blacks are much more likely than whites to say things are worse today: whereas 53% of black adults say things have gotten worse, only 39% of the white adults concur. Although the gap is less pronounced, women (43%) are more likely than men (34%) to say that things have deteriorated.

Perhaps the state of affairs is most clearly delineated by a person's household income and place of residence. Adults living in the northeast—the section of the nation widely regarded to feel the economic decline most acutely—are much more likely than others to claim that the quality of life has declined in the last 12 months. While nearly half of the northeastern adults (46%) say things have gotten worse, just over one-third of all other adults (37%) have come to the same conclusion.

Religious background and perspectives appear to have no impact on perceptions about the state of the union. Born again Christians react the same as non-Christians. Those associated with evangelical, Catholic, and mainline Protestant churches hold similar views. The views of churched and unchurched adults are indistinguishable on this matter.

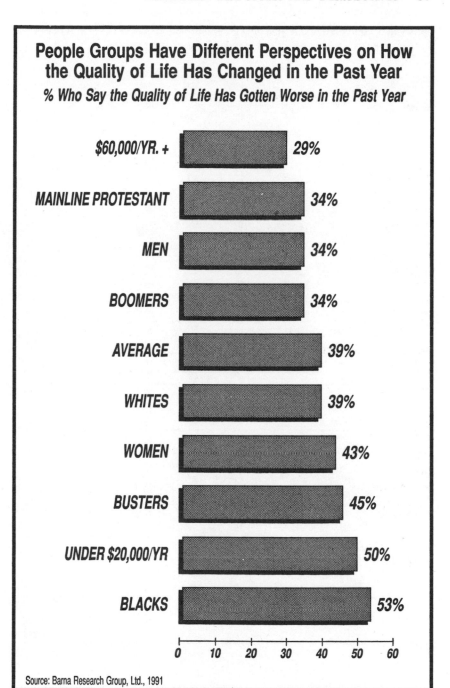

People Groups Have Different Perspectives on How the Quality of Life Has Changed in the Past Year

% Who Say the Quality of Life Has Gotten Worse in the Past Year

$60,000/YR. +   29%

MAINLINE PROTESTANT   34%

MEN   34%

BOOMERS   34%

AVERAGE   39%

WHITES   39%

WOMEN   43%

BUSTERS   45%

UNDER $20,000/YR   50%

BLACKS   53%

0   10   20   30   40   50   60

Source: Barna Research Group, Ltd., 1991

Q: Overall, compared to one year ago, do you think the quality of life in America has gotten better, gotten worse, or remained about the same?

		Better	Same	Worse	Don't Know	N
Total Population		11%	49%	39%	1%	1005
Age:	18 to 25	10	45	45	*	190
	26-44	12	54	34	1	464
	45-54	11	44	45	1	141
	55-64	15	45	38	1	101
	65 or older	6	50	42	2	92
Education:	High school or less	11	46	42	1	453
	Some college	13	49	37	1	242
	College graduate	9	56	35	1	306
Ethnicity:	White	10	50	39	1	744
	Black	12	36	53	*	119
Household Income:	Under $20,000	10	40	50	1	184
	$20,000 to $39,999	10	50	40	*	397
	$40,000 to $59,999	13	53	35	*	186
	$60,000 or more	9	60	29	1	142
Gender:	Male	15	51	34	*	490
	Female	7	48	43	2	515
Married:	Yes	13	50	37	1	570
	No	9	49	42	1	432
Community:	Urban	11	49	40	1	340
	Suburban	8	52	39	1	387
	Rural	16	45	39	*	245
Region:	Northeast	6	47	46	1	227
	Midwest	13	51	36	1	228
	South	11	54	35	1	210
	Mountain	13	46	41	*	171
	Pacific	12	49	37	2	171
Born Again:	Yes	12	47	41	1	355
	No	10	51	38	1	650
Denominational Affiliation:	Evangelical	10	49	39	2	246
	Catholic	11	50	38	1	250
	Mainline	16	49	34	1	178
Church Attender:	Yes	12	51	37	1	762
	No	9	53	37	1	243

WILL LIFE IMPROVE IN THE NEXT YEAR?

 Question: *In your estimation, do you think that the quality of life in America will be better, worse, or about the same one year from now?*

In total, Americans aren't quite sure what to make of the future. Traditionally we have been an optimistic people, believing that the days ahead will bring even better opportunities and new riches. Clearly, that positive attitude is eroding rapidly. While 37% of adults say that the quality of life they experience next year will probably be equivalent to what they have today, 27% say things are likely to get better, and 32% believe things will get worse. On the one hand, that does represent an optimistic perspective when compared to people's experiences over the past year. On the other hand, these figures are less positive than what has typically been measured in past surveys.

The real pessimists in the crowd are the Busters and Boomers. Combined, 34% of the younger generations believe the quality of life will get worse, while 27% expect things to improve. Compare that to the elderly, among whom 30% expect better times in the coming year, and just 25% expect an erosion of the quality of life.

Breaking the usual pattern, we find that the most pessimistic people are those who are college graduates and those with the lowest household incomes. (Usually, educational achievement and higher levels of income go hand in hand.) Men and women also have divergent views on what the future will bring, with men holding the more optimistic perspective.

The future looks comparatively bleak to those individuals who live in the city: they are more likely than suburbanites or rural residents to anticipate a faltering quality of life. Inexplicably, evangelicals are more likely than mainline Protestants or Catholics to expect a decline in the coming year.

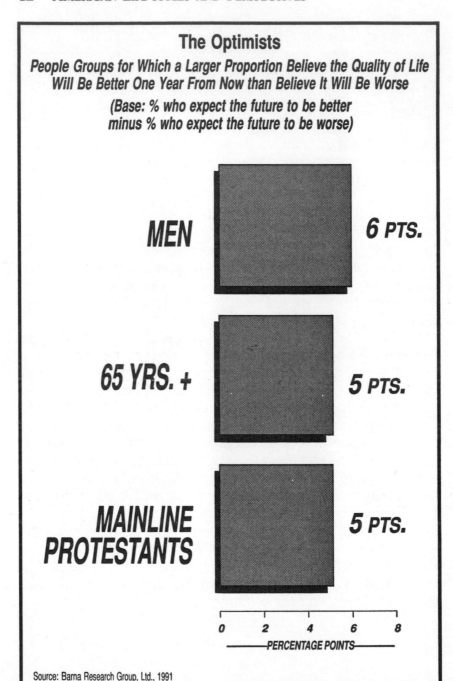

The Optimists

*People Groups for Which a Larger Proportion Believe the Quality of Life
Will Be Better One Year From Now than Believe It Will Be Worse*

*(Base: % who expect the future to be better
minus % who expect the future to be worse)*

MEN   **6** PTS.

65 YRS. +   *5* PTS.

**MAINLINE
PROTESTANTS**   *5* PTS.

0   2   4   6   8
————PERCENTAGE POINTS————

Source: Barna Research Group, Ltd., 1991

Q: In your estimation, do you think that the quality of life in America will be better, worse, or about the same one year from now?

		Better	Same	Worse	Don't Know	N
Total Population		27%	38%	32%	5%	1005
Age:	18 to 25	33	27	38	2	190
	26-44	24	39	32	4	464
	45-54	30	39	28	4	141
	55-64	25	41	29	6	101
	65 or older	30	40	25	5	92
Education:	High school or less	29	37	29	5	453
	Some college	29	33	35	3	242
	College graduate	22	39	33	6	306
Ethnicity:	White	26	41	29	4	744
	Black	26	34	40	1	119
Household Income:	Under $20,000	27	32	40	2	184
	$20,000 to $39,999	27	36	31	6	397
	$40,000 to $59,999	29	39	31	1	186
	$60,000 or more	25	44	24	7	142
Gender:	Male	31	40	25	4	490
	Female	23	34	38	6	515
Married:	Yes	27	36	31	6	570
	No	26	38	33	3	432
Community:	Urban	24	37	35	5	340
	Suburban	27	38	30	6	387
	Rural	30	36	31	3	245
Region:	Northeast	27	36	28	9	227
	Midwest	23	45	30	2	228
	South	28	36	33	3	210
	Mountain	29	36	35	1	171
	Pacific	29	29	34	8	171
Born Again:	Yes	27	36	33	3	355
	No	27	37	31	6	650
Denominational Affiliation:	Evangelical	24	37	33	6	246
	Catholic	31	34	31	4	250
	Mainline	30	44	25	2	178
Church Attender:	Yes	28	37	31	4	762
	No	27	39	29	5	243

2 HOW WE VIEW THE CHANGING ECONOMY

HOW HAS THE WEAKENED ECONOMY AFFECTED OUR LIFE-STYLES?

Question: *Turning to the economy and people's life-styles, some economists are saying that we are now in a recession. Which, if any, of the following changes are you likely to make in your life-style during the next few months as a result of the weakening of the nation's economy?*

You can learn a lot about people based on how they spend their money. When we asked adults to indicate how they plan to cope with the recession, their responses help us to understand their priorities in life.

The first line of defense against the recession is to reduce spending on what many people perceive to be the luxuries in their lives. The luxuries most likely to suffer cutbacks are entertainment (61% plan to decrease such spending) and eating at restaurants (58%).

The second line of financial defense is to reduce spending by doing less driving (mentioned by 36%); setting less money aside for savings (31%); decreasing the amount of money donated to charities (27%); and reducing the money contributed to churches (16%).

The least likely candidates for budget reduction are moving to less expensive housing (anticipated by 8%) and buying more items on credit (7%).

Overall, one out of every five adults (19%) has no intention of cutting back in any of these eight areas.

Reduction in giving to churches is most likely among younger adults: 26% of the Busters and 16% of the Boomers plan to give less, compared to 9% among those 45 or older. Cutbacks in church donations are less likely among households earning $60,000 a year or more (8%) than among other households (17%). Single adults are also more likely than married adults to say they will slice their church gifts (20% vs. 12%, respectively). Not surprisingly, born again Christians are only about half as likely as non-Christians to reduce their giving, but even 11% of the Christian community expects to reduce church donations as a result of the recession.

The segments of the population who are least likely to alter their spending habits due to the changed economic climate are those who are 55 or older (since they have a more comfortable, established life-style less susceptible to external change); people in the upper income brackets; and unchurched adults.

The Groups Most—and Least—Likely to Reduce Contributions to Churches

(Index = 100; Represents 16% of Adults)

130 OR MORE — WAY ABOVE AVERAGE

BABY BUSTERS (167)
UNDER $20,000/YR (131)
SINGLES (130)

129 TO 111 — ABOVE AVERAGE

HIGH SCHOOL OR LESS (118)
NON-CHRISTIANS (116)
MALES (117)

110 TO 90 — AVERAGE

BABY BOOMERS (101)

89 TO 71 — BELOW AVERAGE

MARRIED (77)
COLLEGE GRADUATES (73)
FEMALES (84)

70 OR LESS — WAY BELOW AVERAGE

BORN AGAIN CHRISTIANS (70)
MAINLINE PROTESTANTS (70)
45 OR OLDER (60)
$60,000/YR OR MORE (50)

Indexes are standardized scores. Index scores below the population index (i.e. 100) indicate population segments that are less likely to have the test attribute; segments with scores above the base index are more likely to engage in that behavior. The larger the difference from the base index, the more the segment differs from the norm.

Source: Barna Research Group, Ltd., 1991

Q: Turning to the economy and people's life-styles, some economists are saying that we are now in a recession. Which, if any, of the following changes are you likely to make in your life-style during the next few months as a result of the weakening of the nation's economy? (See next page for column headings.)

		#1	#2	#3	#4	#5	#6	#7	#8	No Change	N
Total Population		27%	61%	58%	8%	7%	36%	16%	31%	19%	1005
Age:	18 to 25	32	59	60	13	11	31	26	30	18	190
	26-44	26	66	64	8	6	39	16	35	16	464
	45-54	23	59	62	4	13	38	10	31	19	141
	55-64	27	55	44	6	2	34	9	20	26	101
	65 or older	28	47	41	7	5	38	10	28	27	92
Education:	High school or less	27	58	58	10	7	38	18	32	18	453
	Some college	29	69	61	6	8	37	15	33	17	242
	College graduate	24	59	56	6	6	33	11	28	23	306
Ethnicity:	White	27	60	58	6	7	36	14	31	20	744
	Black	26	66	61	15	10	36	15	30	14	119
Household Income:	Under $20,000	31	64	60	14	13	43	20	32	19	184
	$20,000 to $39,999	27	61	60	8	7	37	17	36	18	397
	$40,000 to $59,999	25	66	58	6	5	36	13	29	15.	186
	$60,000 or more	19	55	56	4	3	26	8	18	28	142
Gender:	Male	26	53	54	6	7	33	18	30	25	490
	Female	27	68	62	10	7	39	13	33	15	515
Married:	Yes	25	62	59	7	6	39	12	32	18	570
	No	30	59	57	10	8	33	20	31	21	432
Community:	Urban	27	58	56	9	9	33	18	28	20	340
	Suburban	26	62	60	6	7	35	12	32	20	387
	Rural	29	62	60	8	4	42	16	33	17	245
Region:	Northeast	26	62	58	8	10	31	12	27	20	227
	Midwest	29	57	54	7	2	38	17	37	21	228
	South	29	60	59	8	11	39	16	33	18	210
	Mountain	25	57	57	9	8	34	16	27	21	171
	Pacific	24	67	63	8	5	39	17	30	17	169
Born Again:	Yes	26	65	60	9	7	41	11	35	17	355
	No	27	58	57	7	8	34	18	29	21	650
Denominational Affiliation:	Evangelical	28	60	56	8	8	39	14	35	20	246
	Catholic	26	66	67	7	9	38	17	31	12	250
	Mainline	29	57	54	3	3	36	11	32	22	178
Church Attender:	Yes	26	65	60	9	6	38	12	34	16	762
	No	24	52	53	4	5	31	22	27	29	243

Columns:

#1 Reduce the amount of money you are donating to charity.

#2 Spend less money on entertainment. .

#3 Eat meals at restaurants less often.

#4 Move to less expensive housing.

#5 Buy more items on credit.

#6 Reduce the amount of driving you do.

#7 Reduce the amount of money you are donating to churches.

#8 Reduce the amount of money you set aside for savings.

3 HOW WE SPEND OUR TIME: FAMILY, WORK, AND PLAY

HOW MUCH TIME FOR FAMILY?

> ☎ **Question:** *Compared to one year ago, please tell me if you are now spending more time, less time, or about the same amount of time as a year ago on each of the following activities: Time spent at home with your family.*

Family is "in." As Boomers age and find themselves with one or more young ones, the importance of a healthy family has come to the fore. Today's families look and live differently from those of the past few decades, but the notion of nurturing a happy and growing family is on the rise.

This perspective is reflected in the perception held by many adults that compared to a year earlier, they now spend more time with their family than they used to. Among Boomers, especially, this pattern is apparent: while 28% of the Boomers say they are now spending the same amount of time with family as last year, 48% say they're spending more time, while just 13% claim to have reduced their time with the family.

Don't be confused by the response pattern among the Baby Bust generation (the 18-25 year olds). The fact that a high proportion of them (30%) say they're spending less time with family—that's twice the national average—is largely due to the fact that many of these young adults are single and recently separated from their parents, or in a life-style which now provides them with less time to spend with their parents.

And even grandparents are getting into the flow of things. With Boomers increasing their families, and looking for help raising the kids, notice that 33% of those 55 or older are spending more time with family (largely attributable to visits by the grandchildren and increased involvement with their own children who are interested in parenting tips) compared to just 5% who now spend less time with family.

It's still comparatively difficult in suburbia to make the extra time for anything outside of work. Overall, adults are more likely to say they're currently giving more time to family than to say they're devoting less time to family. However, people in cities and in rural areas are significantly more likely than those residing in the suburbs to claim they are apportioning more of their time for family interaction.

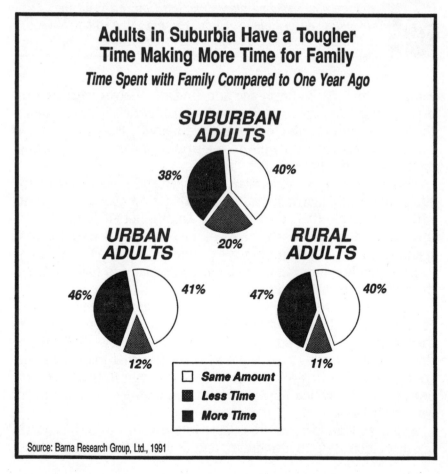

Adults in Suburbia Have a Tougher Time Making More Time for Family

Time Spent with Family Compared to One Year Ago

SUBURBAN ADULTS

38%   40%

20%

URBAN ADULTS   **RURAL ADULTS**

46%   41%   47%   40%

12%   11%

☐ Same Amount
■ Less Time
■ More Time

Source: Barna Research Group, Ltd., 1991

Q: Compared to one year ago, please tell me if you are now spending more time, less time, or about the same amount of time as a year ago on each of the following activities: Time spent at home with your family.

		More Time	Same Amount	Less Time	Don't Know	N
Total Population		43%	41%	14%	2%	1005
Age:	18 to 25	43	28	30	*	190
	26-44	48	39	13	1	464
	45-54	46	39	14	2	141
	55-64	39	51	5	5	101
	65 or older	24	61	5	9	92
Education:	High school or less	45	39	14	2	453
	Some college	44	38	15	3	242
	College graduate	39	46	14	1	306
Ethnicity:	White	40	44	13	3	744
	Black	50	29	21	*	119
Household Income:	Under $20,000	52	29	16	3	184
	$20,000 to $39,999	42	40	15	2	397
	$40,000 to $59,999	40	46	13	1	186
	$60,000 or more	41	45	13	1	142
Gender:	Male	40	41	17	2	490
	Female	46	40	12	2	515
Married:	Yes	50	44	5	1	570
	No	33	37	26	4	432
Community:	Urban	46	41	12	1	340
	Suburban	38	40	20	3	387
	Rural	47	40	11	2	245
Region:	Northeast	38	46	12	4	227
	Midwest	43	40	15	2	228
	South	41	44	14	1	210
	Mountain	49	30	18	3	171
	Pacific	44	41	12	2	171
Born Again:	Yes	45	39	14	2	355
	No	42	41	14	2	650
Denominational Affiliation:	Evangelical	45	40	14	1	246
	Catholic	46	35	15	3	250
	Mainline	44	44	10	3	178
Church Attender:	Yes	44	41	13	2	623
	No	38	44	16	2	243

HOW MUCH TIME ON THE JOB?

Question: *Compared to one year ago, please tell me if you are now spending more time, less time, or about the same amount of time as a year ago on each of the following activities: Time spent working at your job.*

Americans may have an unquenchable thirst for leisure, and a growing interest in family development, but there's also an undeniable move toward increasingly long hours on the job. Roughly two-fifths (39%) say they are spending the same amount of time on the job today as they did a year ago; two-fifths (39%) claim they're putting in longer hours; and about one-fifth (17%) believe they're working fewer hours.

Not surprisingly, Busters (many of whom are entering the job market for the first time) are the segment most likely to claim they're increasing their work schedule (53% say this is their lot), while senior citizens are most likely to note a reduction (24% cite a decreased work week, while just 7% say their hours on-the-job are increasing).

Of more than passing interest is the reality that women are below average when it comes to citing an increased work week. While 47% of the men say they're working longer hours now than last year, only 32% of the women make the same statement. Since 21% of the women say they're working fewer hours than last year, there is still a net gain in the number of women putting in longer hours. However, this might be indicative of a period in which more women are doing whatever they can to cut back on the job in order to devote more time to family matters.

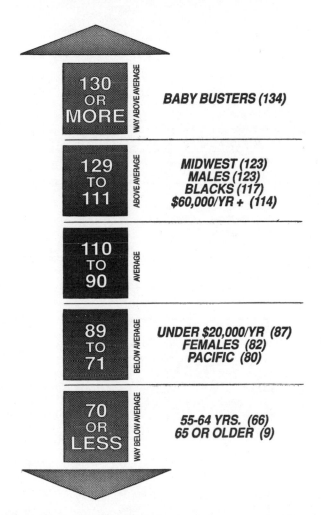

Who's Putting in More—and Fewer—Hours on the Job?

(Index base = 100; Represents 39% of Adults)

Index	Level	Segments
130 OR MORE	WAY ABOVE AVERAGE	*BABY BUSTERS (134)*
129 TO 111	ABOVE AVERAGE	*MIDWEST (123)* *MALES (123)* *BLACKS (117)* *$60,000/YR + (114)*
110 TO 90	AVERAGE	
89 TO 71	BELOW AVERAGE	*UNDER $20,000/YR (87)* *FEMALES (82)* *PACIFIC (80)*
70 OR LESS	WAY BELOW AVERAGE	*55-64 YRS. (66)* *65 OR OLDER (9)*

Indexes are standardized scores. Index scores below the population index (i.e. 100) indicate population segments that are less likely to have the test attribute; segments with scores above the base index are more likely to engage in that behavior. The larger the difference from the base index, the more the segment differs from the norm.

Source: Barna Research Group, Ltd., 1991

Q: Compared to one year ago, please tell me if you are now spending more time, less time, or about the same amount of time as a year ago on each of the following activities: Time spent working at your job.

		More Time	Same Amount	Less Time	Don't Know	N
Total Population		39%	39%	17%	5%	1005
Age:	18 to 25	53	27	19	2	190
	26-44	44	42	13	1	464
	45-54	40	39	18	3	141
	55-64	26	42	17	15	101
	65 or older	7	42	24	28	92
Education:	High school or less	39	36	18	7	453
	Some college	40	36	20	5	242
	College graduate	40	46	11	2	306
Ethnicity:	White	38	39	17	5	744
	Black	46	34	13	7	119
Household Income:	Under $20,000	34	30	28	8	184
	$20,000 to $39,999	42	39	14	5	397
	$40,000 to $59,999	39	45	12	4	186
	$60,000 or more	45	41	13	1	142
Gender:	Male	47	38	11	3	490
	Female	32	39	21	7	515
Married:	Yes	38	40	17	6	570
	No	42	38	16	4	432
Community:	Urban	39	41	16	4	340
	Suburban	39	41	15	5	387
	Rural	42	35	17	6	245
Region:	Northeast	36	44	15	5	227
	Midwest	48	33	13	5	228
	South	38	37	18	7	210
	Mountain	42	38	16	4	171
	Pacific	32	42	22	4	171
Born Again:	Yes	37	39	18	7	355
	No	41	39	16	4	650
Denominational Affiliation:	Evangelical	43	34	16	7	246
	Catholic	41	40	15	4	250
	Mainline	37	40	17	6	178
Church Attender:	Yes	40	38	16	7	623
	No	40	41	15	4	243

HOW MUCH TIME READING FOR PLEASURE?

Question: *Compared to one year ago, please tell me if you are now spending more time, less time, or about the same amount of time as a year ago on each of the following activities: Time spent reading for pleasure.*

In a nation in which functional illiteracy is a major concern, how encouraging it is to hear people state that they are, on balance, spending more time reading materials which are not related to their occupation.

Growth in time spent reading is related to educational achievement: people who have attended college are more likely to be spending greater amounts of time in reading for pleasure than are those with less formal schooling.

Unexpectedly, the greatest gains are among adults in the urban and suburban areas of the nation. Regionally, there is virtually no net gain in pleasure reading in the southwestern and mountain states. Conversely, there are significant net gains in the northeastern and southern states.

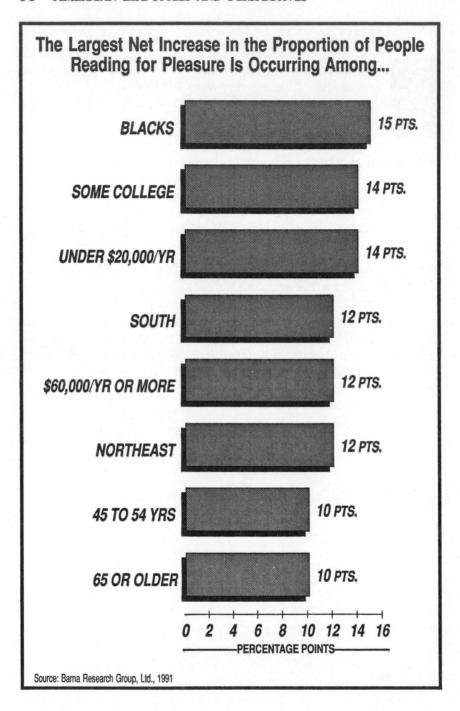

The Largest Net Increase in the Proportion of People Reading for Pleasure Is Occurring Among...

BLACKS — 15 PTS.

SOME COLLEGE — 14 PTS.

UNDER $20,000/YR — 14 PTS.

SOUTH — 12 PTS.

$60,000/YR OR MORE — 12 PTS.

NORTHEAST — 12 PTS.

45 TO 54 YRS — 10 PTS.

65 OR OLDER — 10 PTS.

0 2 4 6 8 10 12 14 16

———PERCENTAGE POINTS———

Source: Barna Research Group, Ltd., 1991

Q: Compared to one year ago, please tell me if you are now spending more time, less time, or about the same amount of time as a year ago on each of the following activities: Time spent reading for pleasure.

		More Time	Same Amount	Less Time	Don't Know	N
Total Population		34%	38%	27%	1%	1005
Age:	18 to 25	42	19	39	1	190
	26-44	33	39	27	*	464
	45-54	35	39	25	1	141
	55-64	29	49	20	2	101
	65 or older	28	52	16	5	92
Education:	High school or less	33	35	30	2	453
	Some college	39	36	25	*	242
	College graduate	33	43	24	*	306
Ethnicity:	White	32	42	25	1	744
	Black	46	22	31	1	119
Household Income:	Under $20,000	40	32	26	3	184
	$20,000 to $39,999	33	40	27	*	397
	$40,000 to $59,999	32	34	34	*	186
	$60,000 or more	35	40	23	1	142
Gender:	Male	34	39	26	1	490
	Female	35	36	28	1	515
Married:	Yes	34	39	27	1	570
	No	35	36	28	1	432
Community:	Urban	37	35	28	*	340
	Suburban	32	41	26	1	387
	Rural	33	37	29	1	245
Region:	Northeast	33	44	21	2	227
	Midwest	33	40	26	*	228
	South	37	36	25	2	210
	Mountain	35	28	37	*	171
	Pacific	33	38	28	2	171
Born Again:	Yes	37	37	26	*	355
	No	33	38	27	2	650
Denominational Affiliation:	Evangelical	31	42	26	1	246
	Catholic	37	33	31	*	250
	Mainline	28	45	26	*	178
Church Attender:	Yes	34	38	28	*	623
	No	30	43	26	1	243

HOW MUCH TIME FOR PHYSICAL EXERCISE?

 Question: *Compared to one year ago, please tell me if you are now spending more time, less time, or about the same amount of time as a year ago on each of the following activities: Time spent exercising or working out physically.*

Sociologists tell us that the fitness craze has passed, with two results. Some people have embraced a healthier life-style—i.e. regular exercise, or eating healthy foods consistently—and thus have a new daily regimen that has become standard operating procedure for them. Others are continuing to dabble in fitness activities, though the prospects of their long-term acceptance of such activity as life-style are dim.

The survey statistics reflect waning interest in fitness-related activity. This year there has been a small net gain in the proportion of adults committed to spending more time on fitness activities (an increase of six percentage points). Again, the life-style changes occurring among the youngest and oldest adults tend to cancel each other out: while the net gain in the numbers of Busters spending more time on fitness efforts was 16 percentage points, the elderly reflected a net loss of 11 points.

Other population segments that demonstrate above average inclination to spend more of their time engaged in exercise are men, single adults, people living west of the Colorado River, non-Christians, and mainline Protestants.

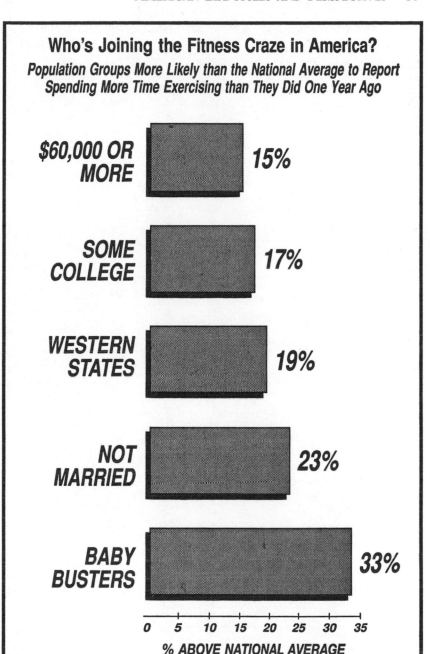

Who's Joining the Fitness Craze in America?

Population Groups More Likely than the National Average to Report Spending More Time Exercising than They Did One Year Ago

$60,000 OR MORE — 15%

SOME COLLEGE — 17%

WESTERN STATES — 19%

NOT MARRIED — 23%

BABY BUSTERS — 33%

0   5   10   15   20   25   30   35

% ABOVE NATIONAL AVERAGE

Source: Barna Research Group, Ltd., 1991

Q: Compared to one year ago, please tell me if you are now spending more time, less time, or about the same amount of time as a year ago on each of the following activities: Time spent exercising or working out physically.

		More Time	Same Amount	Less Time	Don't Know	N
Total Population		34%	37%	28%	1%	1005
Age:	18 to 25	46	24	30	*	190
	26-44	34	37	29	*	464
	45-54	27	45	27	1	141
	55-64	26	45	26	3	101
	65 or older	23	45	25	7	92
Education:	High school or less	33	34	31	2	453
	Some college	40	34	26	*	242
	College graduate	29	46	25	*	306
Ethnicity:	White	32	42	25	2	744
	Black	37	21	42	*	119
Household Income:	Under $20,000	38	29	30	3	184
	$20,000 to $39,999	33	39	28	1	397
	$40,000 to $59,999	28	41	30	1	186
	$60,000 or more	39	39	22	*	142
Gender:	Male	35	40	24	1	490
	Female	32	35	31	2	515
Married:	Yes	27	41	31	1	570
	No	42	33	24	1	432
Community:	Urban	36	36	28	1	340
	Suburban	34	38	26	2	387
	Rural	29	40	31	1	245
Region:	Northeast	28	44	27	2	227
	Midwest	29	42	28	1	228
	South	34	33	31	2	210
	Mountain	41	32	28	*	171
	Pacific	40	34	25	1	171
Born Again:	Yes	32	36	32	1	355
	No	34	38	26	2	650
Denominational Affiliation:	Evangelical	30	34	34	2	246
	Catholic	33	37	30	1	250
	Mainline	36	39	22	3	178
Church Attender:	Yes	33	37	29	1	623
	No	33	44	23	1	243

4 HOW WE SPEND OUR TIME: EDUCATION, RELIGION, TV, AND FRIENDS

HOW MUCH TIME FOR ADDITIONAL EDUCATION?

> ☎ **Question:** *Compared to one year ago, please tell me if you are now spending more time, less time, or about the same amount of time as a year ago on each of the following activities: Time spent seeking additional formal education.*

Compared to last year, fewer adults are spending time in school settings. While 26% said they spend more time pursuing formal education than was true a year ago, 34% say they are spending less time doing so.

The segments most likely to be less actively seeking additional education are those who never attended college; whites; women; low-income adults; married adults; those living in urban areas; residents of the midwest or south; and Catholics.

People groups who are especially likely to be devoting greater amounts of time to educational options are Busters (48% are putting in more time into education); blacks (37%); and individuals in the mountain and southwestern states.

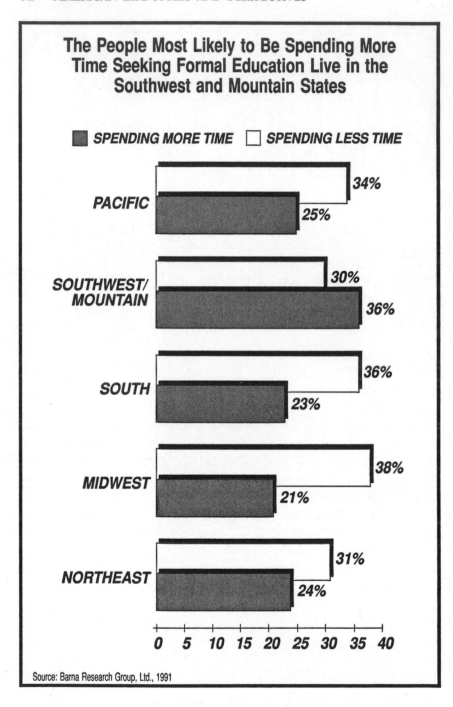

The People Most Likely to Be Spending More Time Seeking Formal Education Live in the Southwest and Mountain States

▨ SPENDING MORE TIME   ☐ SPENDING LESS TIME

PACIFIC — 34% / 25%

SOUTHWEST/MOUNTAIN — 30% / 36%

SOUTH — 36% / 23%

MIDWEST — 38% / 21%

NORTHEAST — 31% / 24%

0 5 10 15 20 25 30 35 40

Source: Barna Research Group, Ltd., 1991

Q: Compared to one year ago, please tell me if you are now spending more time, less time, or about the same amount of time as a year ago on each of the following activities: Time spent seeking additional formal education.

		More Time	Same Amount	Less Time	Don't Know	N
Total Population		30%	37%	34%	4%	1005
Age:	18 to 25	48	22	27	3	190
	26-44	28	37	33	2	464
	45-54	15	41	37	7	141
	55-64	8	44	43	5	101
	65 or older	7	45	44	5	92
Education:	High school or less	23	35	37	5	453
	Some college	29	35	34	3	242
	College graduate	27	41	30	2	306
Ethnicity:	White	22	41	34	4	744
	Black	37	22	36	5	119
Household Income:	Under $20,000	23	29	43	5	184
	$20,000 to $39,999	28	36	33	3	397
	$40,000 to $59,999	26	35	37	2	186
	$60,000 or more	22	47	26	5	142
Gender:	Male	30	35	33	3	490
	Female	22	39	36	4	515
Married:	Yes	21	38	37	4	570
	No	32	35	31	3	432
Community:	Urban	24	37	37	3	340
	Suburban	26	38	34	3	387
	Rural	28	36	32	5	245
Region:	Northeast	24	40	31	4	227
	Midwest	21	38	38	3	228
	South	23	38	36	3	210
	Mountain	36	29	30	5	171
	Pacific	25	38	34	3	171
Born Again:	Yes	28	34	36	3	355
	No	24	38	33	4	650
Denominational Affiliation:	Evangelical	25	32	38	5	246
	Catholic	19	38	39	4	250
	Mainline	27	42	28	3	178
Church Attender:	Yes	25	37	35	3	623
	No	31	37	28	4	243

HOW MUCH TIME FOR VOLUNTEERISM?

 Question: *Compared to one year ago, please tell me if you are now spending more time, less time, or about the same amount of time as a year ago on each of the following activities: Time spent volunteering your time.*

It appears that the claims about Americans being increasingly likely to give their time to worthy organizations may be overblown. The data in this study confirm findings from other recent Barna Research studies suggesting that while many people are happy to donate some of their time to help a worthy cause, the enormous demands on people's time are draining them of the energy and opportunity to offer their time as freely as in the past.

Waning Volunteerism: A Sign of the Times

Overall, there is a net loss noted in the proportion of people who say they are volunteering more time this year than last. While 45% say there is no difference between this year's volunteering and last year's allocation of their schedule to such efforts, 22% say they are spending more time in volunteer work and 32% say they're giving up less of their time.

Surprisingly, the age segment that is least likely to say they're doing less volunteering this year is the Baby Boomers! Although there is a net decrease in the proportion of Boomers saying they're volunteering more hours now than they did last year, that net loss is smaller than is true for any other age group evaluated. Skeptics might propose that this is because Boomers give so little time to begin with that there isn't much to decrease. However, other research indicates that Boomers do give of their time at a level that is on par with other age groups.

Who's Cutting Back?

Substantial reductions in volunteering are also evident among those earning less than $40,000 a year. This may be a move of necessity on the part of the less affluent households, given the impact of the recession.

Born again Christians are less likely to be reducing their volunteer time than are non-Christians. Also notice that while those affiliated with evangelical or Catholic churches are more likely than average to reduce their volunteer hours, those adults associated with mainline Protestant churches show no net change in their volunteer time.

One-third of All Adults Are Spending Less Time than Last Year on Volunteer Activity

Index Base = 100; Represents 32% of the Population Who Say They're Spending Less Time Volunteering

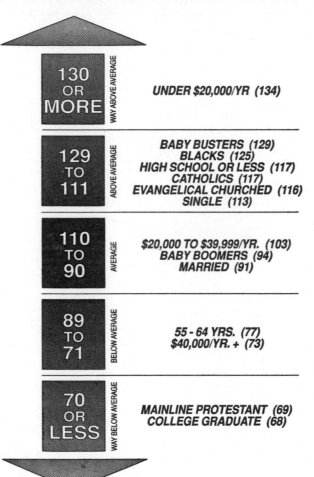

130 OR MORE — WAY ABOVE AVERAGE

UNDER $20,000/YR (134)

129 TO 111 — ABOVE AVERAGE

BABY BUSTERS (129)
BLACKS (125)
HIGH SCHOOL OR LESS (117)
CATHOLICS (117)
EVANGELICAL CHURCHED (116)
SINGLE (113)

110 TO 90 — AVERAGE

$20,000 TO $39,999/YR. (103)
BABY BOOMERS (94)
MARRIED (91)

89 TO 71 — BELOW AVERAGE

55 - 64 YRS. (77)
$40,000/YR. + (73)

70 OR LESS — WAY BELOW AVERAGE

MAINLINE PROTESTANT (69)
COLLEGE GRADUATE (68)

Indexes are standardized scores. Index scores below the population index (i.e. 100) indicate population segments that are less likely to have the test attribute; segments with scores above the base index are more likely to engage in that behavior. The larger the difference from the base index, the more the segment differs from the norm.

Source: Barna Research Group, Ltd., 1991

Q: Compared to one year ago, please tell me if you are now spending more time, less time, or about the same amount of time as a year ago on each of the following activities: Time spent volunteering your time.

		More Time	Same Amount	Less Time	Don't Know	N
Total Population		22%	45%	32%	1%	1005
Age:	18 to 25	26	32	41	1	190
	26-44	25	45	30	1	464
	45-54	18	46	35	1	141
	55-64	17	52	28	2	101
	65 or older	15	57	25	3	92
Education:	High school or less	19	42	38	2	453
	Some college	23	41	34	2	242
	College graduate	25	53	22	1	306
Ethnicity:	White	20	48	30	2	744
	Black	27	33	40	*	119
Household Income:	Under $20,000	15	40	43	2	184
	$20,000 to $39,999	24	42	33	2	397
	$40,000 to $59,999	24	52	23	1	186
	$60,000 or more	24	52	22	1	142
Gender:	Male	21	47	31	1	490
	Female	22	43	33	2	515
Married:	Yes	20	50	29	1	570
	No	24	39	36	2	432
Community:	Urban	19	47	33	1	340
	Suburban	25	44	31	1	387
	Rural	22	44	32	3	245
Region:	Northeast	20	47	31	3	227
	Midwest	20	48	31	*	228
	South	19	47	34	1	210
	Mountain	31	33	35	2	171
	Pacific	21	48	29	2	171
Born Again:	Yes	26	44	29	2	355
	No	20	46	34	1	650
Denominational Affiliation:	Evangelical	23	40	37	1	246
	Catholic	19	43	37	1	250
	Mainline	21	55	22	1	178
Church Attender:	Yes	25	43	30	1	623
	No	16	49	33	2	243

HOW MUCH TIME FOR RELIGIOUS ACTIVITIES?

Question: *Compared to one year ago, please tell me if you are now spending more time, less time, or about the same amount of time as a year ago on each of the following activities: Time spent participating in activities related to your church or place of religious involvement.*

The bad news for churches is that across-the-board people are spending less time participating in church activities. Overall, 44% of adults say they are giving the same amount of time to church endeavors this year as they did last year; 20% are giving more time; 33% are spending less time. This is a net loss of 13 percentage points in the proportion of people giving more to their church's life.

Once again, Boomers trash the prevailing image, emerging as the age group least likely to have reduced their time spent involved with church activities.

The people groups most prone to reducing their time volunteered to churches are Baby Busters; those with low levels of formal education; individuals from low-income households; single adults; urban residents; people in the south; non-Christians; Catholics; and the unchurched.

Born again Christians and mainline Protestants are just as likely to increase their church time as to reduce it. A larger proportion of those attending evangelical churches, on the other hand, exhibit a tendency to be cutting back on church participation.

Shown Below Are the People Groups for Which a Greater Proportion of Adults Are Spending *More* Time in Church-related Activities than Are Spending *Less* Time in Such Endeavors

In Fact, There Are NO People Groups for Which a Greater Proportion of Adults Are Spending More Time in Church-related Activities than Are Spending Less Time in Such Endeavors

Source: Barna Research Group, Ltd., 1991

Q: Compared to one year ago, please tell me if you are now spending more time, less time, or about the same amount of time as a year ago on each of the following activities: Time spent participating in activities related to your church or place of religious involvement.

		More Time	Same Amount	Less Time	Don't Know	N
Total Population		20%	44%	33%	3%	1005
Age:	18 to 25	17	31	46	5	190
	26-44	24	43	32	1	464
	45-54	16	48	31	5	141
	55-64	20	50	25	5	101
	65 or older	18	54	25	3	92
Education:	High school or less	19	38	39	5	453
	Some college	22	43	33	1	242
	College graduate	21	53	25	2	306
Ethnicity:	White	19	48	31	3	744
	Black	30	25	43	2	119
Household Income:	Under $20,000	17	38	41	4	184
	$20,000 to $39,999	20	42	34	4	397
	$40,000 to $59,999	25	47	25	3	186
	$60,000 or more	19	52	26	2	142
Gender:	Male	20	41	36	4	490
	Female	21	46	30	3	515
Married:	Yes	24	47	27	2	570
	No	15	39	41	5	432
Community:	Urban	19	41	35	4	340
	Suburban	22	45	31	2	387
	Rural	20	47	31	3	245
Region:	Northeast	19	48	29	4	227
	Midwest	22	44	33	2	228
	South	17	42	39	2	210
	Mountain	23	38	33	6	171
	Pacific	21	45	31	3	171
Born Again:	Yes	26	45	26	2	355
	No	17	43	36	4	650
Denominational Affiliation:	Evangelical	26	39	33	2	246
	Catholic	19	44	36	1	250
	Mainline	20	54	23	3	178
Church Attender:	Yes	27	46	26	1	623
	No	4	47	42	7	243

HOW MUCH TIME FOR TELEVISION?

 Question: *Compared to one year ago, please tell me if you are now spending more time, less time, or about the same amount of time as a year ago on each of the following activities: Time spent watching television.*

Of the various activities measured, television viewing took the greatest beating. To some degree this may be due to the mood of the nation: i.e. it is not healthy to watch too much television. Studies by Nielsen and Arbitron confirm, though, that people seem to be spending less time in front of the TV set, and more time engaged in other activities. Among those, however, is time spent in front of the TV set watching videos.

By better than a two-to-one margin, adults are more likely to contend that they now spend less time watching television than more time, compared to last year. Two-fifths of the population (42%) say they're spending less time, two-fifths say their total viewing hours are unchanged (40%), while one-fifth (18%) claim increased time devoted to television.

Only one segment of the adult population states that it is watching more hours now than last year: the elderly. In a society ripe with entertainment and leisure opportunities, it seems in some ways incongruous (if not disappointing) to think that the individuals with the most time on their hands would spend that precious resource passively viewing the tube. However, this condition may say more about the ways in which our society cares for its elderly than it says about the life-style choices of the elderly themselves.

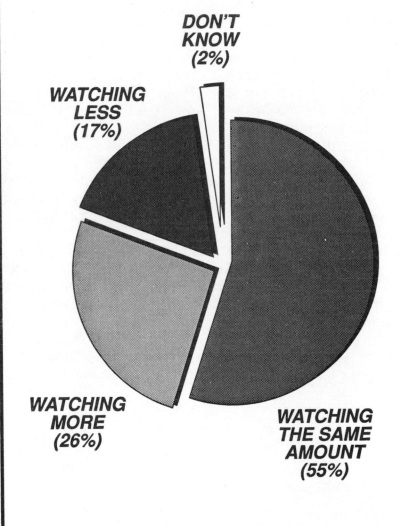

The Elderly Are the *ONLY* Adult Population Segment that Are Watching More Television Today than They Did One Year Ago

Graph Represents Responses of Those 65 Years and Older

DON'T KNOW (2%)

WATCHING LESS (17%)

WATCHING MORE (26%)

WATCHING THE SAME AMOUNT (55%)

Source: Barna Research Group, Ltd., 1991

Q: Compared to one year ago, please tell me if you are now spending more time, less time, or about the same amount of time as a year ago on each of the following activities: Time spent watching television.

		More Time	Same Amount	Less Time	Don't Know	N
Total Population		18%	40%	42%	1%	1005
Age:	18 to 25	20	25	54	1	190
	26-44	14	37	49	*	464
	45-54	18	47	34	2	141
	55-64	21	57	23	*	101
	65 or older	26	55	17	2	92
Education:	High school or less	22	37	40	*	453
	Some college	17	37	44	1	242
	College graduate	11	47	42	*	306
Ethnicity:	White	16	45	39	1	744
	Black	28	24	49	*	119
Household Income:	Under $20,000	27	35	36	2	184
	$20,000 to $39,999	15	40	46	*	397
	$40,000 to $59,999	14	45	41	*	186
	$60,000 or more	14	40	45	1	142
Gender:	Male	17	41	42	*	490
	Female	18	40	41	1	515
Married:	Yes	16	43	40	1	570
	No	19	36	44	*	432
Community:	Urban	17	43	39	1	340
	Suburban	15	40	44	1	387
	Rural	18	38	44	*	245
Region:	Northeast	14	47	38	2	227
	Midwest	18	43	40	*	228
	South	20	37	42	1	210
	Mountain	20	31	48	*	171
	Pacific	16	40	43	1	169
Born Again:	Yes	17	29	43	1	355
	No	18	41	41	*	650
Denominational Affiliation:	Evangelical	19	37	44	*	246
	Catholic	17	40	43	*	250
	Mainline	16	45	38	2	178
Church Attender:	Yes	17	40	44	*	623
	No	17	45	37	1	243

HOW MUCH TIME FOR FRIENDS?

 Question: *Compared to one year ago, please tell me if you are now spending more time, less time, or about the same amount of time as a year ago on each of the following activities: Time spent with your friends.*

Other studies we have conducted document how lonely millions of Americans feel. In fact, sociologists who conduct transitional studies have suggested that Americans are among the loneliest people on earth.

Given this, wouldn't you expect people to spend increasing amounts of time with friends? Sadly, just the opposite is happening. There is actually a net decrease, albeit small, in the proportion of adults who are spending more time with friends than was true one year earlier. While 42% say they spend the same amount of time with friends today as they did one year ago, 26% claim they are spending more time with friends, while 30% are spending less time with friends.

Neither age nor income appear to be a dominant factor in this situation. Racial background is apparently a key, though: while white adults show little difference compared to a year ago, there is a substantial drop in the percentage of blacks who are spending more time with friends. In fact, blacks are twice as likely to say they're allocating less of their time to friendships (46%) as to claim they're giving more of their schedule to friends (24%).

Other subgroups of the population that are particularly likely to say they are spending less time with friends are people from rural areas; residents of the south; and individuals associated with evangelical churches.

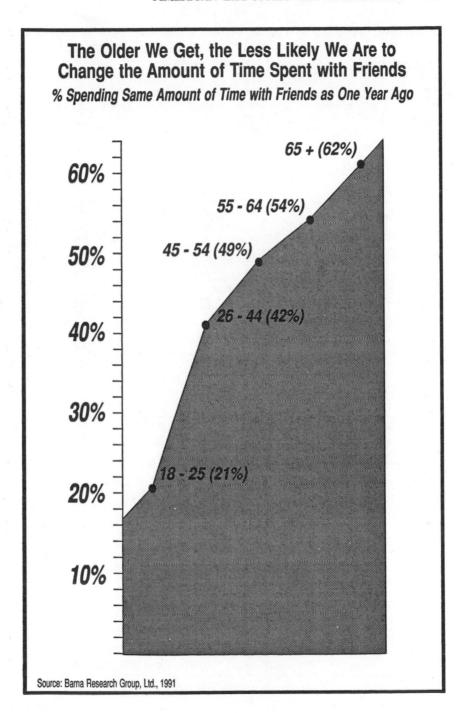

The Older We Get, the Less Likely We Are to Change the Amount of Time Spent with Friends

% Spending Same Amount of Time with Friends as One Year Ago

65 + (62%)

55 - 64 (54%)

45 - 54 (49%)

26 - 44 (42%)

18 - 25 (21%)

60%

50%

40%

30%

20%

10%

Source: Barna Research Group, Ltd., 1991

Q: Compared to one year ago, please tell me if you are now spending more time, less time, or about the same amount of time as a year ago on each of the following activities: Time spent with your friends.

		More Time	Same Amount	Less Time	Don't Know	N
Total Population		26%	42%	30%	1%	1005
Age:	18 to 25	43	21	35	*	190
	26-44	24	42	34	*	464
	45-54	19	49	31	1	141
	55-64	25	54	20	1	101
	65 or older	20	62	13	7	92
Education:	High school or less	27	40	32	1	453
	Some college	27	39	33	1	242
	College graduate	24	49	26	1	306
Ethnicity:	White	26	47	26	1	744
	Black	24	29	46	1	119
Household Income:	Under $20,000	29	34	36	2	184
	$20,000 to $39,999	30	43	27	1	397
	$40,000 to $59,999	20	42	37	1	186
	$60,000 or more	24	50	26	*	142
Gender:	Male	26	40	33	1	490
	Female	27	44	28	1	515
Married:	Yes	21	47	31	1	570
	No	34	37	29	1	432
Community:	Urban	28	41	30	1	340
	Suburban	26	46	27	1	387
	Rural	25	40	35	*	245
Region:	Northeast	23	47	30	1	227
	Midwest	26	45	27	2	228
	South	22	41	36	1	210
	Mountain	33	34	32	1	171
	Pacific	31	42	26	2	169
Born Again:	Yes	24	44	31	*	355
	No	28	41	30	1	650
Denominational Affiliation:	Evangelical	24	39	36	1	246
	Catholic	24	44	31	1	250
	Mainline	27	45	27	1	178
Church Attender:	Yes	25	45	30	1	623
	No	26	40	33	1	243

5 WHAT WE BELIEVE: TRUTH AND RESPONSIBILITY

IS AMERICA A CHRISTIAN NATION?

 Question: *Do you agree strongly, agree somewhat, disagree somewhat, or disagree strongly with the following statement: America is a Christian nation.*

Two-thirds of all adults either agree strongly (22%) or somewhat (44%) that America is a Christian nation. Past research we have conducted suggests that to the typical American, Christianity is a generic term, not necessarily inferring anything about a relationship with Jesus Christ.

Notice that whites are more likely than blacks to describe America as a Christian nation (68% vs. 55%). Remember that blacks, overall, exhibit a greater level of commitment and involvement to Christianity, both in terms of spiritual beliefs and church involvement. Thus, we might interpret their cautious response to this statement to mean that they have a different standard for understanding what it means to be Christian. Upon evaluating the spiritual commitment of Americans, blacks may be indicating that they simply do not view Americans as a people committed to Christ, and therefore are not as likely to consider this to be a Christian nation.

A similar difference may exist among those attending evangelical churches when compared to those affiliated with Catholic or mainline Protestant congregations. Whereas 64% of those aligned with evangelical churches say America is Christian, 70% of Catholics concur, and 75% of the mainliners agree.

Regional differences are among the most striking on this question. While just 59% of the northeastern adults concur that America is a Christian nation, 70% of those living in the midwest and 73% of the adults in the south maintain this view.

Unexpectedly, there is no difference in the views of born again Christians and non-Christians on this matter. Similarly, churched and unchurched adults respond in a similar vein.

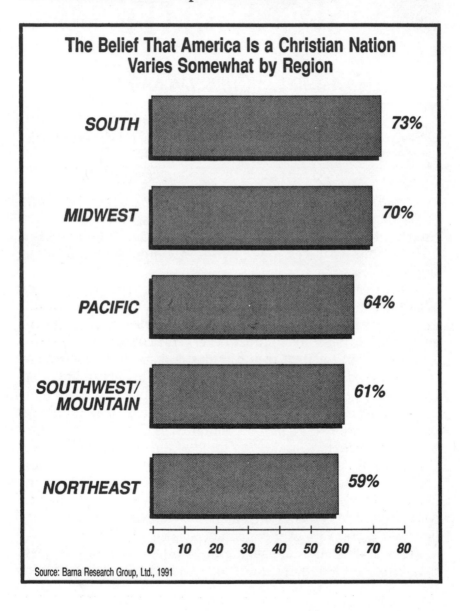

The Belief That America Is a Christian Nation Varies Somewhat by Region

SOUTH — 73%

MIDWEST — 70%

PACIFIC — 64%

SOUTHWEST/ MOUNTAIN — 61%

NORTHEAST — 59%

0   10   20   30   40   50   60   70   80

Source: Barna Research Group, Ltd., 1991

Q: Do you agree strongly, agree somewhat, disagree somewhat, or disagree strongly with the following statement: America is a Christian nation.

		Agree Strongly	Agree Somewhat	Disagree Somewhat	Disagree Strongly	Don't Know	N
Total Population		22%	44%	19%	13%	3	1005
Age:	18 to 25	15	41	24	19	2	190
	26-44	22	46	18	11	3	464
	45-54	23	45	12	15	4	141
	55-64	29	43	15	11	3	101
	65 or older	31	37	16	9	6	92
Education:	High school or less	25	42	19	11	3	453
	Some college	23	45	13	15	3	242
	College graduate	17	45	22	14	3	306
Ethnicity:	White	22	46	18	11	3	744
	Black	21	34	25	17	3	119
Household Income:	Under $20,000	21	44	19	13	4	184
	$20,000 to $39,999	23	45	17	11	3	397
	$40,000 to $59,999	19	45	20	14	3	186
	$60,000 or more	24	41	18	16	1	142
Gender:	Male	23	44	18	14	2	490
	Female	21	43	20	12	4	515
Married:	Yes	25	42	18	13	3	570
	No	19	45	20	13	3	432
Community:	Urban	18	45	19	14	5	340
	Suburban	23	43	20	12	2	387
	Rural	26	44	15	11	3	245
Region:	Northeast	20	39	25	11	5	227
	Midwest	23	47	17	11	3	228
	South	24	49	13	11	4	210
	Mountain	21	40	21	15	3	171
	Pacific	22	42	17	18	1	169
Born Again:	Yes	21	44	19	13	3	355
	No	22	43	18	13	3	650
Denominational Affiliation:	Evangelical	25	39	22	13	2	246
	Catholic	25	45	19	10	2	250
	Mainline	21	54	11	10	4	178
Church Attender:	Yes	23	44	18	11	3	623
	No	20	46	17	14	2	243

DOES GOD HELP THOSE WHO HELP THEMSELVES?

 Question: *Do you agree strongly, agree somewhat, disagree somewhat, or disagree strongly with the following statement: God helps those who help themselves.*

Notice that the majority of Americans strongly believe that the notion "God helps those who help themselves" is accurate. Overall, more than four out of five adults (82%) agree to some extent that this statement is true.

Blacks are more likely to agree strongly with this philosophy (77% strongly agreed, compared to 49% of whites). Geographically, note that adults located in the southern states are more likely than other adults to support this philosophy.

Personal religious background makes little difference on this issue. Four out of five born again Christians agree with the statement—as do four out of five non-Christians. Church affiliation has no apparent impact on this issue, since 84% of those attending an evangelical church, 83% of those who are Catholic, and 87% of those who are aligned with a mainline Protestant church concur. There is, however, a discernible difference between churched and unchurched adults. Eighty-three percent of the churched adults agree that God helps those who help themselves; somewhat fewer unchurched people (75%) agree with that thinking.

It might be instructive to realize that the expression "God helps those who help themselves" is generally credited to Benjamin Franklin. Neither those words nor that thought are found anywhere in the Bible. Most evangelical expositors reject the notion that this viewpoint is consistent with Scripture, noting that human beings are incapable of winning God's favor by their good or mighty deeds, but must instead rely upon the grace of God, shown to those who are truly repentant, for their strength, earthly blessings, and eternal salvation.

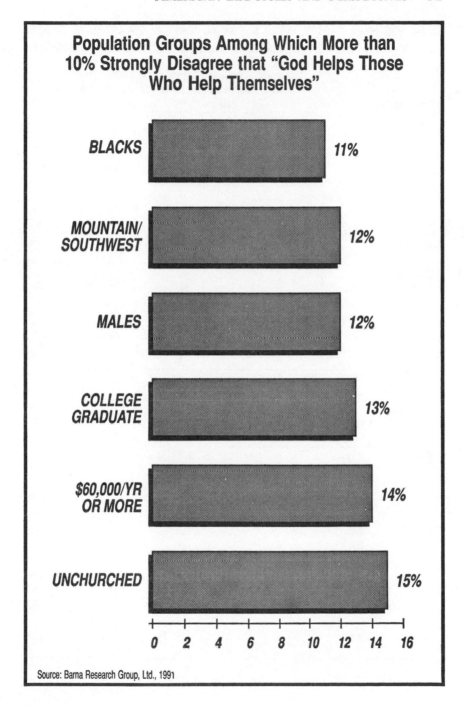

Population Groups Among Which More than 10% Strongly Disagree that "God Helps Those Who Help Themselves"

BLACKS — 11%

MOUNTAIN/SOUTHWEST — 12%

MALES — 12%

COLLEGE GRADUATE — 13%

$60,000/YR OR MORE — 14%

UNCHURCHED — 15%

0 2 4 6 8 10 12 14 16

Source: Barna Research Group, Ltd., 1991

Q: Do you agree strongly, agree somewhat, disagree somewhat, or disagree strongly with the following statement: God helps those who help themselves.

		Agree Strongly	Agree Somewhat	Disagree Somewhat	Disagree Strongly	Don't Know	N
Total Population		54%	27%	8%	9%	2%	1005
Age:	18 to 25	60	23	9	8	*	190
	26-44	53	29	7	10	1	464
	45-54	56	26	9	6	3	141
	55-64	50	29	10	9	3	101
	65 or older	58	22	8	9	3	92
Education:	High school or less	62	21	8	7	2	453
	Some college	56	29	9	6	*	242
	College graduate	45	33	8	13	2	306
Ethnicity:	White	49	32	9	8	2	744
	Black	77	10	2	11	1	119
Household Income:	Under $20,000	64	15	12	8	1	184
	$20,000 to $39,999	55	27	9	8	2	397
	$40,000 to $59,999	48	37	3	10	2	186
	$60,000 or more	52	27	6	14	2	142
Gender:	Male	50	29	9	12	1	490
	Female	60	24	8	6	3	515
Married:	Yes	53	28	9	8	2	570
	No	57	24	7	10	2	432
Community:	Urban	57	25	8	10	1	340
	Suburban	53	27	9	8	3	387
	Rural	56	29	7	7	2	245
Region:	Northeast	51	29	9	10	1	227
	Midwest	54	30	8	6	2	228
	South	61	26	4	6	2	210
	Mountain	58	19	10	12	1	171
	Pacific	53	27	10	9	2	169
Born Again:	Yes	59	21	9	9	1	355
	No	53	30	7	8	2	650
Denominational Affiliation:	Evangelical	62	22	7	6	2	246
	Catholic	58	25	11	4	1	250
	Mainline	53	34	7	5	2	178
Church Attender:	Yes	57	26	9	7	1	623
	No	45	30	8	15	2	243

IS THERE ABSOLUTE TRUTH?

 Question: *Do you agree strongly, agree somewhat, disagree somewhat, or disagree strongly with the following statement: There is no such thing as absolute truth; different people can define truth in conflicting ways and still be correct.*

While it is a minority who wholeheartedly believe this perspective (28%), the majority of adults generally concur with this thinking (66%). Only one out of six adults strongly disagrees with this statement.

Age is clearly related to feelings on this matter. The older people are, the less likely they are to agree with the statement. Almost three-quarters of the Baby Busters (72%) agree that there is no absolute truth; the level declines to 56% among the elderly.

Geography appears to have some impact on these views, too. The bastions of diverse thought—the Pacific coast and the northeast—are home to the greatest concentrations of adults who reject the concept of absolute truth. The areas of the nation traditionally deemed part of the "Bible belt"—states in the midwest and south—have the lowest concentrations of people who dismiss the existence of absolute truth.

Perhaps most disappointing of all is the revelation that adults associated with mainline Protestant churches are more likely than all other adults to agree that there is no such thing as absolute truth (73% compared to 65%). We might expect such conclusions to be drawn from those who reject the Church—and indeed the unchurched segment (81%) is much more likely than the churched population (59%) to deny that there is absolute truth. For such an important and central element of the Christian community as the mainline adherents to dismiss absolute truth is truly an eye-opening statement about the spiritual condition of both the Church and the nation.

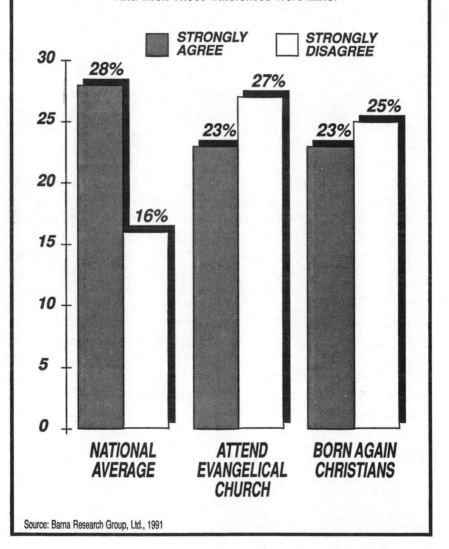

Only Among Born Again Christians and Those People Attending Evangelical Churches Is There a Greater Percentage of Adults Who Strongly Disagree than Strongly Agree that "There Is No Such Thing as Absolute Truth"

—And Even Those Differences Were Minor

STRONGLY AGREE   STRONGLY DISAGREE

NATIONAL AVERAGE: 28% / 16%
ATTEND EVANGELICAL CHURCH: 23% / 27%
BORN AGAIN CHRISTIANS: 23% / 25%

Source: Barna Research Group, Ltd., 1991

Q: Do you agree strongly, agree somewhat, disagree somewhat, or disagree strongly with the following statement: There is no such thing as absolute truth; different people can define truth in conflicting ways and still be correct.

		Agree Strongly	Agree Somewhat	Disagree Somewhat	Disagree Strongly	Don't Know	N
Total Population		28%	39%	13%	16%	5%	1005
Age:	18 to 25	30	42	17	9	2	190
	26-44	29	38	12	17	4	464
	45-54	24	40	11	20	4	141
	55-64	25	34	12	21	9	101
	65 or older	24	32	13	19	12	92
Education:	High school or less	26	37	16	15	7	453
	Some college	27	43	10	17	3	242
	College graduate	30	38	11	18	3	306
Ethnicity:	White	26	41	13	16	4	744
	Black	29	31	14	25	2	119
Household Income:	Under $20,000	26	37	15	17	6	184
	$20,000 to $39,999	29	37	14	16	4	397
	$40,000 to $59,999	26	43	11	17	4	186
	$60,000 or more	27	42	11	16	4	142
Gender:	Male	28	40	13	16	3	490
	Female	27	37	13	17	6	515
Married:	Yes	25	41	11	18	5	570
	No	31	36	15	14	4	432
Community:	Urban	32	38	13	14	3	340
	Suburban	23	44	12	16	5	387
	Rural	28	34	14	20	4	245
Region:	Northeast	30	44	12	13	3	227
	Midwest	31	36	14	15	5	228
	South	24	37	11	22	6	210
	Mountain	24	36	16	20	4	171
	Pacific	31	41	12	13	5	169
Born Again:	Yes	23	29	15	27	5	355
	No	30	44	12	10	5	650
Denominational Affiliation:	Evangelical	23	30	17	25	5	246
	Catholic	31	37	15	12	6	250
	Mainline	27	47	7	15	5	178
Church Attender:	Yes	23	36	14	21	6	623
	No	38	43	10	7	2	243

IS OUR FIRST RESPONSIBILITY TO OURSELVES?

 Question: *Do you agree strongly, agree somewhat, disagree somewhat, or disagree strongly with the following statement: When it comes right down to it, your first responsibility is to yourself.*

A slim majority of Americans (52%) agree that this is true.

Perhaps unexpectedly, among Baby Boomers—the generation that is reportedly the most self-indulgent, self-centered segment ever to represent this nation—a plurality actually disagree with this notion.

One of the largest subgroup differentials occurs in relation to single and married adults. Among married people, 45% agree with the statement while 53% disagree. This may be largely due to the feelings of responsibility toward their children. Single adults, in contrast, generally accept the statement at face value: 63% agree, while only 35% disagree.

Perhaps the "urban jungle" metaphor has some support in this question as well. Fifty-nine percent of urban residents agree with the statement compared to just 42% of rural residents.

Spiritual standing has the greatest impact on this issue. Born again Christians generally reject this idea, as 57% disagree and just 41% agree. Among non-Christians the reverse is true: 39% disagree but 58% agree. Denominationally, evangelicals and mainline Protestants are evenly split, while Catholics agree by a considerable margin (56% agree, 42% disagree). Church presence is related, as we find the churched evenly divided, but the unchurched clearly agreeing with the statement (59%, compared to 39% in disagreement).

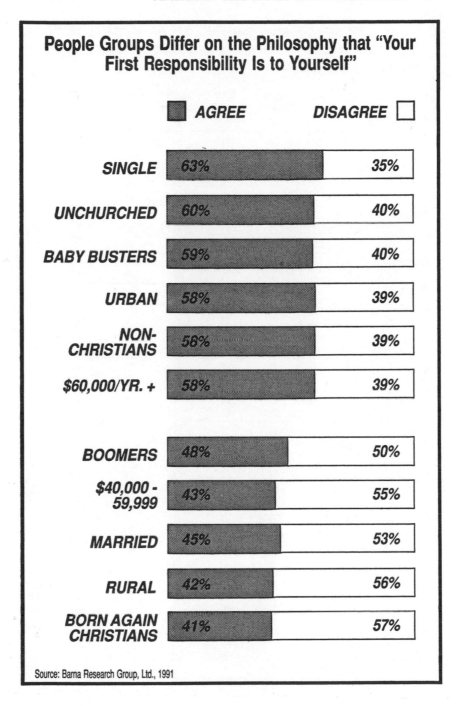

People Groups Differ on the Philosophy that "Your First Responsibility Is to Yourself"

■ AGREE   DISAGREE □

	AGREE	DISAGREE
SINGLE	63%	35%
UNCHURCHED	60%	40%
BABY BUSTERS	59%	40%
URBAN	58%	39%
NON-CHRISTIANS	56%	39%
$60,000/YR. +	58%	39%
BOOMERS	48%	50%
$40,000 - 59,999	43%	55%
MARRIED	45%	53%
RURAL	42%	56%
BORN AGAIN CHRISTIANS	41%	57%

Source: Barna Research Group, Ltd., 1991

Q: Do you agree strongly, agree somewhat, disagree somewhat, or disagree strongly with the following statement: When it comes right down to it, your first responsibility is to yourself.

		Agree Strongly	Agree Somewhat	Disagree Somewhat	Disagree Strongly	Don't Know	N
Total Population		26%	26%	22%	24%	2%	1005
Age:	18 to 25	29	31	16	24	1	190
	26-44	21	27	24	26	2	464
	45-54	31	24	19	23	2	141
	55-64	29	19	29	20	4	101
	65 or older	40	16	20	18	9	92
Education:	High school or less	30	21	22	25	2	453
	Some college	26	24	22	27	2	242
	College graduate	21	36	22	18	3	306
Ethnicity:	White	26	22	24	25	3	744
	Black	36	21	18	25	1	119
Household Income:	Under $20,000	31	24	18	25	3	184
	$20,000 to $39,999	27	26	21	24	2	397
	$40,000 to $59,999	16	27	28	27	2	186
	$60,000 or more	29	29	24	16	3	142
Gender:	Male	23	29	21	26	1	490
	Female	30	23	23	21	3	515
Married:	Yes	22	23	27	26	2	570
	No	33	30	15	20	2	432
Community:	Urban	28	31	21	19	2	340
	Suburban	28	26	20	24	2	387
	Rural	22	20	27	29	2	245
Region:	Northeast	24	26	24	24	2	227
	Midwest	31	22	22	24	1	228
	South	25	25	21	26	3	210
	Mountain	25	27	23	21	3	171
	Pacific	27	20	18	22	3	169
Born Again:	Yes	20	21	24	33	3	355
	No	30	28	21	18	2	650
Denominational Affiliation:	Evangelical	27	22	21	28	2	246
	Catholic	29	27	21	21	2	250
	Mainline	23	26	24	24	4	178
Church Attender:	Yes	24	24	22	27	3	623
	No	29	30	22	18	1	243

WHAT WE BELIEVE: GOODNESS, FULFILLMENT, AND REAL LIFE

6

ARE PEOPLE BASICALLY GOOD?

Question: *Do you agree strongly, agree somewhat, disagree somewhat, or disagree strongly with the following statement: People are basically good.*

More than four out of five adults (83%) contend that people are basically good. As individuals age, they are more likely to strongly believe that sentiment, ranging from 27% of the Busters firmly agreeing, to half of the elderly (50%).

Black adults are much less likely than whites to agree with this statement. Among whites 86% agree that people are basically good. Among blacks just 69% concur.

Born again Christians are less likely to buy into this notion (77%) than are non-Christians (87%), although a strong majority of believers accept the statement as accurate. The major denominational distinctive is between those associated with evangelical churches (74% agree with the statement) and Catholics (89%) and mainline Protestants (90%).

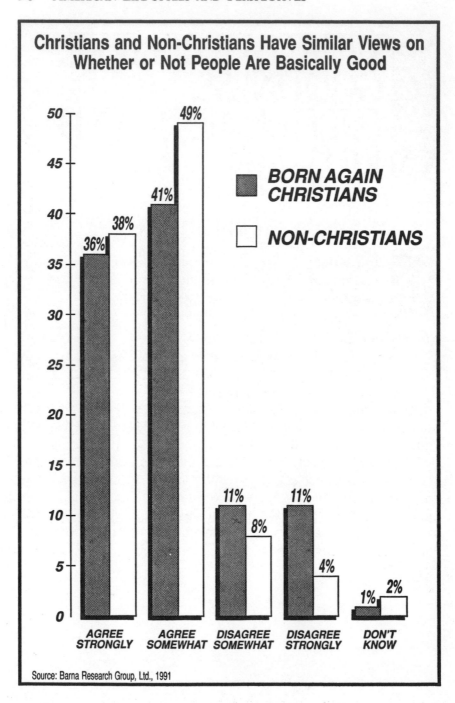

Christians and Non-Christians Have Similar Views on Whether or Not People Are Basically Good

- ■ BORN AGAIN CHRISTIANS
- □ NON-CHRISTIANS

	AGREE STRONGLY	AGREE SOMEWHAT	DISAGREE SOMEWHAT	DISAGREE STRONGLY	DON'T KNOW
Born Again Christians	36%	41%	11%	11%	1%
Non-Christians	38%	49%	8%	4%	2%

Source: Barna Research Group, Ltd., 1991

Q: Do you agree strongly, agree somewhat, disagree somewhat, or disagree strongly with the following statement: People are basically good.

		Agree Strongly	Agree Somewhat	Disagree Somewhat	Disagree Strongly	Don't Know	N
Total Population		37%	46%	9%	6%	2%	1005
Age:	18 to 25	27	55	9	9	*	190
	26-44	36	47	10	6	1	464
	45-54	40	41	10	7	2	141
	55-64	45	45	3	5	2	101
	65 or older	50	36	6	3	4	92
Education:	High school or less	40	44	9	5	2	453
	Some college	35	46	8	10	1	242
	College graduate	35	50	8	5	1	306
Ethnicity:	White	39	47	7	5	1	744
	Black	32	37	18	9	5	119
Household Income:	Under $20,000	34	47	10	6	4	184
	$20,000 to $39,999	38	44	10	7	1	397
	$40,000 to $59,999	33	51	8	7	1	186
	$60,000 or more	44	49	5	3	*	142
Gender:	Male	38	46	8	6	1	490
	Female	36	47	9	6	2	515
Married:	Yes	39	45	9	7	1	570
	No	36	48	9	5	2	432
Community:	Urban	40	45	8	6	2	340
	Suburban	33	52	9	5	2	387
	Rural	42	40	10	7	1	245
Region:	Northeast	39	42	12	5	2	227
	Midwest	42	46	7	5	1	228
	South	35	50	9	6	1	210
	Mountain	32	47	9	9	3	171
	Pacific	37	47	8	7	1	169
Born Again:	Yes	36	41	11	11	1	355
	No	38	49	8	4	2	650
Denominational Affiliation:	Evangelical	30	44	14	12	2	246
	Catholic	44	45	8	3	*	250
	Mainline	46	44	5	4	1	178
Church Attender:	Yes	40	43	9	7	1	623
	No	35	52	7	5	1	243

IS PERSONAL FULFILLMENT MOST IMPORTANT?

 Question: *Do you agree strongly, agree somewhat, disagree somewhat, or disagree strongly with the following statement: The purpose of life is enjoyment and personal fulfillment.*

While a majority do not buy into this philosophy with intensity, two out of three adults gave their assent to this statement (63%).

There are some significant differences among people groups on this matter, although a majority of each group examined accepts this statement as true for them. Men (68%) are more likely than women (58%) to agree; single adults (69%) are more likely than married adults to concur (59%); and people from urban and suburban areas (66%) are more likely than rural adults (57%) to agree.

Although equivalent proportions of the white (63%) and black (64%) populations agreed with the statement, notice that blacks are much more likely to strongly agree with the statement (40%) than are whites (26%).

Religious perspective also impacted views on this statement. Non-Christians are considerably more likely than believers to buy this sentiment (69% vs. 53%, respectively). Those attending evangelical churches (56%) are less likely to accept the statement than are Catholics (65%) or mainline Protestants (62%). An even bigger difference is evident between the churched adults (58% agreed) and the unchurched (77%). The fact remains, however, that even among the groups most involved in religious endeavors, the majority agreed that life is about personal satisfaction and fulfillment.

**The Following Population Groups Are at Least 20%
More Likely than Average to *Strongly Agree*
that the Main Purpose in Life Is Enjoyment
and Personal Fulfillment**

BLACKS
(43% MORE LIKELY)

UNCHURCHED
(35% MORE LIKELY)

**$20,000/YR.
OR LESS**
(23% MORE LIKELY)

**HIGH SCHOOL
OR LESS**
(21% MORE LIKELY)

Source: Barna Research Group, Ltd., 1991

Q: Do you agree strongly, agree somewhat, disagree somewhat, or disagree strongly with the following statement: The purpose of life is enjoyment and personal fulfillment.

		Agree Strongly	Agree Somewhat	Disagree Somewhat	Disagree Strongly	Don't Know	N
Total Population		28%	35%	21%	14%	2	1005
Age:	18 to 25	32	33	22	11	2	190
	26-44	25	36	22	16	1	464
	45-54	31	37	17	13	2	141
	55-64	31	33	18	17	1	101
	65 or older	33	28	25	11	3	92
Education:	High school or less	34	34	19	12	2	453
	Some college	24	36	23	17	1	242
	College graduate	24	36	23	15	2	306
Ethnicity:	White	26	37	21	14	2	744
	Black	40	24	20	14	1	119
Household Income:	Under $20,000	35	32	18	13	2	184
	$20,000 to $39,999	28	37	21	13	2	397
	$40,000 to $59,999	27	31	22	19	1	186
	$60,000 or more	22	38	26	13	1	142
Gender:	Male	32	36	17	14	1	490
	Female	24	34	26	15	2	515
Married:	Yes	26	33	22	18	2	570
	No	31	38	19	10	1	432
Community:	Urban	32	35	20	12	1	340
	Suburban	24	40	21	14	2	387
	Rural	27	30	23	19	2	245
Region:	Northeast	27	39	21	10	3	227
	Midwest	26	33	25	15	2	228
	South	29	36	20	13	2	210
	Mountain	31	29	20	20	*	171
	Pacific	29	37	18	15	1	169
Born Again:	Yes	25	28	22	23	2	355
	No	30	39	21	9	2	650
Denominational Affiliation:	Evangelical	26	30	21	22	2	246
	Catholic	29	36	23	12	*	250
	Mainline	23	39	21	15	2	178
Church Attender:	Yes	25	33	23	18	1	623
	No	38	39	15	8	*	243

DO MATERIAL POSSESSIONS DEFINE SUCCESS?

 Question: *Do you agree strongly, agree somewhat, disagree somewhat, or disagree strongly with the following statement: You can usually tell how successful a person is by examining what they own.*

The bumper sticker which reads "he who dies with the most toys wins" may be popular but it does not appear to fit with the prevailing image that people have of success. Only one out of five adults (20%) asserts that you can tell how successful persons are by examining what they own. Just 6% agree strongly with that notion. A majority of adults (51%) feel strongly that this statement is incorrect.

Unexpectedly, adults living in the Midwest are more than twice as likely as other Americans to agree strongly with this philosophy. There were no other demographic distinctions worthy of note, though. So while people strive for success, and our penchant for possessing material goods remains unquenched, relatively few people say that they would tally the value of another's possessions and assign the "success" label simply as a consequence of that bottom line.

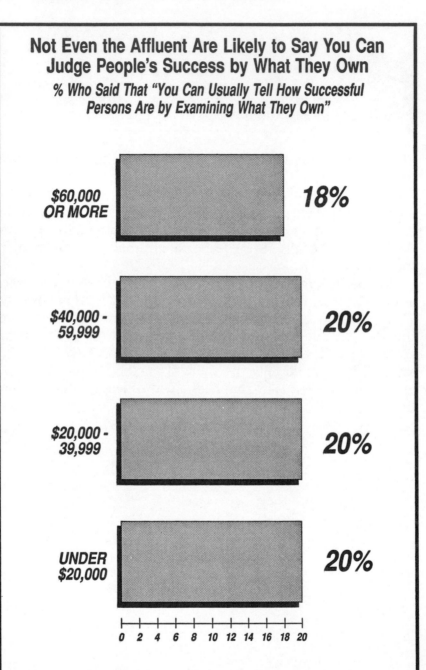

Not Even the Affluent Are Likely to Say You Can Judge People's Success by What They Own

% Who Said That "You Can Usually Tell How Successful Persons Are by Examining What They Own"

$60,000 OR MORE — **18%**

$40,000 - 59,999 — **20%**

$20,000 - 39,999 — **20%**

UNDER $20,000 — **20%**

0 2 4 6 8 10 12 14 16 18 20

Source: Barna Research Group, Ltd., 1991

Q: Do you agree strongly, agree somewhat, disagree somewhat, or disagree strongly with the following statement: You can usually tell how successful a person is by examining what they own.

		Agree Strongly	Agree Somewhat	Disagree Somewhat	Disagree Strongly	Don't Know	N
Total Population		6%	14%	28%	51%	1%	1005
Age:	18 to 25	10	14	20	56	1	190
	26-44	4	14	31	50	*	464
	45-54	4	15	27	54	1	141
	55-64	10	11	29	49	1	101
	65 or older	4	9	31	51	5	92
Education:	High school or less	10	14	26	49	1	453
	Some college	3	11	28	57	1	242
	College graduate	2	16	32	49	1	306
Ethnicity:	White	6	14	29	51	1	744
	Black	3	16	22	58	1	119
Household Income:	Under $20,000	7	13	26	53	2	184
	$20,000 to $39,999	6	13	25	55	1	397
	$40,000 to $59,999	5	15	31	49	*	186
	$60,000 or more	3	15	40	41	1	142
Gender:	Male	7	15	26	51	1	490
	Female	4	13	30	52	2	515
Married:	Yes	6	13	30	49	1	570
	No	6	15	25	54	1	432
Community:	Urban	5	12	27	55	1	340
	Suburban	5	17	32	46	1	387
	Rural	8	12	25	54	2	245
Region:	Northeast	4	16	26	53	1	227
	Midwest	11	11	34	44	1	228
	South	5	15	26	52	2	210
	Mountain	3	17	20	59	1	171
	Pacific	4	12	34	50	1	169
Born Again:	Yes	7	12	26	54	1	355
	No	5	15	29	50	1	650
Denominational Affiliation:	Evangelical	6	12	23	58	1	246
	Catholic	7	12	31	50	1	250
	Mainline	3	16	27	53	*	178
Church Attender:	Yes	6	15	27	51	1	623
	No	5	13	28	54	*	243

DO MOVIES AND TELEVISION REFLECT REAL LIFE?

Question: *Do you agree strongly, agree somewhat, disagree somewhat, or disagree strongly with the following statement: The values and life-styles shown in movies and television programs generally reflect the way most people live and think.*

People just don't buy this concept. The characters on the big and little screens may be fascinating, instructive, and entertaining, but only three out of ten adults agree that the people portrayed in the entertainment media are truly representative of the typical American.

By a substantial margin, Baby Busters are much more likely than older Americans to buy into this belief. Overall, 43% of Busters agreed with the statement, compared to just 28% of the remainder of the adult population.

Similarly, blacks (48%) are twice as likely as whites (24%) to agree that the people seen in movies and TV provide an accurate portrayal of life these days.

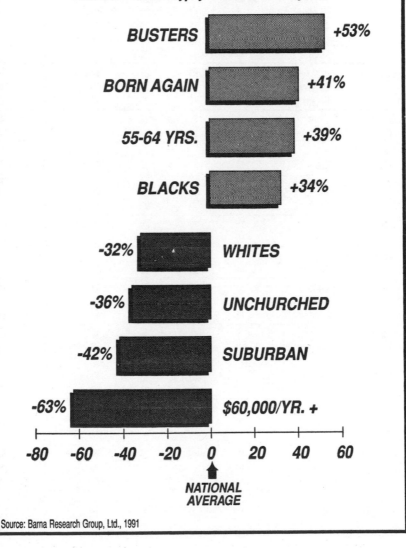

Do Movies and Television Really Reflect the Way We Live? Most People Say "No," But There Are Differences Among Population Segments

% of People in a Segment, Compared to the National Average, Who Agree Strongly That Movies and Television Shows Typify American Life-styles

BUSTERS   +53%

BORN AGAIN   +41%

55-64 YRS.   +39%

BLACKS   +34%

-32%   WHITES

-36%   UNCHURCHED

-42%   SUBURBAN

-63% $60,000/YR. +

-80 -60 -40 -20   0   20   40   60

NATIONAL AVERAGE

Source: Barna Research Group, Ltd., 1991

Q: Do you agree strongly, agree somewhat, disagree somewhat, or disagree strongly with the following statement: The values and life-styles shown in movies and television programs generally reflect the way most people live and think.

		Agree Strongly	Agree Somewhat	Disagree Somewhat	Disagree Strongly	Don't Know	N
Total Population		10%	19%	27%	41%	2%	1005
Age:	18 to 25	16	27	25	32	1	190
	26-44	8	21	29	41	1	464
	45-54	9	16	26	49	2	141
	55-64	15	10	21	51	3	101
	65 or older	9	14	33	37	7	92
Education:	High school or less	13	21	26	37	3	453
	Some college	8	21	27	44	1	242
	College graduate	9	15	29	45	2	306
Ethnicity:	White	7	17	29	45	3	744
	Black	24	24	24	27	1	119
Household Income:	Under $20,000	13	21	22	41	3	184
	$20,000 to $39,999	10	20	25	43	2	397
	$40,000 to $59,999	13	16	29	41	1	186
	$60,000 or more	4	17	35	43	1	142
Gender:	Male	11	19	28	40	2	490
	Female	10	20	26	43	2	515
Married:	Yes	10	18	27	43	2	570
	No	11	22	26	39	3	432
Community:	Urban	13	19	24	43	2	340
	Suburban	6	18	31	43	2	387
	Rural	13	22	25	39	2	245
Region:	Northeast	9	18	25	45	3	227
	Midwest	10	16	27	45	3	228
	South	11	24	30	32	3	210
	Mountain	10	18	22	48	2	171
	Pacific	12	21	30	35	2	169
Born Again:	Yes	15	18	24	42	1	355
	No	8	20	28	41	3	650
Denominational Affiliation:	Evangelical	12	19	27	39	3	246
	Catholic	10	17	27	45	1	250
	Mainline	10	16	29	43	3	178
Church Attender:	Yes	13	17	27	41	2	623
	No	7	20	27	45	2	243

IS IT BETTER TO GET EVEN THAN TO GET MAD?

 Question: *Do you agree strongly, agree somewhat, disagree somewhat, or disagree strongly with the following statement: It's better to get even than to get mad.*

This is a cute expression, perhaps, but not one which most people admit to living by. Only 15% of the public say they agree with this notion. The vast majority (60%) strongly disagree with the concept.

Baby Busters are twice as likely as the rest of the adult population to strongly agree with this philosophy. On the one hand, this attitude might be written off to their relative youth and lack of experience. On the other hand, if this expression does represent a belief deeply embraced, the nation may be in for an interesting, if potentially dangerous, era.

Born again Christians are considerably more likely than non-believers to strongly disagree with this approach (69% versus 54%, respectively). Adults associated with evangelical churches are also more likely than those attending Catholic or mainline churches to strongly disagree with this philosophy.

BE CAREFUL!

*These People Groups Are Much More Likely
than Average to Agree It's Better to
Get Even than to Get Mad*

MEN - 87% ABOVE AVERAGE

BABY BUSTERS - 53% ABOVE AVERAGE

CATHOLICS - 40% ABOVE AVERAGE

BLACKS - 27% ABOVE AVERAGE

SINGLES - 20% ABOVE AVERAGE
HIGH SCHOOL EDUCATION OR LESS - 20% ABOVE AVERAGE

← AVERAGE

Source: Barna Research Group, Ltd., 1991

Q: Do you agree strongly, agree somewhat, disagree somewhat, or disagree strongly with the following statement: It's better to get even than to get mad.

		Agree Strongly	Agree Somewhat	Disagree Somewhat	Disagree Strongly	Don't Know	N
Total Population		6%	9%	22%	60%	3%	1005
Age:	18 to 25	14	9	25	52	1	190
	26-44	4	9	21	63	3	464
	45-54	4	7	23	61	4	141
	55-64	5	9	22	61	3	101
	65 or older	6	11	25	51	7	92
Education:	High school or less	9	9	21	59	3	453
	Some college	4	7	26	61	3	242
	College graduate	4	10	22	60	4	306
Ethnicity:	White	6	8	24	60	3	744
	Black	9	10	18	60	4	119
Household Income:	Under $20,000	6	8	21	63	3	184
	$20,000 to $39,999	8	6	19	63	4	397
	$40,000 to $59,999	3	10	26	60	2	186
	$60,000 or more	1	16	31	50	2	142
Gender:	Male	18	10	24	54	4	490
	Female	5	7	20	65	3	515
Married:	Yes	5	8	22	63	3	570
	No	8	10	23	55	4	432
Community:	Urban	6	8	23	59	4	340
	Suburban	7	9	24	58	3	387
	Rural	6	8	20	64	3	245
Region:	Northeast	6	7	26	55	6	227
	Midwest	8	9	18	63	2	228
	South	6	9	26	56	3	210
	Mountain	5	7	22	65	1	171
	Pacific	5	11	18	61	5	169
Born Again:	Yes	5	6	19	69	1	355
	No	7	10	24	54	5	650
Denominational Affiliation:	Evangelical	6	9	15	68	2	246
	Catholic	7	14	18	59	2	250
	Mainline	3	8	29	57	3	178
Church Attender:	Yes	6	9	19	64	2	623
	No	6	8	27	56	3	243

7 OUR DAILY OUTLOOK, PROSPERITY, AND QUALITY TIME

HOW DO AMERICANS VIEW A NEW DAY—BETTER THAN THE DAY BEFORE?

> **Question:** Do you agree strongly, agree somewhat, disagree somewhat, or disagree strongly with the following statement: When you wake up in the morning you usually feel that the new day will be better than the day before.

More than four out of five adults adhere to a day-to-day optimism as described by this statement. In fact, two-fifths of adults (42%) strongly agree with the statement, while another two-fifths agree less intensely.

Observe the dramatic difference in perspective between those who are in the 55-64 age group and those who are 65 or older. While we frequently refer to retirement as the "golden years," these statistics suggest that many people living out their retirement years may not hold quite as sanguine a view. The 55-64-year-old group represents the most optimistic segment of all: more than half of them (55%) agree strongly that they usually believe the new day will be even better than the old. Among the senior citizens, however, the outlook is much different. Only 34%—the lowest total of any age group—strongly agree with this statement.

A gap of similar proportions exists between whites and blacks. About 37% of the whites strongly believe that each new day will be better than the next. That pales in comparison to the 61% among blacks who share that same conviction.

Faith may have an impact in this arena, as well. Notice that while born again Christians are no more likely than non-believers to admit to such optimism (86% vs. 83%, respectively), they are more likely to strongly ascribe to this viewpoint (47% vs. 39%, respectively). Interestingly, those aligned with evangelical churches (81%) are less likely than either Catholics (88%) or mainline Protestants (88%) to maintain this perspective.

When They Wake Up Each Morning, at Least Half of These Groups Usually Feel that the New Day Will Be Better than the Day Before

BLACKS (61%)

55 - 64 YEARS (55%)

RESIDENTS OF THE PACIFIC STATES (50%)

Source: Barna Research Group, Ltd., 1991

Q: Do you agree strongly, agree somewhat, disagree somewhat, or disagree strongly with the following statement: When you wake up in the morning you usually feel that the new day will be better than the day before.

		Agree Strongly	Agree Somewhat	Disagree Somewhat	Disagree Strongly	Don't Know	N
Total Population		42%	42%	10%	3%	3%	1005
Age:	18 to 25	40	47	8	4	2	190
	26-44	41	43	12	3	2	464
	45-54	42	41	11	3	4	141
	55-64	55	33	6	2	4	101
	65 or older	34	38	13	3	11	92
Education:	High school or less	48	37	11	3	3	453
	Some college	40	45	10	3	2	242
	College graduate	34	49	11	2	4	306
Ethnicity:	White	37	46	11	3	3	744
	Black	61	21	13	3	3	119
Household Income:	Under $20,000	43	39	9	4	5	184
	$20,000 to $39,999	41	41	12	3	3	397
	$40,000 to $59,999	42	45	10	3	1	186
	$60,000 or more	39	49	9	1	3	142
Gender:	Male	38	44	12	2	3	490
	Female	45	40	9	3	3	515
Married:	Yes	44	42	9	2	3	570
	No	39	43	12	3	3	432
Community:	Urban	43	42	10	2	4	340
	Suburban	40	47	9	2	2	387
	Rural	43	37	14	4	3	245
Region:	Northeast	36	42	16	3	4	227
	Midwest	40	48	9	2	2	228
	South	42	40	10	3	4	210
	Mountain	42	44	7	3	3	171
	Pacific	50	36	9	3	2	169
Born Again:	Yes	47	39	10	2	2	355
	No	39	44	11	3	4	650
Denominational Affiliation:	Evangelical	41	40	12	4	3	246
	Catholic	48	40	8	3	1	250
	Mainline	43	45	6	*	5	178
Church Attender:	Yes	45	42	9	2	2	623
	No	33	47	14	3	4	243

DOES EVERYONE HAVE A RIGHT TO FREEDOM AND PROSPERITY?

 Question: *Do you agree strongly, agree somewhat, disagree somewhat, or disagree strongly with the following statement: Everyone has a right to freedom and prosperity.*

For years, the "prosperity doctrine" ("prosperity is your divine right") has been popular among a certain segment of the public. Initially popularized by New Age leaders like Terry Cole-Whitaker, and quickly picked up and minimally adapted by some Christian televangelists, social analysts have lampooned this perspective as a self-styled mixture of ideas drawn from the Constitution of the United States, the Bible, and hearts filled with greed.

It may come as a disappointment to some—but apparently not many—that the vast majority of American adults accept this statement as truth. Four out of five people agree strongly with the sentiment expressed in this statement. More than nine out of ten people (96%) agree to some extent with it. This is about as close to a consensus as you'll find when examining attitudinal data.

The extreme level of agreement renders it difficult to identify differences across population subgroups. Notice, though, that the elderly are the least likely age segment to strongly agree with this statement (66%), while blacks are more likely than whites to strongly affirm the notion (88%, compared to 77% among whites).

Born again Christians hold the same views as non-Christians on this matter. Neither church affiliation nor church attendance makes any difference in people's attitudes on this issue.

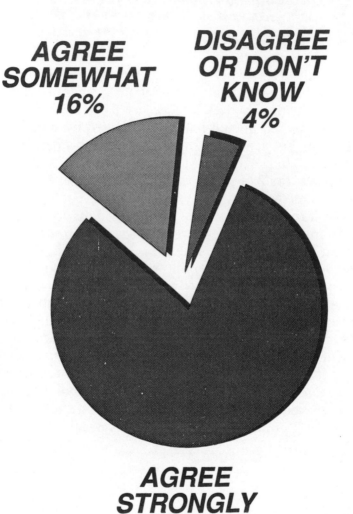

Most People Strongly Agree That "Everyone Has a Right to Freedom and Prosperity"

AGREE SOMEWHAT 16%

DISAGREE OR DON'T KNOW 4%

AGREE STRONGLY 80%

Source: Barna Research Group, Ltd., 1991

Q: Do you agree strongly, agree somewhat, disagree somewhat, or disagree strongly with the following statement: Everyone has a right to freedom and prosperity.

		Agree Strongly	Agree Somewhat	Disagree Somewhat	Disagree Strongly	Don't Know	N
Total Population		80%	16%	2%	1%	1%	1005
Age:	18 to 25	85	14	1	*	*	190
	26-44	80	17	2	1	1	464
	45-54	81	15	2	1	1	141
	55-64	76	17	5	*	2	101
	65 or older	66	19	7	3	5	92
Education:	High school or less	81	16	1	*	1	453
	Some college	80	16	3	1	1	242
	College graduate	77	16	3	1	2	306
Ethnicity:	White	77	18	3	1	1	744
	Black	88	8	2	1	1	119
Household Income:	Under $20,000	76	20	2	2	1	184
	$20,000 to $39,999	83	13	2	1	1	397
	$40,000 to $59,999	79	18	1	1	2	186
	$60,000 or more	81	17	2	*	*	142
Gender:	Male	81	15	2	1	*	490
	Female	78	17	2	1	2	515
Married:	Yes	76	18	3	1	1	570
	No	83	13	2	1	1	432
Community:	Urban	82	15	2	1	1	340
	Suburban	80	15	3	*	1	387
	Rural	77	18	2	2	1	245
Region:	Northeast	80	14	4	1	1	227
	Midwest	78	19	2	*	1	228
	South	81	15	1	2	2	210
	Mountain	80	14	4	1	2	171
	Pacific	81	17	1	1	*	169
Born Again:	Yes	79	16	3	2	1	355
	No	80	16	2	1	2	650
Denominational Affiliation:	Evangelical	79	17	2	1	1	246
	Catholic	82	16	2	*	*	250
	Mainline	77	17	4	1	1	178
Church Attender:	Yes	78	17	3	1	1	623
	No	84	14	*	1	1	243

WHAT'S MORE IMPORTANT IN A RELATIONSHIP—QUANTITY OR QUALITY OF TIME?

Question: *Do you agree strongly, agree somewhat, disagree somewhat, or disagree strongly with the following statement: The important thing in a relationship is not how much time you spend together but the quality of time spent together.*

Once again, adults overwhelmingly indicate that this statement represents a true perspective for them. Two-thirds (67%) strongly agree with the statement; the cumulative proportion who agree to some extent with this philosophy is 90%.

The only distinctions between subgroups relate to the intensity with which this statement is supported. Blacks are more likely than whites to strongly agree (79% compared to 66%, respectively). Adults living in the southwest and mountain states are the least likely to strongly concur with this statement (61%).

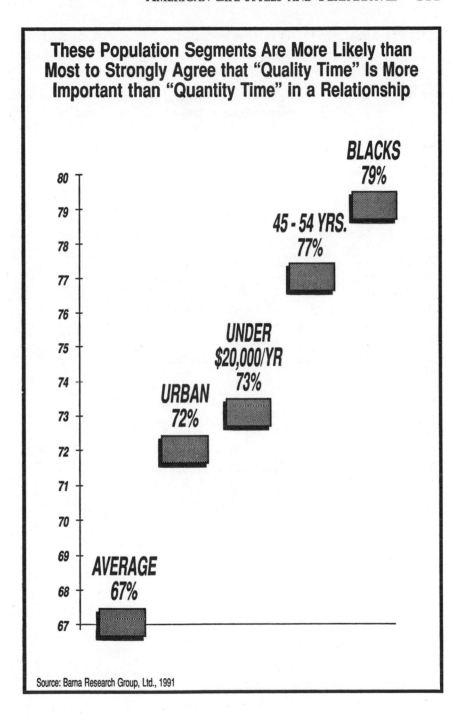

These Population Segments Are More Likely than Most to Strongly Agree that "Quality Time" Is More Important than "Quantity Time" in a Relationship

BLACKS
79%

45 - 54 YRS.
77%

UNDER
$20,000/YR
73%

URBAN
72%

AVERAGE
67%

Source: Barna Research Group, Ltd., 1991

Q: Do you agree strongly, agree somewhat, disagree somewhat, or disagree strongly with the following statement: The important thing in a relationship is not how much time you spend together but the quality of time spent together.

		Agree Strongly	Agree Somewhat	Disagree Somewhat	Disagree Strongly	Don't Know	N
Total Population		67%	23%	7%	2%	1%	1005
Age:	18 to 25	64	23	8	4	1	190
	26-44	64	26	7	3	1	464
	45-54	77	18	3	1	1	141
	55-64	68	20	9	2	2	101
	65 or older	70	20	6	1	3	92
Education:	High school or less	69	20	5	4	2	453
	Some college	69	24	6	2	*	242
	College graduate	62	26	10	2	1	306
Ethnicity:	White	66	24	7	2	1	744
	Black	79	11	5	1	4	119
Household Income:	Under $20,000	73	17	5	4	2	184
	$20,000 to $39,999	66	24	8	1	1	397
	$40,000 to $59,999	64	25	6	4	*	186
	$60,000 or more	69	23	6	2	*	142
Gender:	Male	64	25	6	3	2	490
	Female	70	21	7	2	1	515
Married:	Yes	67	23	7	3	1	570
	No	67	22	6	2	2	432
Community:	Urban	72	21	6	1	1	340
	Suburban	62	26	7	4	1	387
	Rural	68	22	8	1	2	245
Region:	Northeast	70	20	8	1	1	227
	Midwest	65	28	4	3	*	228
	South	68	22	6	3	1	210
	Mountain	61	24	8	5	2	171
	Pacific	71	19	7	1	2	169
Born Again:	Yes	70	20	7	2	1	355
	No	66	24	6	3	2	650
Denominational Affiliation:	Evangelical	68	21	7	3	1	246
	Catholic	67	26	6	1	*	250
	Mainline	67	23	8	2	1	178
Church Attender:	Yes	67	22	7	2	1	623
	No	67	25	5	3	*	243

MEDIA AND ELECTRONICS

SECTION HIGHLIGHTS:

◆ While Christians are just as likely as non-Christians to own an answering machine, a VCR, a cellular car phone, or satellite dish, they are somewhat less likely to own a compact disc player or a home computer.

◆ Among VCR owners, the most popular types of videos to rent or purchase are movies. About one out of six VCR owners claimed they had rented or bought a "Christian teaching or entertainment" video within the past year.

◆ Between one-half and one-third of the adult population who consider themselves to be Christian had engaged in each of the five Christian media forms tested: watched religious television, listened to Christian music on the radio, read a Christian magazine, listened to Christian teaching or preaching on the radio, and read a Christian book other than the Bible.

IN BRIEF

MEDIA AND HOUSEHOLD ELECTRONIC EQUIPMENT PLAY AN increasingly important role in the lives of Americans. While we appear to be shifting our loyalties between media, and shifting our leisure habits accordingly, there can be little argument with the notion that America is "wired."

Technology Growth Patterns

After several years of explosive growth, VCR ownership has plateaued. Not quite four out of five households (78%) own at least one VCR. Telephone answering machines have found their way into half of the nation's homes (49%). Although they have been in the consumer market for just a few years, compact disc players are now in 30% of all households, while personal computers for home use are owned by one-quarter of the population (26%).

Some of the newer, more exotic equipment is much less commonly owned. Cellular car telephones, for instance, are possessed by just 7% of the population. Satellite dishes used for television reception are owned by 6% of U.S. households, while only 2% currently have a fax machine for home use.

Who Owns What?

Born again Christians are somewhat less likely to own a compact disc player than are non-Christians. They are also somewhat less likely to have a home computer. The other pieces of electronic equipment studied are equally likely to be in the homes of Christians and non-Christians.

As might be expected, older adults are less likely than younger adults to own any given piece of electronic equipment. People who have lower levels of education and income are also less likely than others to own such equipment. People in the suburbs are more inclined than either urban or rural residents to own such items.

Popular Videos

Among VCR owners, the most popular type of pre-recorded videos to rent or purchase are movies. Over the course of the last year, almost nine out of ten VCR owners have either rented or purchased a movie. For each of the four other video genres evaluated, roughly one-fifth of the VCR owners had obtained cassettes of that type of recording. Those genres included sports events, musical performances, exercise or fitness, and Christian teaching or entertainment.

Despite the high overall appeal of movies, the older a person is, the less likely he or she is to view movies on video. Born again Christians were also less likely than non-Christians to see movies on videotape.

Christian Videos and Christian Media

When it comes to Christian teaching or entertainment, blacks, low-income adults, born again Christians, and those associated with evangelical churches are the most prolific audience segments. Less than one out of ten Catholics had watched Christian videos in the past year, compared to three out of ten among those who attend an evangelical church.

Among adults who call themselves "Christian" (as opposed to Jewish, Buddhist, Muslim, or some other religious label), about half (48%) had watched a religious television program in the past year. Slightly fewer people (44%) had listened to Christian music on the radio or say they read a Christian magazine (42%). Two-fifths say they have listened to radio programming featuring Christian teaching or preaching within the past year, while 36% of the self-described Christians say they have read a Christian book other than the Bible during the preceding 12 months.

Among those who say they are Christian but who do not attend a church, large proportions claim exposure to Christian media. For instance, one-third say they have watched religious television; one-quarter have read a Christian magazine; the same proportion have heard Christian teaching or preaching on the radio; one-fifth have listened to Christian music on the radio; and one-fifth have read a Christian book other than the Bible.

Overall, the people groups most likely to engage in the Christian media are older adults (pre-Boomers); those with lower levels of education and income; blacks; born again Christians; residents of the southern and mountain states; and those associated with evangelical churches.

On average, born again Christians are twice as likely to have exposure to any of these sources of spiritual content as are non-Christians. (The average proportion of Christians exposed to any of these five religious-oriented media is 60%; among non-believers the average is 30%.)

8 WHAT WE OWN: VCRs TO VIDEOTAPES

WHAT ELECTRONIC GOODS ARE WE BUYING?

Question: *Which, if any, of the following types of equipment does your household own? A VCR; a cellular telephone for your car; a fax machine for your home; a home computer; a compact disc player; a satellite dish for television reception; a telephone answering machine.*

VCRs

VCR ownership has plateaued after nearly a decade of strong, rapid growth. Three-quarters of all households now contain at least one VCR. Ownership appears related to the life stage of the user, though. Only seven out of ten Busters own a VCR, despite their penchant for movies and entertainment.

Boomers and those in the 45-54 age bracket are more likely to own a VCR: 85% have a unit. Ownership levels then decline with age, to 69% among the 55-64 age group, and 57% among seniors. Note, however, that this represents a dramatic increase among the elderly.

Socioeconomic status is also related to VCR ownership: people from households earning more than $20,000 are 45% more likely than less affluent individuals to own a VCR, while those who have either attended or graduated from college are 22% more likely than those who have not done so to own a video machine.

As has been true for years, married adults are more likely to own a VCR primarily because of their children and their higher household income level.

Religious beliefs or affiliations have little apparent relation to VCR ownership.

Answering Machine

Telephone answering machines are found in about half of all households (49%). The types of homes in which they are least common are those headed by an elderly person (only 19% have a machine); those headed by people with lower levels of education and income; and people living outside of suburbia.

Households in the Pacific coast region are the most likely, geographically speaking, to have an answering machine (57%).

Compact Disc Player

Although it has only been around for a few years, the compact disc player can now be found in 30% of all households. Not surprisingly, the people most likely to have adopted this music machine are Busters (44%), the affluent, and people living in the suburbs.

Also worthy of note is the fact that CD players are having a tougher time gaining entry into the homes of born again Christians. Just 25% of the born again Christian population own a CD player, compared to 33% among the non-Christian public.

Home Computer

Home computers are taking longer to penetrate the market than many electronic experts initially predicted. To date, only one out of every four homes (26%) contains a personal computer.

Relatively few people over 55 years of age own one; college graduates are twice as likely as those who never attended college to have a PC; and adults from households whose earnings top $60,000 a year are more than twice as likely as people from households with cumulative incomes of under $40,000 to own a computer. Born again Christians were also significantly less likely than non-Christians to own PCs.

Cellular Phone

Among the less widespread technologies, 7% of all adults own a cellular car phone. This instrument is definitely a resource of the upper class: 20% of those earning $60,000 or more have such a telephone, compared to just 5% among all other adults.

Satellite Dish and Fax Machine

Satellite dishes used for television reception are owned by 6% of the populace. Fax machines are currently found in only 2% of all homes. Once again, income is the dominant distinguishing factor: those from homes earning $60,000 or more per year are more than four times as likely as other adults to have a fax unit in their residence.

Behind the Times?

Interestingly, the evidence points to born again Christians as "late adopters." Past research showed that Christians were slower than others to embrace VCRs, although they have since caught up. The same pattern appears to be in evidence regarding ownership of CD players and personal computers. If the pattern holds true, Christians will reach ownership levels comparable to that of non-Christians within the next few years.

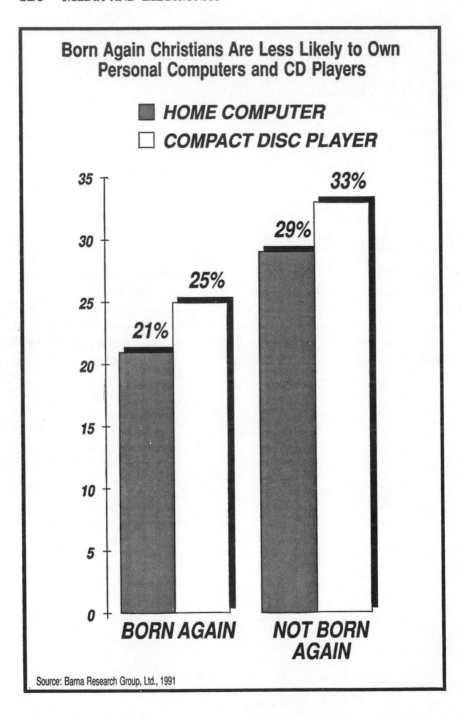

Born Again Christians Are Less Likely to Own
Personal Computers and CD Players

■ *HOME COMPUTER*
□ *COMPACT DISC PLAYER*

Source: Barna Research Group, Ltd., 1991

Q: Which, if any, of the following types of equipment does your household own? (See next page for column headings.)

		#1	#2	#3	#4	#5	#6	#7	N
Total Population		78%	7%	2%	26%	30%	6%	49%	1005
Age:	18 to 25	70	8	3	31	44	12	53	190
	26-44	87	7	3	30	32	4	53	464
	45-54	78	9	3	26	22	6	51	141
	55-64	69	4	2	16	22	4	48	101
	65 or older	57	6	1	8	13	4	19	92
Education:	High school or less	69	5	1	17	25	6	38	453
	Some college	88	7	2	26	35	8	56	242
	College graduate	82	8	5	40	34	5	58	306
Ethnicity:	White	77	7	2	26	27	4	50	744
	Black	72	7	2	17	32	8	48	119
Household Income:	Under $20,000	58	1	2	13	17	5	34	184
	$20,000 to $39,999	78	5	2	20	28	5	47	397
	$40,000 to $59,999	89	8	1	34	33	4	57	186
	$60,000 or more	94	20	9	52	53	9	72	142
Gender:	Male	80	7	2	28	36	7	49	490
	Female	76	6	3	24	25	5	48	515
Married:	Yes	84	7	2	27	27	5	48	570
	No	70	6	3	25	35	8	49	432
Community:	Urban	79	7	2	26	28	7	48	340
	Suburban	80	9	4	31	39	3	56	387
	Rural	74	5	*	21	19	8	41	245
Region:	Northeast	76	6	4	25	35	2	47	227
	Midwest	78	8	1	26	25	2	47	228
	South	78	5	2	23	26	10	48	210
	Mountain	73	8	1	28	32	7	45	171
	Pacific	86	8	5	28	32	10	57	169
Born Again:	Yes	76	7	2	21	25	6	46	355
	No	79	7	3	29	33	6	50	650
Denominational Affiliation:	Evangelical	74	6	1	19	27	6	46	246
	Catholic	81	7	3	26	32	4	44	250
	Mainline	80	8	2	26	24	3	49	178
Church Attender:	Yes	79	8	3	24	28	5	47	623
	No	76	6	2	31	34	6	53	243

Columns:

#1 A VCR

#2 A cellular telephone for your car

#3 A home fax machine

#4 A home computer

#5 A compact disc player

#6 A satellite dish for TV reception

#7 A telephone answering machine

WHAT TYPES OF VIDEOS DO AMERICANS RENT AND PURCHASE?

Question: *Which, if any, of the following types of pre-recorded videotapes did you or other members of your household either rent or purchase during the last 12 months? Movies; sports; music; exercise or fitness; Christian teaching or entertainment. (Note: based on responses of VCR owners.)*

Movies

Movies are, of course, the most popular category of pre-recorded videos for people to rent or purchase. Almost nine out of ten VCR owners (85%) have rented or bought such a video in the last 12 months. The probability of having done so decreases the older a person gets: while 94% of Busters have obtained a pre-recorded movie to see at home, the proportions decrease consistently to the point where barely half of senior citizens who own a VCR (54%) had done so.

Sports

Sports events have been acquired by one-fifth of the VCR owners in the past year (22%). Among the most likely segments to have gotten a sports video are men, blacks, single adults, and those who attend church services.

Music

Music videos, rented or purcnased by one-fifth of the aggregate audience (21%), are most popular among Busters (29%), blacks (29%), singles (26%), and residents of the northeast (26%). Again, churched adults are more likely than the unchurched to seek out music videos (22% versus 14%, respectively).

Exercise or Fitness

One-fifth of all adults who own a VCR (19%) say they have obtained an exercise or physical fitness video within the past year. The people groups most likely to do so are women (24%) and those from households earning $60,000 or more annually (27%).

Christian Teaching or Entertainment

Pre-recorded videotapes of Christian teaching or entertainment have been rented or bought by 17% of the universe of VCR owners within the last year. These tapes are more appealing to individuals with comparatively low levels of education and income; to black adults; born again Christians; those attending evangelical churches; and churched adults overall. Of particular interest is the finding that Catholic adults are only half as likely as the population at-large to get a Christian video (9%, compared to the 17% aggregate). Also worthy of note is the fact that those attending evangelical churches were twice as likely as those associated with mainline congregations to view a Christian video (29% vs. 13%, respectively).

Who Is the Most Likely to Rent Christian Videotapes?

Score Range	Level	Segments
130 OR MORE	WAY ABOVE AVERAGE	*BORN AGAIN CHRISTIANS (171)* *ATTEND EVANGELICAL CHURCH (171)* *BLACKS (165)* *UNDER $20,000/YR. (147)* *65 OR OLDER (141)*
129 TO 111	ABOVE AVERAGE	*HIGH SCHOOL OR LESS (124)* *MARRIED (112)* *RURAL (111)*
110 TO 90	AVERAGE	*URBAN (100)*
89 TO 71	BELOW AVERAGE	*SUBURBAN (88)* *ATTEND MAINLINE PROT. CHURCH (76)* *SINGLE (76)* *COLLEGE GRADUATES (71)*
70 OR LESS	WAY BELOW AVERAGE	*$60,000/YR. OR MORE (53)* *ATTEND CATHOLIC CHURCH (53)*

Indexes are standardized scores. Index scores below the population index (i.e. 100) indicate population segments that are less likely to have the test attribute; segments with scores above the base index are more likely to engage in that behavior. The larger the difference from the base index, the more the segment differs from the norm.

Source: Barna Research Group, Ltd., 1991

Q: Which, if any, of the following types of pre-recorded videotapes did you or other members of your household either rent or purchase during the last 12 months? Movies; sports; music; exercise or fitness; Christian teaching or entertainment. (Note: based on responses of VCR owners.)

		Movies	Sports	Music	Exercise/ Fitness	Christian Teaching or Entertainment	N
Total Population		85%	22%	21%	19%	17%	781
Age:	18 to 25	94	26	29	16	14	132
	26-44	90	22	19	21	17	403
	45-54	81	20	23	20	20	111
	55-64	68	23	19	14	12	70
	65 or older	54	12	16	15	22	52
Education:	High school or less	83	23	18	17	21	314
	Some college	87	19	26	21	16	213
	College graduate	86	21	20	20	12	252
Ethnicity:	White	85	21	20	19	13	569
	Black	79	30	29	21	28	86
Household Income:	Under $20,000	85	18	18	11	25	107
	$20,000 to $39,999	84	24	23	18	17	311
	$40,000 to $59,999	87	21	22	22	17	166
	$60,000 or more	89	25	17	27	9	133
Gender:	Male	84	26	17	14	17	391
	Female	86	17	24	24	17	390
Married:	Yes	84	19	18	17	19	477
	No	86	25	26	21	13	304
Community:	Urban	86	18	19	16	17	268
	Suburban	84	24	21	22	15	309
	Rural	87	22	22	19	19	181
Region:	Northeast	90	18	26	20	15	172
	Midwest	89	22	18	22	16	178
	South	85	25	20	15	18	162
	Mountain	82	23	21	20	21	124
	Pacific	78	20	19	18	14	145
Born Again:	Yes	80	19	20	20	29	271
	No	88	23	21	18	10	511
Denominational Affiliation:	Evangelical	83	21	19	18	29	183
	Catholic	91	22	22	20	9	201
	Mainline	80	23	22	20	13	142
Church Attender:	Yes	85	23	22	19	20	489
	No	84	13	14	18	6	184

9 RELIGIOUS TV, MAGAZINES, BOOKS, AND RADIO

ARE WE WATCHING RELIGIOUS TELEVISION?

 Question: *During the past year, have you watched a religious television program?*

Among people who call themselves "Christian" (as opposed to Jewish, Muslim, Buddhist, or some other broad-based faith label), nearly half (48%) say they have watched a religious television program during the past year.

Marked Distinctions

There is a clear dividing line between those under 45 (i.e. Boomers and Busters) and those who are 45 or older. Among the younger group, 44% have watched such programming in the past year; among the older adults 58% have done so. This correlates to the stronger levels of interest and activity related to religion that is consistently evident among older adults.

Viewing of religious television by self-described "Christians" is also most prolific among those with lower levels of education, among married people, and among people living in the south, southwest, and mountain states. Blacks (67%) are nearly 50% more likely than whites (44%) to view such programming.

Relationship Between Viewership and Religiosity

Religious involvement also relates strongly to watching religious television. Born again Christians (66%) are almost twice as likely to

watch such programming as non-Christians (36%). People attending evangelical churches (64%) are twice as likely as Catholics (34%)
and considerably more likely than those attending mainline Protestant churches (48%) to watch such programming. Church attenders
(53%) are also more likely than the unchurched (33%) to spend
time absorbing this type of programming.

   Not to be overlooked is the fact that among people who are
"nominally" Christian—i.e. think of themselves as Christian but are
not active in the Christian faith—one-third or so have exposure to
religious input through television. While past studies have revealed
that religious television does not generally act as a substitute for
involvement in a church, there remain many adults (perhaps as
many as 50 million adults) who utilize televised religious teaching
and services as one of their major inputs about their faith.

Religious Television Reaches People Who Call Themselves "Christian" but Who Are Not Integrally Involved in Their Faith

Source: Barna Research Group, Ltd., 1991

Q: During the past year, have you watched a religious television program? (Among those who describe themselves as "Christian.")

		Yes	No	Don't Know	N
Total Population		48%	52%	*	825
Age:	18 to 25	43	58	*	136
	26-44	44	56	*	400
	45-54	56	44	*	116
	55-64	56	44	*	87
	65 or older	58	42	*	83
Education:	High school or less	53	47	*	388
	Some college	46	54	*	203
	College graduate	43	57	*	233
Ethnicity:	White	44	56	*	625
	Black	67	33	*	100
Household Income:	Under $20,000	52	49	*	154
	$20,000 to $39,999	48	52	*	328
	$40,000 to $59,999	53	47	*	153
	$60,000 or more	40	60	*	110
Gender:	Male	46	54	*	387
	Female	50	50	*	438
Married:	Yes	51	49	*	496
	No	44	56	*	329
Community:	Urban	45	55	*	267
	Suburban	49	51	*	317
	Rural	52	48	*	216
Region:	Northeast	39	61	1	164
	Midwest	41	59	*	201
	South	62	38	*	183
	Mountain	60	40	*	144
	Pacific	39	61	*	133
Born Again:	Yes	66	34	*	338
	No	36	64	*	487
Denominational Affiliation:	Evangelical	64	36	*	246
	Catholic	34	66	*	250
	Mainline	48	52	*	178
Church Attender:	Yes	53	48	*	623
	No	33	67	*	170

ARE WE LISTENING TO CHRISTIAN RADIO STATIONS?

 Question: *During the past year, have you listened to a radio station that was playing Christian music?*

About two out of every five adults (44%) who call themselves Christian claim they have listened to Christian music on the radio during the past year.

The segments most likely to listen to Christian music broadcast over the airwaves are those in the 45-64 age bracket (53%); adults who have not graduated from college (48%); blacks (76%); rural residents (51%); and people living in the southern (51%) or south-west/mountain areas (50%). The data also point out that the higher a person's household income is, the less likely they are to listen to Christian music played on the radio.

It is interesting that while young adults are generally those who are the most prolific audience for music broadcast on the radio, they are among the *least* likely to listen to *Christian* music on the radio. This can be interpreted not so much as a rejection of Christian music as a reflection of the fact that comparatively few markets have stations that feature Christian music (and especially few that emphasize contemporary Christian music).

Not surprisingly, among the religious segments of the population, those who are born again (66%), who attend evangelical churches (66%), and who regularly attend church services (50%) are much more likely than other religious subgroups (e.g. Catholics, mainline Protestants, non-Christians, the unchurched) to listen to Christian music on radio.

Christian Music on the Radio Is Listened to in the South, Southwest, and Mountain States More than Elsewhere

% of Self-described Christians Who Listened to Christian Music on the Radio in the Past 12 Months

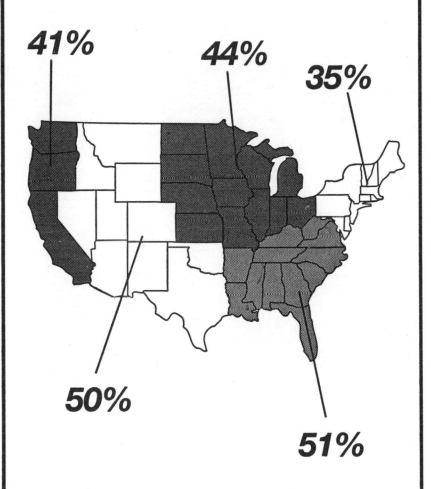

41%

44%

35%

50%

51%

Source: Barna Research Group, Ltd., 1991

Q: During the past year, have you listened to a radio station that was playing Christian music? (Among those who describe themselves as "Christian.")

		Yes	No	Don't Know	N
Total Population		44%	56%	*	825
Age:	18 to 25	38	62	*	136
	26-44	41	58	1	400
	45-54	52	48	*	116
	55-64	53	47	*	87
	65 or older	46	54	*	83
Education:	High school or less	48	52	*	388
	Some college	45	55	*	203
	College graduate	38	62	1	233
Ethnicity:	White	41	58	1	625
	Black	76	24	*	100
Household Income:	Under $20,000	52	48	*	154
	$20,000 to $39,999	46	54	*	328
	$40,000 to $59,999	44	55	1	153
	$60,000 or more	27	72	1	110
Gender:	Male	43	57	1	387
	Female	46	54	*	438
Married:	Yes	45	54	1	496
	No	43	57	*	329
Community:	Urban	39	61	*	267
	Suburban	43	57	*	317
	Rural	51	48	1	216
Region:	Northeast	35	64	1	164
	Midwest	44	56	*	201
	South	51	49	*	183
	Mountain	50	50	1	144
	Pacific	41	59	*	133
Born Again:	Yes	66	34	*	338
	No	29	70	1	487
Denominational Affiliation:	Evangelical	66	34	*	246
	Catholic	26	74	*	250
	Mainline	36	63	1	178
Church Attender:	Yes	50	50	*	623
	No	22	78	*	170

ARE WE LISTENING TO RELIGIOUS TEACHING ON THE RADIO?

 Question: *During the past year, have you listened to Christian preaching or teaching on the radio?*

About two out of five people who call themselves Christian indicate that they have heard Christian preaching or teaching programs on the radio during the past year (38%).

The segments of the population most likely to have heard such programming are those 45 or older; those who have not attended college; blacks (who are twice as likely as whites to listen to these types of broadcasts); lower income households; and residents of the south, southwest, and mountain states.

As might be expected, we also learned that born again Christians (59%) are more likely than people who call themselves Christian but are not born again to listen to such programming (26%). Adults attending evangelical churches (61%) are three times as likely as those attending Catholic churches (21%) and nearly twice as likely as those aligned with mainline congregations (35%) to tune in such broadcasts. Churched adults (43%) are also somewhat more likely than unchurched people who consider themselves to be Christian (25%) to hear these broadcasts.

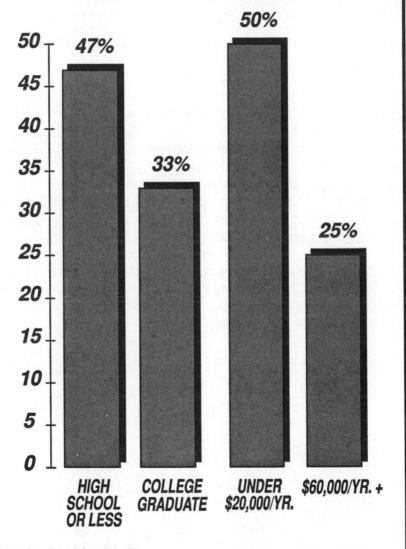

Christian Teaching and Preaching on Radio Appeals to the "Downscale" Audience

% of Self-described Christians Who Listened to Christian Preaching and Teaching on the Radio in the Last 12 Months

Source: Barna Research Group, Ltd., 1991

Q: During the past year, have you listened to Christian preaching or teaching on the radio? (Among those who describe themselves as "Christian.")

		Yes	No	Don't Know	N
Total Population		38%	62%	*	825
Age:	18 to 25	38	62	*	136
	26-44	34	66	1	400
	45-54	49	51	1	116
	55-64	52	49	*	87
	65 or older	44	56	*	63
Education:	High school or less	47	53	*	388
	Some college	33	67	*	203
	College graduate	33	67	*	233
Ethnicity:	White	35	64	*	625
	Black	70	30	*	100
Household Income:	Under $20,000	50	50	*	154
	$20,000 to $39,999	42	58	*	328
	$40,000 to $59,999	36	64	*	153
	$60,000 or more	25	75	1	110
Gender:	Male	41	59	*	387
	Female	38	62	*	438
Married:	Yes	40	59	*	496
	No	38	62	*	329
Community:	Urban	35	65	*	267
	Suburban	40	61	*	317
	Rural	44	55	1	216
Region:	Northeast	30	69	1	164
	Midwest	36	64	*	201
	South	50	50	*	183
	Mountain	46	54	1	144
	Pacific	34	66	*	133
Born Again:	Yes	59	41	*	338
	No	26	74	1	487
Denominational Affiliation:	Evangelical	61	40	*	246
	Catholic	21	79	*	250
	Mainline	35	64	1	178
Church Attender:	Yes	43	56	*	623
	No	25	75	1	170

ARE WE READING CHRISTIAN MAGAZINES?

 Question: *During the past year, have you read a Christian magazine?*

The proportion of self-described Christians who say they have read a Christian magazine is startlingly high (42%). This may well have to do with what people consider to be a Christian magazine. In many cases, this includes not just the subscription-based Christian publications (e.g. *Moody, Christian Herald*), but also includes the free, mass distribution magazines from parachurch ministries (such as *Focus on the Family* magazine, *World Vision* magazine, and *Decision* from the Billy Graham Evangelistic Association). We are aware of some instances in which individuals consider some secular-based magazines (particularly *Reader's Digest*) to be a "Christian" magazine.

The individuals most likely to cite having read a Christian magazine in the past year are those in the 45 and older age group; people earning less than $60,000 a year; women; married adults; and individuals in the midwest and southern states. Born again Christians (56%), and churched adults are also among the most common readers of Christian magazines, although barely half of the born again audience (56%) admits to reading such literature (even using this very broad-based definition of a Christian magazine).

Even with the meaning of "Christian magazine" somewhat uncertain, notice that significant proportions of those who are either outside of or not active within the community of believers (i.e. non-Christians and the unchurched) say they have exposure to such publications.

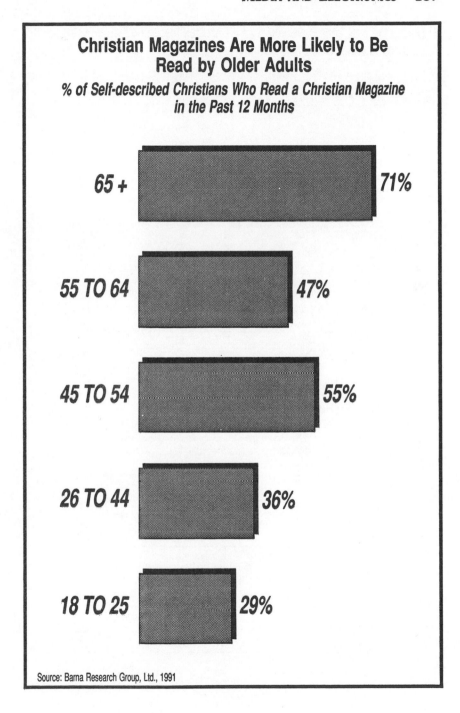

Christian Magazines Are More Likely to Be Read by Older Adults

% of Self-described Christians Who Read a Christian Magazine in the Past 12 Months

65 +   71%

55 TO 64   47%

45 TO 54   55%

26 TO 44   36%

18 TO 25   29%

Source: Barna Research Group, Ltd., 1991

Q: During the past year, have you read a Christian magazine? (Among those who describe themselves as "Christian.")

		Yes	No	Don't Know	N
Total Population		42%	57%	*	825
Age:	18 to 25	29	71	*	136
	26-44	36	64	*	400
	45-54	55	45	*	116
	55-64	47	52	1	87
	65 or older	71	28	1	83
Education:	High school or less	41	58	1	388
	Some college	44	55	*	203
	College graduate	42	58	*	233
Ethnicity:	White	43	57	1	625
	Black	50	50	*	100
Household Income:	Under $20,000	43	56	1	154
	$20,000 to $39,999	43	57	*	328
	$40,000 to $59,999	43	57	*	153
	$60,000 or more	30	70	*	110
Gender:	Male	37	63	*	387
	Female	47	52	1	438
Married:	Yes	46	54	1	496
	No	37	63	*	329
Community:	Urban	44	56	1	267
	Suburban	38	62	*	317
	Rural	47	53	*	216
Region:	Northeast	38	61	2	164
	Midwest	47	53	*	201
	South	50	49	*	183
	Mountain	42	59	*	144
	Pacific	31	69	*	133
Born Again:	Yes	56	44	*	338
	No	33	66	1	487
Denominational Affiliation:	Evangelical	50	50	*	246
	Catholic	30	70	1	250
	Mainline	44	56	*	178
Church Attender:	Yes	48	52	*	623
	No	24	75	1	170

ARE WE READING CHRISTIAN BOOKS?

 Question: During the past year, did you read a Christian book, other than the Bible?

Just more than one-third of the people calling themselves Christian (36%) say they have read a Christian book, other than the Bible, during the past year.

The reading of such books is most common among people in the 45-54 and the 65 or older age groups (49% and 50%, respectively, have done so in the past year). Other segments more likely to engage in such reading are blacks (57%), women (41%), married adults (40%), born again Christians (53%), those at evangelical churches (47%), and the churched (41%).

The segments that stand out as particularly unlikely to read Christian books are individuals living in the northeast (27%), Catholics (22%), Baby Busters (25%), and self-professed Christians who are unchurched (19%).

Only Half of All Born Again Christians Read a Christian Book, Other than the Bible, Last Year

53% READ A CHRISTIAN BOOK

46% DID NOT READ A CHRISTIAN BOOK

Source: Barna Research Group, Ltd., 1991

Q: During the past year, did you read a Christian book, other than the Bible? (Among those who describe themselves as "Christian.")

		Yes	No	Don't Know	N
Total Population		36%	64%	*	825
Age:	18 to 25	25	76	*	136
	26-44	33	67	1	400
	45-54	49	50	1	116
	55-64	37	63	*	87
	65 or older	50	50	*	83
Education:	High school or less	33	66	1	388
	Some college	40	60	*	203
	College graduate	37	63	*	233
Ethnicity:	White	33	67	*	625
	Black	57	43	*	100
Household Income:	Under $20,000	37	62	1	154
	$20,000 to $39,999	36	65	*	328
	$40,000 to $59,999	39	61	*	153
	$60,000 or more	24	76	*	110
Gender:	Male	31	69	*	387
	Female	41	59	1	438
Married:	Yes	40	60	1	496
	No	30	70	*	329
Community:	Urban	36	63	1	267
	Suburban	36	64	*	317
	Rural	35	65	*	216
Region:	Northeast	27	73	1	164
	Midwest	40	60	*	201
	South	42	58	*	183
	Mountain	37	62	1	144
	Pacific	32	68	1	133
Born Again:	Yes	53	46	1	338
	No	24	76	*	487
Denominational Affiliation:	Evangelical	47	52	1	246
	Catholic	22	78	*	250
	Mainline	33	66	*	178
Church Attender:	Yes	41	58	*	623
	No	19	81	*	170

WHAT TYPES OF BOOKS ARE WE BUYING?

Question: *Which, if any, of the following types of books did you buy during the last 12 months? Fiction novels; children's books; business or career; self-help or self-improvement; biographies; Christian books, other than the Bible; the Bible.*

Despite the ever-present allure of technology, and the on-going battle to protect our time and use it efficiently, reading books is not a thing of the past. Overall, close to two-thirds of all adults (65%) say that they have purchased at least one book during the past 12 months. The people most likely to do so are 26-54 years of age (68%), those who have attended college (77%), people who earn $40,000 or more (74%), and adults currently living in the suburbs (70%).

Fiction Tops the List

What kinds of books do they buy? Among the seven topical categories posed to people, the most popular was fiction novels, which almost two-fifths of all adults (39%) claim to have purchased in the past year. Not far behind are children's books, bought by one-third of all adults in the last 12 months. Next are business or career-oriented books (29%), self-help or self-improvement titles (26%), then biographies (20%). Low on this non-exhaustive topical list are Christian books other than the Bible (bought by 18%) and the Bible (8%).

Be aware that this is a relatively strong showing for Christian books. Since these titles are geared to a relatively limited niche audience, having such books purchased by about 32 million adults during the past year represents a large pool of buyers. The people who are most likely to buy Christian books are 45 or older; college-educated; middle-income households; and individuals who are married.

As for the sales of the Bible, considering its deep penetration among American households, the fact that 8% say they purchased a Bible in the past year is remarkable. More than nine out of ten households already own at least one Bible, and more than half own more than one. Also understand that the number of households in America expanded by just 1% last year. Thus, in this context, for Bibles to have been bought by 8% of the population constitutes a significant penetration into a saturated market.

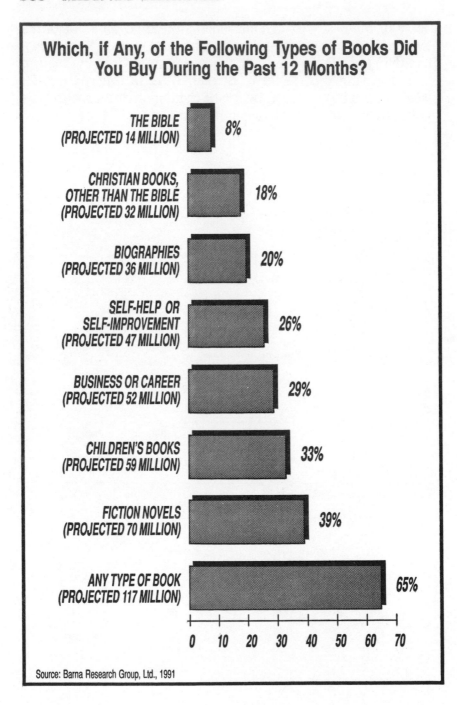

Which, if Any, of the Following Types of Books Did You Buy During the Past 12 Months?

THE BIBLE
(PROJECTED 14 MILLION) 8%

CHRISTIAN BOOKS,
OTHER THAN THE BIBLE
(PROJECTED 32 MILLION) 18%

BIOGRAPHIES
(PROJECTED 36 MILLION) 20%

SELF-HELP OR
SELF-IMPROVEMENT
(PROJECTED 47 MILLION) 26%

BUSINESS OR CAREER
(PROJECTED 52 MILLION) 29%

CHILDREN'S BOOKS
(PROJECTED 59 MILLION) 33%

FICTION NOVELS
(PROJECTED 70 MILLION) 39%

ANY TYPE OF BOOK
(PROJECTED 117 MILLION) 65%

0   10   20   30   40   50   60   70

Source: Barna Research Group, Ltd., 1991

Q: Which, if any, of the following types of books did you buy during the last 12 months? (See next page for column headings.)

		#1	#2	#3	#4	#5	#6	#7	N
Total Population		39%	33%	29%	26%	20%	18%	8%	1005
Age:	18 to 25	38	17	26	18	20	11	6	190
	26-44	43	47	35	28	21	19	10	464
	45-54	34	28	31	30	22	26	7	141
	55-64	29	19	18	26	17	16	6	101
	65 or older	28	18	9	17	13	26	11	92
Education:	High school or less	28	22	14	18	14	14	8	453
	Some college	42	39	31	33	23	21	7	242
	College graduate	52	45	50	31	25	23	9	306
Ethnicity:	White	42	34	28	26	21	19	6	744
	Black	23	23	28	23	15	21	14	119
Household Income:	Under $20,000	32	22	13	19	13	15	7	184
	$20,000 to $39,999	35	33	26	24	13	19	8	397
	$40,000 to $59,999	39	41	38	32	27	22	9	186
	$60,000 or more	58	42	51	28	31	11	8	142
Gender:	Male	33	27	36	25	19	17	8	490
	Female	44	39	23	26	20	20	9	515
Married:	Yes	39	41	28	29	20	22	10	570
	No	39	23	30	22	19	13	7	432
Community:	Urban	41	31	27	25	20	15	9	340
	Suburban	43	36	34	28	20	22	9	387
	Rural	32	33	26	27	20	19	8	245
Region:	Northeast	51	38	38	26	23	13	4	227
	Midwest	34	35	24	27	15	20	11	228
	South	34	28	25	24	16	21	10	210
	Mountain	35	31	31	26	21	24	7	171
	Pacific	38	35	28	25	25	15	8	169
Born Again:	Yes	32	37	29	31	17	35	16	355
	No	42	31	29	23	21	9	4	650
Denominational Affiliation:	Evangelical	29	31	26	25	18	29	12	246
	Catholic	45	35	31	22	21	10	6	250
	Mainline	42	36	27	22	21	20	8	178
Church Attender:	Yes	37	35	29	28	19	25	12	623
	No	41	31	30	20	17	6	2	243

Columns:

#1   Fiction novels

#2   Children's books

#3   Business or career

#4   Self-help or self-improvement

#5   Biographies

#6   Christian books, other than the Bible

#7   The Bible

WHAT AMERICANS VALUE

◆ Most Americans say religion is very important to them. A majority also say the Bible is very important to them. However, these factors are less important in the mental hierarchy of values to American adults than a number of other elements.

◆ People have a greater degree of confidence in Christian churches than in most other social institutions.

◆ Among the conditions that people desire for their lives, by far the most desirous is having good health. The next most important aspects are being known as a person of integrity, having close personal friendships, and having a close relationship with God.

◆ Being part of a local church is very desirable to about half of all adults.

▶ IN BRIEF

AMERICA CONTINUES TO EXPERIENCE A SHIFT IN THE VALUES structure that undergirds our society. Led by the curious and skeptical minds of the Post-World War II generations, every facet of our lives gets placed under the microscope and is evaluated according to a new set of rules and expectations.

Does religion play a role in this new values structure? How does family fit into the developing mold? What types of efforts and conditions are held in highest esteem?

Family Matters

Family, despite its changing contours, is at the top of the list of dearly held values. Better than nine out of ten adults (94%) say that family is very important to them. Almost as many people (87%) say having good health is a similarly important reality for them.

Time Is of the Essence

People are increasingly protective of, and sensitive to, the importance of their time. Three out of four adults (74%) say that their time, in general, is very important. More specifically, two-thirds of adults (63%) indicate that their free time is of great importance to them.

As many organizations have learned, it is more difficult than ever to get people to invest time in ideas, people, and organizations they support. The people groups who place the highest degree of value upon their free time are those who are 45 or older, upscale, and worship in churches other than evangelical ones.

Relationships and Religion

Relationships outside of family ties are also of major importance to a majority of adults. Two-thirds (67%) say having close friends is very important. Of greatest interest is the fact that Boomers are least insistent on the value of having close friends; blacks are 35% less likely than whites to say close friendships are very important to them; and people in evangelical churches are less likely to underscore the importance of friendships than are people affiliated with other types of churches.

The importance of religion has not varied greatly over the past decade. Today, about six out of ten adults say religion is very important to them. This represents a small increase from a few years ago, and is likely attributable to the Persian Gulf War. Religion is more important to people as they age, and seems less important to adults as they achieve financial security. As expected, women tend to attach greater importance to religion than do men.

The Bible, the most owned—and perhaps least read —book in America, is considered very important to half of all adults (55%). The same people groups who appreciate the value of religion, in general, show the greatest support for the Bible.

Career and Standard of Living

Also appealing to half of the public are career interests. In total, 53% call their career very important. There is a very clear correlation between the groups who value religion highly and those who value career highly. That is, the segments that are more likely to value religion highly are lowest in the degree of importance they ascribe to career, while those who place high value upon career are the lowest in terms of the importance they assign to religion.

Half of all adults also consider living comfortably to be very important. However, only one-third say money is very important to them.

Society

Confidence in public institutions also reflects some of the values to which we cling. In examining our reactions to nine major public institutions, Christian churches place second, trailing only the military. While 58% say they have a lot of confidence in the military, 43% say they have a similar level of confidence in Christian churches.

Note that, as a reflection of our high standards and skepticism, only one of the institutions monitored carries a high degree of confidence among at least half of our adults. Not even Christian churches, which were formerly revered as worthy of considerable trust and as being greatly influential, reach the half-way mark.

On the other hand, while the absolute levels of confidence people have in institutions is declining, the comparative context remains relatively unchanged. Most institutions lag behind the Church in their ability to inspire confidence. Among those that trail are hospitals and health care organizations (40% are very confident in these); the Supreme Court (28%); public schools (27%); charities and non-profit institutions (23%); private business (20%); Congress (16%); and the media (10%).

Born again Christians have significantly higher levels of confidence in Christian churches, somewhat more confidence in hospitals and health care organizations, and somewhat less confidence in the Supreme Court than do non-believers. Surprisingly, Christians do not differ from non-Christians in the degrees of confidence they have in the public schools (a frequent target of the evangelical movement), Congress, or the media. Similarly, despite their tendency to donate more money to charity, they do not possess distinguished levels of confidence in charitable and non-profit organizations.

Building the Perfect World

Given the chance to build their ideal world, what would Americans seek? We get a glimpse of this by examining what people consider to be a desirable condition in their life. By far the most desirable condition for adults is to have good health; 93% say this is a very desirable condition.

There is quite a gap between the proportion who say good health is very desirable and those who indicate that any of the 12 other conditions tested are very desirable. Three-quarters of adults (76%)

believe that being known as a person of integrity is very desirable. Similar proportions of adults say that having close personal friendships (73%) and having a close relationship with God (72%) are very desirable.

The next highest item is a bit surprising: living close to family (67%). After that comes living comfortably (59%), living to an old age (51%), being part of a local church (50%), and being able to influence other people's lives (40%). The remaining conditions examined are highly desirable to just one-third or less of the adult populace. Those conditions include having a high-paying job (36%), not having to work for a living (35%), owning a large home (23%), and achieving fame or recognition (10%).

Born again Christians differ appreciably from non-believers principally in that they are substantially more desirous of having a close personal relationship with God, being a member of a local church, and having an influence in other people's lives.

WHAT WE VALUE: 10 FAMILY, HEALTH, AND TIME

WHO AND WHAT DO WE VALUE?

Question: *I'm going to name several things that are important in life. For each one that I mention, please tell me how important that thing is to you, personally: very, somewhat, not too, or not at all important. (Elements tested: family; health; your time; having close friends; your free time; religion; the Bible; your career; living comfortably; money.)*

Family and Health

By far the two most important elements in life to people are their family (considered very important by 94%) and their health (87%). Regarding family, there are no people groups in which less than 90% say family is very important. The only segments which consider anything else to be of equivalent or greater importance are the elderly (among whom an equivalent proportion say their health and having close friends are very important) and residents of the northeast (among whom the same proportion cite their health as very important).

Time and Friends

The next most important elements in people's lives, after family and health, relate to time and relationships. Three-quarters of adults (74%) believe that their time is very important. In fact, to many people perhaps the most important time is that reserved for leisure. Two-thirds of all adults (63%) say their free time is very important.

That's more people than say that money, religion, or career are very important to them. Intriguingly, the population groups who are least likely to say their free time is very important are the Baby Busters and Boomers. For Busters, note that career matters and having close friends are deemed very important by higher proportions. Among Boomers, although free time is considered very important by a lower percentage of people than the national norm, it remains ahead of most other life aspects in terms of relative importance to adults in the Boomer cohort.

Religion and the Bible

Religion (59%) and the Bible (55%) rank in the middle range of the list of priorities. The older persons are, the more likely they are to view both of these elements as very important. The largest shift in the degree of importance occurs upon reaching age 65. Notice that 67% of adults in the 45-64 age class say religion is very important to them. That figure jumps to 84% among the senior citizens.

Another pattern that occurs is that the higher a person's socioeconomic status—i.e. educational achievement and household income—the less likely they are to rate religion or the Bible as very important. Blacks and women are about 50% more likely than whites and men, respectively, to view religion and the Bible as very important. Other segments of the population that hold religion and Bible in high regard are individuals who live outside of the urban and suburban areas, those who live outside of the Pacific and northeastern states, regular church attenders, and adults who attend evangelical churches.

Career

About half of all American adults (53%) view their careers as very important. Tellingly, this importance declines steadily as people age. Other adults who are more likely than average to describe their careers as very important include men (59%), singles (64%), and blacks (73%).

Living Comfortably and Money

Living comfortably (48%) and money (33%) are lowest on the list of priorities. Of course, this varies by subgroup. Among the more interesting revelations is the fact that the only thing deemed less important to Baby Busters than money is religion. Geographically, people living in the Pacific states are least likely to rate money as a very important factor in life.

Rankings Across Population Groups

There are a number of people groups whose values differ radically. For instance, the relative priorities of blacks bear little resemblance to those of whites. Young adults and old adults also pursue different ends. Perhaps most surprising, though, is the finding that if religion and the Bible are removed from the mix of factors, born again Christians and non-Christians have identical values patterns. These two groups of adults rank the other eight elements exactly the same.

The only areas of true difference in relative priorities in life, among those measured, pertain to the importance of religion. How interesting that the influence of religious beliefs is not discernible in people's ranking of other factors.

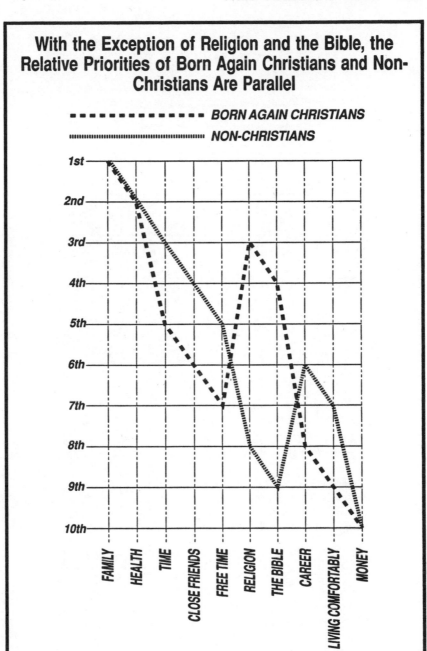

With the Exception of Religion and the Bible, the Relative Priorities of Born Again Christians and Non-Christians Are Parallel

- - - - - - - - - - - - BORN AGAIN CHRISTIANS

IIIIIIIIIIIIIIIIIIIIIIIIIIIIIIIIIIIIIIIIIIIIII NON-CHRISTIANS

Source: Barna Research Group, Ltd., 1991

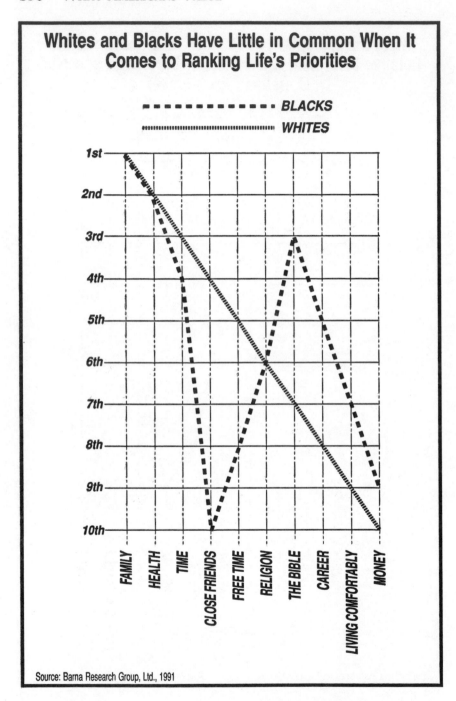

Whites and Blacks Have Little in Common When It Comes to Ranking Life's Priorities

Source: Barna Research Group, Ltd., 1991

Q: I'm going to name several things that some people may feel are important in life. For each one that I mention, please tell me how important that thing is to you, personally: very, somewhat, not too, or not at all important. (Proportion who said the element is very important. Please see next page for column headings.)

		#1	#2	#3	#4	#5	#6	#7	#8	#9	#10	N
Total Population		94%	87%	74%	67%	63%	59%	55%	53%	48%	33%	1005
Age:	18 to 25	93	87	67	71	54	42	48	70	51	43	190
	26-44	95	86	74	62	62	57	53	56	43	30	464
	45-54	98	91	81	66	71	66	57	45	44	26	141
	55-64	93	87	76	75	66	68	60	38	56	31	101
	65 or older	91	92	74	89	68	84	76	28	59	26	92
Education:	High school or less	95	89	74	67	60	61	63	52	54	40	453
	Some college	92	83	72	67	63	59	54	46	44	28	242
	College graduate	93	88	76	67	68	54	43	58	43	26	306
Ethnicity:	White	94	86	72	72	62	56	51	47	45	28	744
	Black	96	91	80	47	60	73	86	73	67	52	119
Household Income:	Under $20,000	95	87	67	65	54	65	70	45	45	32	184
	$20,000 to $39,999	93	88	75	71	62	59	57	56	51	34	397
	$40,000 to $59,999	95	89	72	62	65	56	50	52	44	28	186
	$60,000 or more	93	84	78	70	71	49	35	60	47	34	142
Gender:	Male	90	86	73	61	64	48	47	59	50	37	490
	Female	97	88	75	72	62	69	62	47	46	29	515
Married:	Yes	96	87	75	64	62	65	59	44	44	29	570
	No	91	87	71	71	64	51	50	64	53	37	432
Community:	Urban	93	88	74	66	61	51	49	56	47	33	340
	Suburban	95	88	71	69	65	60	53	54	47	30	387
	Rural	94	85	77	66	63	65	65	48	48	34	245
Region:	Northeast	90	90	73	68	65	49	38	54	54	34	227
	Midwest	96	87	74	70	60	61	60	54	44	35	228
	South	94	87	77	62	66	61	67	52	53	33	210
	Mountain	98	86	76	66	58	67	62	55	40	36	171
	Pacific	91	84	67	69	66	57	47	49	48	25	169
Born Again:	Yes	96	87	76	67	62	84	83	52	43	29	355
	No	92	87	72	67	64	45	39	53	51	35	650
Denominational Affiliation:	Evangelical	98	86	76	61	59	77	85	51	47	32	246
	Catholic	95	84	66	73	68	59	38	53	48	32	250
	Mainline	96	90	75	69	65	59	56	46	46	29	178
Church Attender:	Yes	97	87	74	70	63	73	67	51	46	29	762
	No	90	85	78	64	64	30	30	58	50	41	243

Columns:

#1 Family

#2 Health

#3 Your time

#4 Having close friends

#5 Your free time

#6 Religion

#7 The Bible

#8 Your career

#9 Living comfortably

#10 Money

11 OUR CONFIDENCE LEVEL: INSTITUTIONS AND ORGANIZATIONS

HOW MUCH CONFIDENCE DO AMERICANS HAVE IN SOCIAL INSTITUTIONS AND ORGANIZATIONS?

Question: *For each of the social institutions or organizations I mention, please tell me how much confidence you have in that institution or organization: a lot, some, not much, or none. (Institutions tested: the public schools; Christian churches; Congress; the Supreme Court; the military; hospitals and health care organizations; the media; private business; charities and non-profit organizations.)*

The Military

Of the nine major types of entities evaluated, the military was ranked, by far, the institution in which people have the most confidence. This ranking could well have been influenced by the timing of the survey (during the initial two weeks of the massive and widely-applauded air strike against Iraq). In total, 58% say they have a lot of confidence in the military. Levels are much higher among adults 55 or older (75%), among the least educated adults (65%), whites (62%), and rural Americans (65%).

Christian Churches

Christian churches are the next highest-rated among the institutions studied. Forty-three percent of adults have a lot of confidence in Christian churches. Recognize that this represents less than half of the nation's adult population expressing a high level of faith in our churches.

The only subgroups that demonstrate a higher-than-average degree of confidence in Christian churches are the elderly (64%), blacks (55%), women (49%), and people who live outside of either the northeast or west coast.

Other Organizations

Health care organizations have the confidence of two out of five adults (40%). The confidence levels drop considerably after that, down to the 28% who hold the Supreme Court in the highest regard, and 27% who have a lot of confidence in the public schools.

Charities and non-profit organizations (23%) along with private business (20%) reap the trust of similar proportions of adults.

The lowest confidence levels are reserved for Congress (16%) and the media (10%).

Comparing Christians and Non-Christians

The perspectives of born again Christians and non-Christians differ little. The major difference relates to confidence in Christian churches. While 60% of the Christians have a lot of confidence in the churches, that level is matched by only 34% among the non-Christians.

Do not lose sight of the fact that even among the subgroups that are, theoretically, the most committed to the Church there are nevertheless sizable proportions who do not maintain high degrees of confidence in our churches.

Among key church-related segments, the confidence levels were 60% among born again Christians, 61% among those associated with evangelical churches, 41% among Catholics, 51% among mainline Protestants, and 56% among regular church-goers.

Low Confidence Levels

Some people may be fascinated to learn that the institutions that have some of the most profound degrees of influence over the attitudes and values of the nation—i.e. private business, the media, and Congress—receive very low confidence ratings.

The Public Schools

Further, the public schools, which often come under attack from conservative Christians, receive the same confidence ratings from born again Christians as from non-Christians. In fact, the aggregate ratings awarded by both groups to the public schools—i.e. the percentages of people who rated the schools excellent, good, only fair, or poor—are statistically identical.

Charities and Non-profit Organizations

Given the considerable amounts of money donated by Christians to charities, even apart from churches, it is somewhat surprising to see that Christians and non-Christians give charities and non-profit organizations equivalent ratings. In fact, breaking the prevailing pattern, adults associated with evangelical churches were not more positive in their ratings of such organizations than were Catholics and mainline Protestants. Not even the adults who attend church regularly possess more positive views of charities.

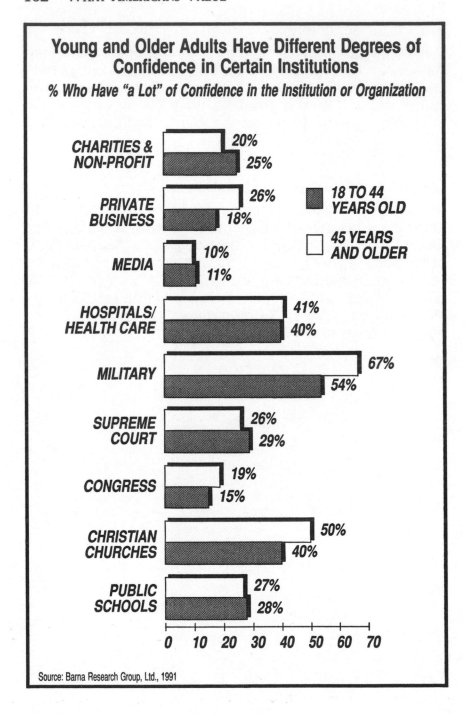

Young and Older Adults Have Different Degrees of Confidence in Certain Institutions

% Who Have "a Lot" of Confidence in the Institution or Organization

CHARITIES & NON-PROFIT — 20% / 25%

18 TO 44 YEARS OLD

PRIVATE BUSINESS — 26% / 18%

45 YEARS AND OLDER

MEDIA — 10% / 11%

HOSPITALS/ HEALTH CARE — 41% / 40%

MILITARY — 67% / 54%

SUPREME COURT — 26% / 29%

CONGRESS — 19% / 15%

CHRISTIAN CHURCHES — 50% / 40%

PUBLIC SCHOOLS — 27% / 28%

0 10 20 30 40 50 60 70

Source: Barna Research Group, Ltd., 1991

Q: For each of the social institutions or organizations I mention, please tell me how much confidence you have in that institution or organization: a lot, some, not much, or none. (Proportion who said they have a lot of confidence in each institution. Please see next page for column headings.)

		#1	#2	#3	#4	#5	#6	#7	#8	#9	N
Total Population		27%	43%	16%	28%	58%	40%	10%	20%	23%	1005
Age:	18 to 25	28	42	20	37	60	50	13	18	36	190
	26-44	28	40	13	26	52	36	10	18	21	464
	45-54	20	45	17	26	57	35	6	26	17	141
	55-64	28	47	24	29	73	44	14	31	23	101
	65 or older	40	64	18	22	79	45	13	20	22	92
Education:	High school or less	32	47	19	27	65	47	13	19	25	453
	Some college	23	43	13	23	59	35	10	24	21	242
	College graduate	23	38	15	32	48	33	8	20	21	306
Ethnicity:	White	26	43	16	27	62	39	10	23	23	744
	Black	34	55	16	30	42	51	7	17	25	119
Household Income:	Under $20,000	31	45	16	23	57	43	14	12	27	184
	$20,000 to $39,999	27	44	19	29	64	42	11	20	24	397
	$40,000 to $59,999	25	46	12	33	58	38	10	22	24	186
	$60,000 or more	25	37	16	31	48	31	5	28	17	142
Gender:	Male	24	37	16	31	58	38	10	27	18	490
	Female	30	49	17	25	58	41	11	14	28	515
Married:	Yes	28	45	18	29	61	40	10	22	22	570
	No	27	41	15	26	55	39	11	19	25	432
Community:	Urban	29	41	17	30	56	38	11	19	25	340
	Suburban	25	44	16	28	56	38	10	22	21	387
	Rural	28	45	16	23	65	43	10	21	23	245
Region:	Northeast	27	35	17	26	56	38	9	21	24	227
	Midwest	33	48	19	30	59	42	11	18	25	228
	South	26	51	17	26	61	45	9	23	23	210
	Mountain	26	48	18	31	62	40	11	22	22	171
	Pacific	22	32	11	26	55	32	13	17	21	169
Born Again:	Yes	27	60	17	24	60	45	9	20	23	355
	No	28	34	16	30	57	40	11	21	23	650
Denominational Affiliation:	Evangelical	28	61	17	25	62	43	8	18	22	246
	Catholic	27	41	19	31	56	41	10	21	26	250
	Mainline	28	51	15	28	62	39	11	26	22	178
Church Attender:	Yes	30	56	18	28	59	42	10	22	25	762
	No	21	20	11	27	59	34	11	19	20	243

Columns:

#1 The public schools

#2 Christian churches

#3 Congress

#4 The Supreme Court

#5 The military

#6 Hospitals and health care organizations

#7 The media

#8 Private business

#9 Charities and non-profit organizations

12 OUR HOPE FOR THE FUTURE: FRIENDS, FAITH, AND FAME

WHAT DO AMERICANS DESIRE FOR THE FUTURE?

Question: *I'm going to read some conditions that you could possibly have in your life in the future. For each condition that I read, please tell me if you find that to be very desirable, somewhat desirable, not too desirable, or not at all desirable. (Conditions tested: to have close, personal friendships; to have a close relationship with God; to be known as a person of integrity; to have a high-paying job; to be part of a local church; to influence other people's lives; to own a large home; to live close to family; to achieve fame or public recognition; to live comfortably; to not have to work for a living; to have good health; to live to an old age.)*

Good Health

The overall response of adults is again consistent with earlier findings regarding life priorities. Given the list of 13 potential life circumstances, by far the most desirable condition of all is having good health (deemed very desirable by 93%).

Integrity, Relationships, and God Rate Highly

The next echelon of desirable conditions is deemed very desirable by about three-fourths of all adults. Those conditions include being known as a person of integrity (76%), having close personal friendships (73%) and having a close relationship with God (72%). Somewhat less appealing is the prospect of living close to family, although two-thirds say this would be very desirable (67%). The only other potential conditions that are very attractive to at least half of all adults are living comfortably (59%), living to an old age (51%), and being part of a local church (50%).

Low Ratings

The conditions that are less motivating for adults include influencing other people's lives (40%); having a high-paying job (36%); not having to work for a living (35%); owning a large home (23%); and achieving fame or public recognition (10%).

God Among Population Groups

The expected population groups emerge as those most likely to express a high level of interest in a close relationship with God. Those segments include older people; blacks; women; married adults; rural adults; born again Christians; people attending evangelical churches; and regular church-goers.

Also realize that people in the northeast, especially, exhibit a very limited interest in having closer ties with God: only 56% described this as a very desirable condition (compared to 76% among adults from all other regions). Do not overlook the fact that half of the unchurched also have a strong desire to have a closer relationship with God.

Frequently, we have a tendency to look at Boomers or Busters and write them off as people who turn their backs on God. These data, however, tell another story. True, the youngest adults are least likely to make the building of a deeper relationship with God a top priority. However, two-thirds of those generations say that such a relationship is very desirable. For the Buster crowd, notice that only two conditions outweighed the importance of a better relationship with God: good health and living comfortably. Boomers, too, have just two items of stronger appeal: good health and being known as a person of integrity.

Being Part of a Local Church

The possibility of being part of a local church is much less appealing to people than the prospect of having a close relationship with God. Integrating into the life of a church is most appealing to people 45 or older (61%); blacks (69%); women (60%); married adults (57%); rural residents (58%); born again Christians (75%); adults attending evangelical churches (71%); and those who attend church regularly (69%).

Perhaps the most striking realizations, however, pertain to the limited desire among the most committed segments of the Christian community to be part of a local church in the days ahead. One out of four born again Christians does *not* have a strong desire to be part of a church. Almost half of the adults associated with mainline Protestant churches, and more than half of all Catholics, do *not* have a strong desire to be an integral part of the church in the future. One out of three people who currently attend church services regularly does *not* have a high degree of interest in remaining part of the local church.

Among the unchurched, there is some interest in getting involved with a local church. About one out of every eight unchurched adults who call themselves Christian would very much like to be part of a local congregation in the future.

Some People Groups Have a Strong Desire to Have a Close Relationship with God—and Others Don't

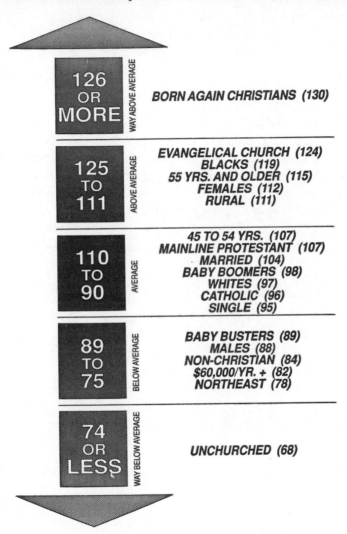

126 OR MORE — WAY ABOVE AVERAGE

BORN AGAIN CHRISTIANS (130)

125 TO 111 — ABOVE AVERAGE

EVANGELICAL CHURCH (124)
BLACKS (119)
55 YRS. AND OLDER (115)
FEMALES (112)
RURAL (111)

110 TO 90 — AVERAGE

45 TO 54 YRS. (107)
MAINLINE PROTESTANT (107)
MARRIED (104)
BABY BOOMERS (98)
WHITES (97)
CATHOLIC (96)
SINGLE (95)

89 TO 75 — BELOW AVERAGE

BABY BUSTERS (89)
MALES (88)
NON-CHRISTIAN (84)
$60,000/YR. + (82)
NORTHEAST (78)

74 OR LESS — WAY BELOW AVERAGE

UNCHURCHED (68)

Indexes are standardized scores. Index scores below the population index (i.e. 100) indicate population segments that are less likely to have the test attribute; segments with scores above the base index are more likely to engage in that behavior. The larger the difference from the base index, the more the segment differs from the norm.

Source: Barna Research Group, Ltd., 1991

Q: I'm going to read some conditions that you could possibly have in your life in the future. For each condition that I read, please tell me if you find that to be very desirable, somewhat desirable, not too desirable, or not at all desirable. (Proportion who said they found that condition to be very desirable. "N" = 1,005. Please see next page for column headings.)

		#1	#2	#3	#4	#5	#6	#7	#8	#9	#10	#11	#12	#13
Total Population		73%	72%	76%	36%	50%	40%	23%	67%	10%	59%	35%	93%	51%
Age:	18 to 25	80	64	65	56	38	49	43	62	18	69	30	89	55
	26-44	69	70	79	34	48	39	19	64	7	53	33	92	48
	45-54	73	77	77	31	57	36	19	71	11	51	34	99	45
	55-64	77	81	81	24	58	41	15	79	12	66	42	97	51
	65 or older	83	85	70	15	75	33	16	83	8	76	41	88	61
Education:	High school or less	73	76	67	43	53	41	31	72	13	67	40	94	57
	Some college	69	74	78	34	51	42	16	64	8	58	33	91	44
	College graduate	76	65	86	27	46	39	16	62	8	49	29	92	47
Ethnicity:	White	75	70	77	31	48	38	18	66	8	57	32	92	48
	Black	59	85	78	63	69	51	41	71	22	78	42	94	66
Household Income:	Under $20,000	72	79	68	38	53	43	29	69	16	63	35	92	55
	$20,000 to $39,999	73	72	75	40	50	40	24	65	10	61	37	93	51
	$40,000 to $59,999	71	74	78	26	53	41	19	69	7	58	30	95	45
	$60,000 or more	76	59	86	32	45	39	17	65	7	51	35	93	52
Gender:	Male	72	63	75	39	40	39	26	60	11	60	35	91	52
	Female	74	80	76	32	60	42	21	73	9	59	34	94	50
Married:	Yes	70	75	77	29	57	42	19	69	7	57	36	94	53
	No	77	68	74	45	42	39	29	65	15	63	33	92	48
Community:	Urban	72	69	73	37	44	43	24	64	10	61	30	93	54
	Suburban	74	69	81	34	50	38	16	65	10	56	38	92	45
	Rural	72	80	73	35	58	41	28	73	8	59	35	94	51
Region:	Northeast	73	56	77	37	40	34	24	60	9	61	31	94	51
	Midwest	77	76	74	35	54	40	20	72	10	56	33	91	46
	South	65	74	74	39	55	47	25	66	13	64	39	94	54
	Mountain	73	80	83	37	54	42	26	67	8	58	36	92	56
	Pacific	77	76	70	29	48	40	21	71	9	56	34	92	47
Born Again:	Yes	75	93	81	36	75	54	21	72	12	57	38	94	56
	No	71	60	73	36	37	33	25	64	9	60	33	92	48
Denominational Affiliation:	Evangelical	68	89	79	41	71	55	28	70	11	63	38	93	56
	Catholic	74	69	73	33	46	30	21	71	10	55	37	91	49
	Mainline	75	77	80	27	56	35	13	68	6	65	33	94	50
Church Attender:	Yes	76	84	79	34	69	45	21	72	10	57	36	93	51
	No	66	49	72	42	13	30	27	58	8	60	34	91	48

Columns:

#1   To have close, personal friendships

#2   To have a close relationship with God

#3   To be known as a person of integrity

#4   To have a high-paying job

#5   To be part of a local church

#6   To influence other people's lives

#7   To own a large home

#8   To live close to family

#9   To achieve fame or public recognition

#10   To live comfortably

#11   Not to have to work for a living

#12   To have good health

#13   To live to an old age

PERSPECTIVES ON RELIGION

SECTION HIGHLIGHTS:

◆ Two-thirds of adults consider themselves to be religious, while one-third call themselves born again Christians.

◆ Based on stated beliefs, one-third of the adult population can be classified as born again Christians. They are not necessarily the same people who describe themselves with the term "born again."

◆ People are almost twice as likely to say that the Christian faith is relevant to the way they live today as to say that the local Christian churches in their area are relevant to their life.

◆ A minority of adults believe that most Christian churches are tolerant of people who hold different beliefs than those taught by the church.

◆ Most adults believe in God, but not in Satan; they believe in the power of prayer, but also in self-determination; they are divided on whether or not people have a responsibility to share their religious beliefs with others; most people claim that people from different religions (i.e. Christian and non-Christian faiths) are all seeking the same God.

▶ *IN BRIEF*

ISN'T IT INTERESTING THAT IN A NATION WHERE TWO OUT OF EVERY three adults (64%) describe themselves as "religious," a widely accepted matter of etiquette is that the two items you should not discuss in "polite company" are religion and politics?

The Politics of Religion

The label "religious" undoubtedly means different things to different people. There is no denying, however, that most Americans feel comfortable describing themselves with that adjective. The older a person becomes, the more likely they are to view themselves as "religious." The likelihood of using the term as a self-description was related to a person's age, gender, marital status, region, and religious affiliations and activity.

Born Again? A Matter of Perspective

The label "born again Christian" is even more interesting. One-third of adults claim to be born again. However, when we look at the perspectives on eternal salvation held by those people, we find that roughly one-third of the self-described born again Christians believe that they will gain entry into Heaven as a consequence of their good works, rather than God's grace through Jesus Christ. Instead, if we rely upon a person's beliefs to classify them as a Christian, we still find that one-third are classified as such—but it is a different one-third of the population than that which calls itself "born again."

The major differences between the two segments—those who call themselves born again and those who might be classified as born again according to what they believe—relate to church affiliation and region.

Specifically, people who associate with mainline Protestant churches are more likely to call themselves born again than to hold beliefs that would confirm that label. Likewise, people in the northeastern states are more likely to be born again according to their faith commitment than to use that terminology to describe themselves.

Relevancy and Impact

Overall, four out of five adults agree at least somewhat that the Christian faith is relevant to the way they live these days. In fact, half of all adults strongly agree with that sentiment.

Why, then, does the Church have such difficulty penetrating this culture? Partially because of the manner in which adults perceive the local Christian churches. Only about one-quarter of all adults (28%) strongly agree that the Christian churches in their area are relevant to the way people live these days. Thus, the issue is not the relevance of Christianity, as a faith; the issue is how people gain exposure to and involvement with that faith, i.e. the ministry of the local church.

Similarly, note that people generally do not view local Christian churches as tolerant of people who have ideas that differ from those taught by the church. Note an important distinction: the perception is not simply that churches reject different ideas, but that they reject the people who hold those ideas, as well.

This varies considerably from Jesus' approach to dealing with people: while He rejected their sins, He did not reject the sinners, but exhibited a burning desire to see them made whole in spite of their sin. Again, the image of our churches suffers significantly when people perceive Christian congregations to be judgmental and closed to those who approach life differently.

Finding the Christians

In fitting with the fact that most Americans view themselves to be Christian (although not "born again"), six out of ten adults say they have made a personal commitment to Jesus Christ that is important in their lives. About half of those individuals can be classified as born again (that is, they believe that they will have eternal salvation as a result of their own confession of sins and personal reliance upon Christ as their Savior), while the remaining half are relying upon their behavior and achievements to earn entry into Heaven.

We Are Not Lacking for Religion

Most people in America (more than nine out of ten) believe in a god or gods that have power over the universe. The question is, what god do they believe in? After analyzing various surveys, we have concluded that about two-thirds of the population believe in the God worshipped by the Christian church. Acceptance of other gods is growing slowly but steadily in America, as true Christianity loses its foothold in our culture.

God, god, and gods

Three-quarters of all adults strongly agree that there is only one true God, whose attributes include holiness and perfection, and who created the world and continues to rule over it today. There are dramatic differences in opinion on this matter according to socioeconomic status. Holding such views is much more likely among "downscale" individuals: those with lower levels of education and income.

Three-quarters of all adults also strongly agree that there is a god who watches over them and answers their prayers. The same socioeconomic patterns are evident in responses to this question.

Satan as a Symbol

At the same time that increasing numbers of people are questioning the existence of a holy and omnipotent God, even greater numbers question the existence of Satan. Only one-fourth of the adult public strongly disagree that Satan is simply a symbol of evil—that is, a representation of evil, but not actually a living being or spirit. What makes this revelation all the more chilling is to recognize that even within the Christian community, the majority do not embrace the belief that Satan is a real being.

Syncretism and Works-based Theology

Confusion over spiritual matters is evident when examining perspectives on the relationship between Christianity and other faiths.

About four out of every ten adults strongly concurred that when Christians, Jews, Buddhists, and others pray to their god, all of those individuals are actually praying to the same god, but simply use different names for that deity. Only one out of every six adults strongly disagreed with this view. Larger proportions of born again Christians and people who attend evangelical churches concur with this sentiment than reject it.

Self-determination is also catching on in a big way across the nation. Accepting the philosophy that a person can determine his or her own destiny is one of the central—and most appealing—tenets of many of the New Age sects. The survey discovered that a majority of Americans (56%) strongly agreed that each of us has the power to determine our own destiny.

In a related matter, note that a plurality of adults believe that the notion that "God helps those who help themselves" is drawn directly from the Bible. In fact, a larger proportion of born again Christians than non-Christians strongly affirmed the Bible as the source of this statement. It is, of course, neither from the Bible (Benjamin Franklin originally penned the statement) nor consistent with the teaching in the Bible.

Spreading the Word

Evangelism also raises questions among people. Adults were about evenly split between agreeing and disagreeing that individuals have a responsibility to share their religious convictions with people who hold different beliefs. It was instructive to discover that less than half of the born again Christians and those who attend evangelical churches strongly agreed that they have such a responsibility.

13 HOW WE VIEW OUR RELIGIOUS IDENTITY

HOW MANY AMERICANS CALL THEMSELVES "RELIGIOUS"?

> **Question:** *Please tell me whether or not the word "religious" accurately describes you.*

Overall, 64% of the adults in America believe they are religious. This represents a significant decline from the 72% level achieved in 1985.

Age is clearly related to this factor. The older persons are, the more likely they are to describe themselves as religious. Among Baby Busters, only half (49%) embrace this term. The proportions rise to the point where almost nine out of ten seniors (88%) say they are religious.

Blacks are also somewhat more likely than whites to view themselves as being religious (76% vs. 64%, respectively), and women are much more likely than men to use this expression (71% vs. 57%).

The more removed from an urban environment persons are, the more likely they are to say they are religious. Among people who live in urban areas, 57% say they are religious. In contrast, 65% of suburbanites and 74% of rural residents make the same claim.

Not surprisingly, the two regions that have traditionally proven most difficult for the Church to penetrate—the northeast and the Pacific states—were home to the people least likely to say they are religious.

While more than four out of five born again Christians say they are religious, the most surprising factor is that 15% of the Christian community claim they are not religious. The broad definition of the term *religious* is underscored by noting that even one-third of the unchurched call themselves religious. Those aligned with Protestant churches were also more likely to do so than were adults who are affiliated with the Catholic church.

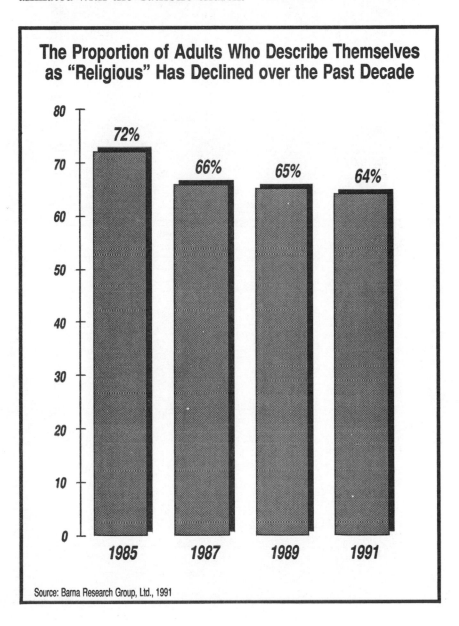

The Proportion of Adults Who Describe Themselves as "Religious" Has Declined over the Past Decade

Source: Barna Research Group, Ltd., 1991

Q: Please tell me whether or not the word "religious" accurately describes you.

		Yes	No	Don't Know	N
Total Population		64%	35%	1%	1005
Age:	18 to 25	49	51	*	190
	26*44	62	36	2	464
	45*54	73	27	*	141
	55*64	79	20	1	101
	65 or older	88	12	*	92
Education:	High school or less	65	33	2	453
	Some college	67	32	1	242
	College graduate	61	39	*	306
Ethnicity:	White	64	35	1	744
	Black	76	24	*	119
Household Income:	Under $20,000	67	30	3	184
	$20,000 to $39,999	62	37	*	397
	$40,000 to $59,999	66	33	1	186
	$60,000 or more	57	42	1	142
Gender:	Male	57	42	1	490
	Female	71	27	2	515
Married:	Yes	71	28	2	570
	No	56	43	*	432
Community:	Urban	57	42	1	340
	Suburban	65	34	1	387
	Rural	74	25	1	245
Region:	Northeast	57	42	1	227
	Midwest	70	29	1	228
	South	69	30	*	210
	Mountain	67	32	1	171
	Pacific	57	41	2	171
Born Again:	Yes	84	15	1	355
	No	54	45	1	650
Denominational Affiliation:	Evangelical	81	18	1	246
	Catholic	66	32	2	250
	Mainline	76	23	1	178
Church Attender:	Yes	75	24	1	762
	No	32	68	2	243

HOW MANY AMERICANS CALL THEMSELVES "BORN AGAIN"?

 Question: *Please tell me whether or not the phrase "born again" accurately describes you.*

One-third of all adults (34%) classify themselves as born again Christians. (Remember that throughout this research, when reference is made to "born again Christians," it is not these individuals who are being described; instead, the report alludes to individuals whose religious beliefs are closely aligned with the biblical meaning of the term.)

The people most likely to view themselves as born again Christians are those 45 or older (i.e. pre-Boomers); those who have not graduated from college; and individuals whose household incomes are below $60,000. Married adults and those living in rural areas are more likely to choose this term than are their counterparts. People living in the south, southwestern, and mountain states are also far above average in their use of this phrase.

Blacks (55%) are much more likely than whites (32%) to accept this label. Gender, however, appears to make no difference.

The inconsistency of this phrase is demonstrated by the finding that among those who call themselves born again Christians, only 65% actually believe that they will have eternal life because they have confessed their sins and have accepted Jesus Christ as their Savior. This means that one-third of the people who, according to their beliefs, are likely to be born again Christians do not call themselves by this term.

There is a distinct hierarchy of usage of this term according to denominational affiliation, too. Two-thirds of those who attend evangelical churches (69%) state that they are born again. Half as many (32%) who attend mainline Protestant churches claim to be born again. Among Catholics, 14% say they are born again.

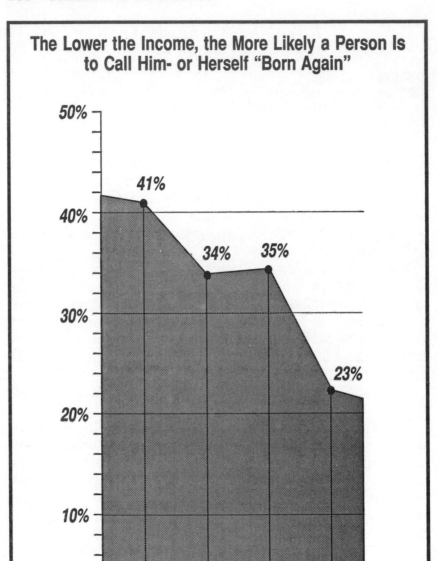

The Lower the Income, the More Likely a Person Is to Call Him- or Herself "Born Again"

Source: Barna Research Group, Ltd., 1991

Q: Please tell me whether or not the word "born again" accurately describes you.

		Yes	No	Don't Know	N
Total Population		34%	64%	2%	1005
Age:	18 to 25	22	77	1	190
	26-44	34	65	1	464
	45-54	42	57	2	141
	55-64	38	59	3	101
	65 or older	45	52	3	92
Education:	High school or less	38	60	2	453
	Some college	35	64	1	242
	College graduate	27	72	1	306
Ethnicity:	White	32	66	2	744
	Black	55	45	*	119
Household Income:	Under $20,000	41	58	1	184
	$20,000 to $39,999	34	64	2	397
	$40,000 to $59,999	35	65	*	186
	$60,000 or more	23	76	1	142
Gender:	Male	32	66	2	490
	Female	36	63	2	515
Married:	Yes	40	58	2	570
	No	27	73	1	432
Community:	Urban	29	69	2	340
	Suburban	30	68	2	387
	Rural	45	55	*	245
Region:	Northeast	17	82	1	227
	Midwest	33	64	3	228
	South	48	50	2	210
	Mountain	46	53	1	171
	Pacific	29	70	1	169
Born Again:	Yes	65	33	2	355
	No	17	81	1	650
Denominational Affiliation:	Evangelical	69	29	2	246
	Catholic	14	86	*	250
	Mainline	32	66	2	178
Church Attender:	Yes	41	57	2	762
	No	13	86	1	243

14 THE RELEVANCE OF CHRISTIANITY IN OUR LIVES

IS THE CHRISTIAN FAITH RELEVANT?

 Question: *"The Christian faith is relevant to the way you live today."* Do you agree strongly, agree somewhat, disagree somewhat, or disagree strongly with that statement?

Overall, almost half of all adults (47%) strongly agree with this statement. Such agreement is related to a number of factors.

Age is an important correlate. Fewer than half of all Boomers and Busters strongly agree, while a majority of their elders do so. Women (52%) were more likely than men (42%) to concur, while married adults (51%) were more likely than single adults to strongly agree (43%). Adults living in urban areas were also less likely than other individuals to indicate strong agreement.

Born again Christians were more than twice as likely as non-believers to accept this statement (73% vs. 34%, respectively). Interestingly, those who attend church regularly were more likely than non-attenders to buy into this perception (55% vs. 24%), but notice that the level of strong agreement among those who attend church services was barely above the 50% mark. As might have been expected, evangelicals (62%) were more likely than mainline Protestants (55%) to endorse the statement, and both of those groups were considerably more likely than Catholics (42%) to strongly agree.

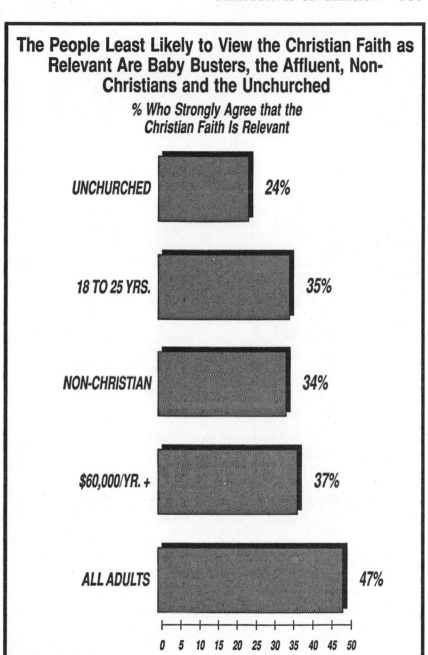

The People Least Likely to View the Christian Faith as Relevant Are Baby Busters, the Affluent, Non-Christians and the Unchurched

% Who Strongly Agree that the Christian Faith Is Relevant

UNCHURCHED — 24%

18 TO 25 YRS. — 35%

NON-CHRISTIAN — 34%

$60,000/YR. + — 37%

ALL ADULTS — 47%

0   5   10   15   20   25   30   35   40   45   50

Source: Barna Research Group, Ltd., 1991

Q: "The Christian faith is relevant to the way you live today." Do you agree strongly, agree somewhat, disagree somewhat, or disagree strongly with that statement?

		Agree Strongly	Agree Somewhat	Disagree Somewhat	Disagree Strongly	Don't Know	N
Total Population		47%	34%	9%	8%	3%	1005
Age:	18 to 25	35	37	11	15	3	190
	26-44	46	39	8	6	2	141
	45-54	53	27	7	10	3	141
	55-64	55	26	8	8	3	101
	65 or older	69	19	4	3	5	92
Education:	High school or less	45	34	8	8	4	453
	Some college	54	32	8	5	1	242
	College graduate	45	34	10	10	2	306
Ethnicity:	White	47	35	8	8	3	744
	Black	56	29	8	4	2	119
Household Income·	Under $20,000	52	28	9	7	4	184
	$20,000 to $39,999	45	36	9	7	2	397
	$40,000 to $59,999	55	31	6	8	1	186
	$60,000 or more	37	44	8	10	1	142
Gender:	Male	42	36	10	10	2	490
	Female	52	31	7	6	4	515
Married:	Yes	51	33	9	5	2	570
	No	43	34	8	12	4	432
Community:	Urban	40	38	9	11	3	340
	Suburban	50	32	9	7	3	387
	Rural	56	30	8	6	1	245
Region:	Northeast	42	35	11	10	3	227
	Midwest	45	39	7	7	3	228
	South	51	31	9	5	4	210
	Mountain	54	31	5	10	*	171
	Pacific	47	30	11	9	3	169
Born Again:	Yes	73	22	2	2	2	355
	No	34	40	12	11	4	650
Denominational Affiliation:	Evangelical	62	28	5	3	2	246
	Catholic	42	44	7	3	3	250
	Mainline	55	41	2	1	1	178
Church Attender:	Yes	55	31	6	5	3	762
	No	24	41	16	16	3	243

ARE CHRISTIAN CHURCHES RELEVANT?

Question: *"The Christian churches in your area are relevant to the way you live today." Do you agree strongly, agree somewhat, disagree somewhat, or disagree strongly with that statement?*

Compared to people's responses to the statement about the relevance of the Christian faith, the lower levels of agreement with this statement underscore the unflattering image of the local church that many people possess. Overall, just 28% strongly agreed with this statement, with an additional 38% agreeing somewhat.

Age was, again, an important factor, but in a different way. This time, it was primarily senior citizens who were distinguished from others. Among seniors, 49% strongly agreed; among all other adults, just 26% gave a similar response.

Women expressed slightly more confidence in the relevance of local churches than did men (32% vs. 24%), while married adults (32%) again rated the church more favorably than did single adults (23%).

Born again Christians were twice as likely as other adults to strongly agree (41% vs. 21%). Those associated with evangelical and mainline churches were more likely than Catholics to concur. Naturally, those who regularly attend church services were more likely than the unchurched to agree strongly (34% vs. 10%).

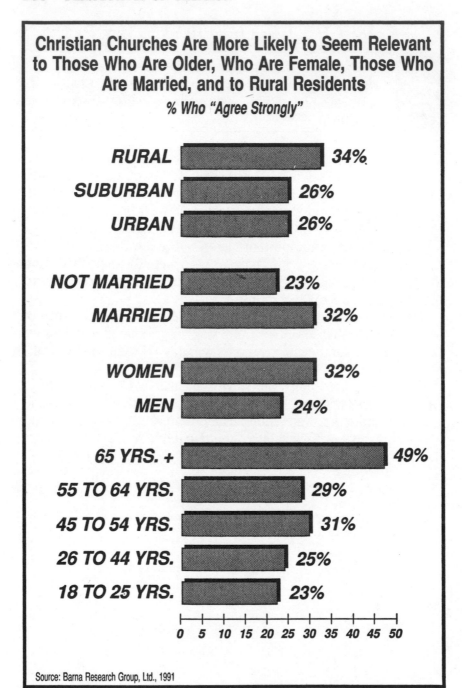

Christian Churches Are More Likely to Seem Relevant to Those Who Are Older, Who Are Female, Those Who Are Married, and to Rural Residents

% Who "Agree Strongly"

RURAL — 34%
SUBURBAN — 26%
URBAN — 26%

NOT MARRIED — 23%
MARRIED — 32%

WOMEN — 32%
MEN — 24%

65 YRS. + — 49%
55 TO 64 YRS. — 29%
45 TO 54 YRS. — 31%
26 TO 44 YRS. — 25%
18 TO 25 YRS. — 23%

0 5 10 15 20 25 30 35 40 45 50

Source: Barna Research Group, Ltd., 1991

Q: "The Christian churches in your area are relevant to the way you live today." Do you agree strongly, agree somewhat, disagree somewhat, or disagree strongly with that statement?

		Agree Strongly	Agree Somewhat	Disagree Somewhat	Disagree Strongly	Don't Know	N
Total Population		28%	38%	14%	11%	9%	1005
Age:	18 to 25	23	35	24	15	3	190
	26-44	25	42	12	12	9	464
	45-54	31	35	12	11	10	141
	55-64	29	40	14	4	13	101
	65 or older	49	33	3	7	8	92
Education:	High school or less	30	38	13	9	10	453
	Some college	27	42	15	10	6	242
	College graduate	26	35	15	15	10	306
Ethnicity:	White	29	40	13	10	9	744
	Black	35	30	11	15	10	119
Household Income:	Under $20,000	31	37	13	10	9	184
	$20,000 to $39,999	25	40	15	10	10	397
	$40,000 to $59,999	30	40	13	12	5	186
	$60,000 or more	27	38	16	15	5	142
Gender:	Male	24	38	17	13	8	490
	Female	32	38	11	9	10	515
Married:	Yes	32	39	12	8	9	570
	No	23	38	17	15	8	432
Community:	Urban	26	37	16	14	8	340
	Suburban	26	37	16	12	10	387
	Rural	34	43	11	6	7	245
Region:	Northeast	29	32	15	16	8	227
	Midwest	31	39	15	8	8	228
	South	30	40	12	10	9	210
	Mountain	29	36	14	12	8	171
	Pacific	21	44	15	9	11	169
Born Again:	Yes	41	38	7	4	10	355
	No	21	38	18	15	8	650
Denominational Affiliation:	Evangelical	40	38	10	7	5	246
	Catholic	28	50	11	5	5	250
	Mainline	36	46	8	3	6	178
Church Attender:	Yes	34	41	9	8	8	762
	No	10	29	31	20	10	243

ARE CHRISTIAN CHURCHES TOLERANT OF DIFFERENT IDEAS?

Question: *"Christian churches are tolerant of people who have different ideas than those taught by the Church." Do you agree strongly, agree somewhat, disagree somewhat, or disagree strongly?*

Just 19% strongly agreed with this statement, while another 40% agreed somewhat.

Look at the segments of society that are least likely to acknowledge that the Church is tolerant of folks with different perspectives. Boomers and Busters lead the way. The upscale audience—those with college education and with higher income levels—are also among the most skeptical. Men (16%) were nearly twice as likely as women (9%) to express strong disagreement with the statement. Single adults (16%) were also more dubious than were married individuals (10%).

Whether or not a person is a born again Christian appears to have no impact on reaction to this statement, since both groups provided similar response distributions. However, people who do not attend church services were much more likely than those who attend regularly to reject this statement.

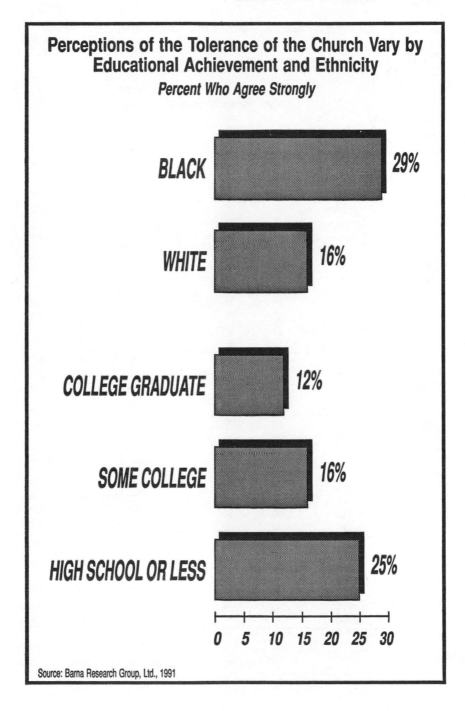

Perceptions of the Tolerance of the Church Vary by Educational Achievement and Ethnicity

Percent Who Agree Strongly

BLACK — 29%

WHITE — 16%

COLLEGE GRADUATE — 12%

SOME COLLEGE — 16%

HIGH SCHOOL OR LESS — 25%

0   5   10   15   20   25   30

Source: Barna Research Group, Ltd., 1991

Q: "Christian churches are tolerant of people who have different ideas than those taught by the Church." Do you agree strongly, agree somewhat, disagree somewhat, or disagree strongly with that statement?

		Agree Strongly	Agree Somewhat	Disagree Somewhat	Disagree Strongly	Don't Know	N
Total Population		19%	40%	20%	12%	9%	1005
Age:	18 to 25	16	44	22	13	4	190
	26-44	18	39	22	12	8	464
	45-54	21	43	12	15	8	141
	55-64	22	40	14	15	10	101
	65 or older	23	35	20	7	15	92
Education:	High school or less	25	37	16	9	12	453
	Some college	16	44	20	14	6	242
	College graduate	12	41	24	15	8	306
Ethnicity:	White	16	44	19	13	9	744
	Black	29	37	18	11	5	119
Household Income:	Under $20,000	24	37	20	10	9	184
	$20,000 to $39,999	18	44	16	13	9	397
	$40,000 to $59,999	18	42	22	11	7	186
	$60,000 or more	18	35	29	13	6	142
Gender:	Male	18	36	22	16	8	490
	Female	20	44	18	9	10	515
Married:	Yes	21	42	19	10	9	570
	No	17	37	21	16	9	432
Community:	Urban	20	39	19	13	10	340
	Suburban	19	38	23	12	8	387
	Rural	15	47	16	13	9	245
Region:	Northeast	20	35	22	12	11	227
	Midwest	19	45	18	11	8	228
	South	21	42	16	10	11	210
	Mountain	20	37	21	16	7	171
	Pacific	14	40	23	15	9	169
Born Again:	Yes	23	42	15	11	8	355
	No	17	39	22	13	10	650
Denominational Affiliation:	Evangelical	24	41	18	10	8	246
	Catholic	20	40	23	11	6	250
	Mainline	17	51	15	10	8	178
Church Attender:	Yes	21	43	17	9	9	762
	No	12	30	26	21	11	243

15 HOW WE VIEW CHRIST AND LIFE AFTER DEATH

HOW MANY AMERICANS HAVE MADE A PERSONAL COMMITMENT TO CHRIST?

 Question: *Have you ever made a personal commitment to Jesus Christ that is still important in your life today?*

Levels of Commitment

Three out of every five adults (62%) claim that they have made a personal commitment to Christ. Related research conducted during the past several years clearly suggests that the nature of that commitment traverses the spectrum from a light, intellectual assent to the divinity of Christ to a wholehearted, life-changing submission to the lordship of Christ.

The Generation Gap

While Boomers and Busters share a relatively skeptical view of Christianity, their levels of commitment to Christ differ. While less than half of the Busters claimed to have made a personal commitment to Jesus (48%), two-thirds of the Boomers made such a claim (66%). In this matter, Boomers were more in line with their seniors than they were with their successors.

Those with higher levels of education and income were the least likely to commit to Christ. In comparison to blacks (76%), white adults (60%) were also much less likely to make such a commitment.

Other segments that generally showed a greater inclination to support Christianity—women, married adults, rural residents—again emerged as much more likely than others to claim they have a commitment to Christ.

Commitment to Christ Among the Unsaved

Realize that among individuals who are not deemed to be born again, two out of five (41%) state that they have made a personal commitment to Jesus. The challenge to churches is clearly to help these individuals understand that while their commitment represents a start, they have yet to reach the fullness of a true relationship with Christ. Ancillary studies have shown that literally millions of adults who have made such a commitment believe they have forged as deep a faith as is possible, and thus feel no further need to pursue the development of their relationship with God.

Perhaps amazingly, one-quarter of regular church attenders, one-third of those aligned with mainline churches, and half of those associated with the Catholic church claim they have not established a personal commitment to Christ that bears any significance in their life. What is the purpose of engaging in religious activity through those churches, if not to develop that deeper relationship with Christ? What kind of community of faith would allow such a circumstance to continue over time?

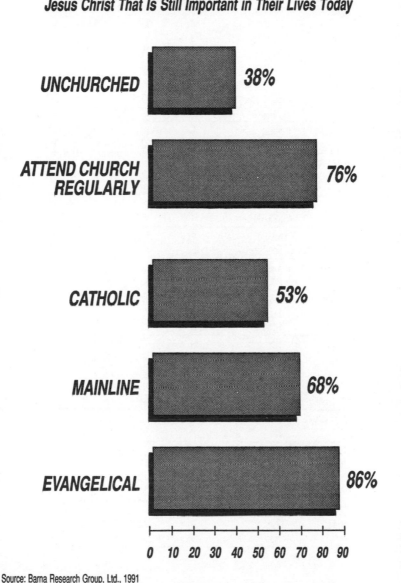

Levels of Personal Commitment to Jesus Christ Differ According to Church Affiliation

% Who Say They Have Made a Personal Commitment to Jesus Christ That Is Still Important in Their Lives Today

UNCHURCHED — 38%

ATTEND CHURCH REGULARLY — 76%

CATHOLIC — 53%

MAINLINE — 68%

EVANGELICAL — 86%

0 10 20 30 40 50 60 70 80 90

Source: Barna Research Group, Ltd., 1991

Q: Have you ever made a personal commitment to Jesus Christ that is still important in your life today?

		Yes	No	Don't Know	N
Total Population		62%	37%	2%	1005
Age:	18 to 25	48	51	*	190
	26-44	66	32	2	464
	45-54	68	30	1	141
	55-64	60	35	5	101
	65 or older	66	30	5	92
Education:	High school or less	63	35	2	453
	Some college	66	33	1	242
	College graduate	56	42	2	306
Ethnicity:	White	60	38	2	744
	Black	76	22	2	119
Household Income:	Under $20,000	67	32	2	184
	$20,000 to $39,999	63	35	2	397
	$40,000 to $59,999	62	35	3	186
	$60,000 or more	51	49	*	142
Gender:	Male	56	43	1	490
	Female	67	30	3	515
Married:	Yes	69	29	2	570
	No	52	46	2	432
Community:	Urban	61	39	*	340
	Suburban	59	38	4	387
	Rural	69	29	1	245
Region:	Northeast	51	47	3	227
	Midwest	62	36	2	228
	South	68	30	2	210
	Mountain	72	26	2	171
	Pacific	57	42	1	169
Born Again:	Yes	100	*	*	355
	No	41	56	3	650
Denominational Affiliation:	Evangelical	86	12	2	246
	Catholic	53	45	2	250
	Mainline	68	30	3	178
Church Attender:	Yes	76	22	2	762
	No	38	61	1	243

WHAT DO AMERICANS BELIEVE ABOUT LIFE AFTER DEATH?

 Question: *I'm going to read six statements about life after death. Please tell me which one of these statements comes closest to describing your own belief about life after death.*

Barely more than half of the people who have made a personal commitment to Jesus Christ are dependent upon that relationship as their means to salvation (56%). Overall, 35% of the adult population could be described as born again, using this definition.

Are We Gaining Ground?

This figure has remained unchanged over the past six years. While the aggregate number of born again Christians is growing, because the adult population is expanding, the "market share" of true believers has not increased. If these figures are projected, we can assume that there are approximately 63 million born again adults.

Differences Among Age and Race Categories

Busters show the greatest resistance to accepting Christ as their Savior. Less than one-quarter of the Busters interviewed had done so (23%). In contrast 37% of the Boomers had accepted Christ, while 41% of their seniors had made a similar decision.

Blacks were noticeably more likely than whites to accept Christ (51% vs. 35%). Others who were most likely to have accepted Christ were married adults (42%), those living in rural areas (46%), and residents of the south, southwest, and mountain regions (43%). Education and income, the signs of secularization, appeared to offer somewhat of a barrier to acceptance of Christ.

Church Affiliation and Acceptance of Christ

Not quite two-thirds of those associated with evangelical churches (63%) had accepted Christ as their Savior. In dramatic contrast, just

39% of those affiliated with mainline churches had the same commitment, and only 16% of those in the Catholic church were similarly aligned. Another perspective on the latter figure, however, is that there does appear to be a growing contingent of born again Christians within the Catholic church. In fact, if we were to look at the born again community and divide it by denominational affiliation, the Catholic church actually produces the second largest number of Christian adults (behind Baptist churches).

What People Groups Are Most Likely to Be Christian?

(Index: 100 = Population Mean)

126 OR MORE	WAY ABOVE AVERAGE	*EVANGELICAL AFFILIATION (180)* *BLACKS (146)* *ATTEND CHURCH REGULARLY (134)* *RURAL (131)* *SOUTH (126)* *55 TO 64 YRS. (126)*
125 TO 111	ABOVE AVERAGE	*45 TO 54 YRS. (123)* *MARRIED (120)* *MOUNTAIN/SOUTHWEST (120)* *SOME COLLEGE (117)* *$40,000 TO $59,999/YR. (114)* *MAINLINE PROTESTANT (111)*
110 TO 90	AVERAGE	*FEMALE (109)* *BOOMERS (106)* *SENIORS (103)* *LESS THAN $20,000/YR. (103)* *HIGH SCHOOL OR LESS (100)* *$20,000 TO $39,999/YR. (100)* *WHITE (100)* *SUBURBAN (97)* *MALE (91)* *MIDWEST (91)* *PACIFIC (91)*
89 TO 75	BELOW AVERAGE	*COLLEGE GRADUATE (86)* *$60,000/YR. + (86)* *URBAN (83)* *NOT MARRIED (77)*
74 OR LESS	WAY BELOW AVERAGE	*BUSTERS (66)* *CATHOLICS (46)* *UNCHURCHED (40)*

Note: "Christians" are defined as having made a personal commitment to Jesus Christ that is still important in their lives today; and believing that they will go to Heaven when they die because they confessed their sins and have accepted Jesus Christ as their Savior.

Indexes are standardized scores. Index scores below the population index (i.e. 100) indicate population segments that are less likely to have the test attribute; segments with scores above the base index are more likely to engage in that behavior. The larger the difference from the base index, the more the segment differs from the norm.

Source: Barna Research Group, Ltd., 1991

Q: I'm going to read six statements about life after death. Please tell me which one comes closest to describing your own belief about what will happen to you when you die. (Please see next page for column headings.)

		#1	#2	#3	#4	#5	#6	#7	Don't Know	N
Total Population		5%	6%	35%	5%	1%	7%	38%	3%	1005
Age:	18 to 25	5	6	23	3	1	11	52	*	190
	26-44	4	8	37	6	1	7	34	3	464
	45-54	6	6	43	6	2	5	3i	2	141
	55-64	3	2	44	5	*	1	40	5	101
	65 or older	8	3	36	4	*	11	34	3	92
Education:	High school or less	7	5	35	5	1	7	37	2	453
	Some college	3	7	41	4	1	7	34	3	242
	College graduate	2	7	31	6	1	7	44	3	306
Ethnicity:	White	5	7	35	5	1	6	40	3	744
	Black	1	3	51	3	3	8	24	2	119
Household Income:	Under $20,000	1	5	36	5	2	9	33	2	184
	$20,000 to $39,999	6	8	35	5	1	6	37	3	397
	$40,000 to $59,999	3	5	40	4	*	7	38	3	186
	$60,000 or more	1	6	30	9	*	4	49	1	142
Gender:	Male	4	6	32	5	1	7	44	2	490
	Female	6	7	38	5	1	7	33	3	515
Married:	Yes	5	6	42	6	1	7	31	3	570
	No	5	6	27	4	1	8	48	2	432
Community:	Urban	5	7	29	8	1	8	39	3	340
	Suburban	4	8	34	3	1	6	41	2	387
	Rural	4	4	46	5	*	7	31	2	245
Region:	Northeast	2	9	28	4	2	5	49	2	227
	Midwest	7	6	32	7	*	5	38	4	228
	South	4	7	44	4	*	7	32	2	210
	Mountain	5	6	42	4	1	11	28	2	171
	Pacific	4	2	32	8	1	8	43	2	169
Born Again:	Yes	*	*	100	*	*	*	*	*	355
	No	7	10	*	8	1	11	59	4	650
Denominational Affiliation:	Evangelical	7	6	63	3	1	5	14	2	246
	Catholic	6	11	16	8	1	10	47	2	250
	Mainline	5	7	39	9	*	6	32	2	178
Church Attender:	Yes	6	8	47	6	1	6	24	2	762
	No	2	4	14	4	1	8	62	4	243

Columns:

#1 "When you die, you will go to Heaven because you have tried to obey the ten commandments."

#2 "When you die, you will go to Heaven because you are basically a good person."

#3 "When you die, you will go to Heaven because you have confessed your sins and accepted Jesus Christ as your Savior."

#4 "When you die, you will go to Heaven because God loves all people and will not let them perish."

#5 "When you die, you will not go to Heaven."

#6 "You do not know what will happen after you die."

#7 Column 7 represents all people who said "no" to the question, "Have you ever made a personal commitment to Jesus Christ that is still important in your life today?" These people were NOT asked the question about life after death.

16 HOW WE VIEW GOD AND SATAN

DO AMERICANS BELIEVE IN ONE TRUE, PERFECT CREATOR?

 Question: *"There is only one true God, who is holy and perfect, and who created the world and rules it today." Do you agree strongly, agree somewhat, disagree somewhat, or disagree strongly with that statement?*

Three-quarters of all adults (74%) strongly affirmed this statement. Realize, of course, that respondents were not necessarily referring to the God who is worshipped in Christian churches, but simply affirming that there is a holy and omnipotent God that exists and has power over the universe.

Exploring Belief

Once again, both educational achievement and wealth seemed to have an adverse effect on a person's willingness to believe in a holy, perfect, and all-powerful deity. People with a college degree were 25% less likely to strongly agree with this statement than were those with no more than a high school education. Individuals from households earning $60,000 or more were 28% less likely than those making under $20,000 to strongly support the statement. Some of the difference can be ascribed to the fact that seniors are least likely to have a college degree and are more likely than the average to be living on a modest annual income. Given the higher tendency of seniors to embrace Christianity and traditional Christian viewpoints, the difference may not be wholly unexpected. However, not all of the variation between the "haves" and the "have nots" can explain the gap.

Regional Differences

As has generally been the case, people living in the northeast and in the far west are those who are least convinced of the existence of a perfect God. Less than two-thirds of the residents of the northeast strongly agreed with this statement, while 70% of the

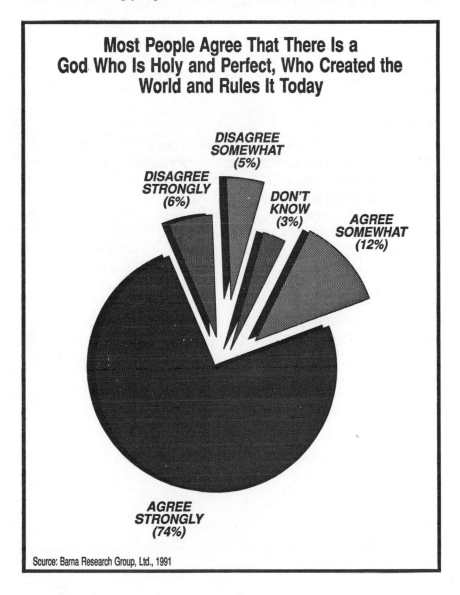

Most People Agree That There Is a God Who Is Holy and Perfect, Who Created the World and Rules It Today

DISAGREE SOMEWHAT (5%)

DISAGREE STRONGLY (6%)

DON'T KNOW (3%)

AGREE SOMEWHAT (12%)

AGREE STRONGLY (74%)

Source: Barna Research Group, Ltd., 1991

adults in the Pacific states concurred. Compare that to the 82% affirmation level among southern adults, 78% among people in the midwest, and 77% of those in the southwest and mountain states.

Racial and Gender Differences

Black adults were nearly 20% more likely than whites to strongly agree with this statement. Also following the established pattern, women (80%) were considerably more likely than men (67%) to strongly support the sentiment of this statement.

In-roads

On an encouraging note for Christians, realize that almost two-thirds (62%) of the non-believers strongly agreed with this statement. Thus, while non-believers may not have a true commitment to, or relationship with Jesus Christ, most people seem to possess a foundational interest in religion and a basic commitment to the notion of a perfect, holy, and powerful God of the universe.

On a challenging note, also see that among people who attend Catholic and mainline Protestant churches, there are many who do not accept the truths included in the statement. Among people who associate with the Catholic church, 28% did not strongly agree with the statement. Among those who affiliate with mainline churches, about one out of every five (18%) did not strongly affirm the perspective of the statement.

Q: "There is only one true God, who is holy and perfect, and who created the world and rules it today." Do you agree strongly, agree somewhat, disagree somewhat, or disagree strongly with that statement?

		Agree Strongly	Agree Somewhat	Disagree Somewhat	Disagree Strongly	Don't Know	N
Total Population		74%	12%	5%	6%	3%	1005
Age:	18 to 25	69	13	5	11	3	190
	26-44	73	15	5	4	3	464
	45-54	76	10	3	8	3	141
	55-64	81	11	1	5	2	101
	65 or older	82	5	5	2	6	92
Education:	High school or less	81	8	3	4	3	453
	Some college	76	14	4	6	1	242
	College graduate	61	17	9	9	5	306
Ethnicity:	White	72	13	5	5	4	744
	Black	88	8	3	*	1	119
Household Income:	Under $20,000	82	10	3	3	2	184
	$20,000 to $39,999	74	12	6	5	3	397
	$40,000 to $59,999	74	13	6	4	4	186
	$60,000 or more	59	19	5	15	3	142
Gender:	Male	67	13	7	9	3	490
	Female	80	12	3	3	3	515
Married:	Yes	77	11	5	4	3	570
	No	69	14	5	8	3	432
Community:	Urban	69	14	7	6	4	340
	Suburban	73	12	5	7	3	387
	Rural	79	12	2	4	2	245
Region:	Northeast	62	16	10	8	4	227
	Midwest	78	13	4	3	4	228
	South	82	9	4	3	3	210
	Mountain	77	10	4	7	2	171
	Pacific	70	14	3	10	3	169
Born Again:	Yes	94	5	1	*	*	355
	No	62	17	7	9	5	650
Denominational Affiliation:	Evangelical	95	3	1	1	*	246
	Catholic	72	19	3	3	3	250
	Mainline	82	14	2	*	1	178
Church Attender:	Yes	85	11	2	1	1	762
	No	55	14	10	16	5	243

IS THE DEVIL FOR REAL?

 Question: *"The devil, or Satan, is not a living being but is a symbol of evil." Do you agree strongly, agree somewhat, disagree somewhat, or disagree strongly with that statement?*

One-third of all adults strongly agree that Satan is merely symbolic of evil, but does not exist as a true presence. Overall, three out of five adults are inclined to disbelieve in the existence of Satan. Only one out of four adults strongly disagreed that Satan is symbolic rather than real.

There was surprising unity of perception on this matter. Only a few people groups stand out as having different views. Those segments include Baby Busters and residents of the northeast. Others included born again Christians, those who regularly attend church services, and adults associated with evangelical churches.

Note that adults who attend Catholic and mainline Protestant churches are considerably less likely than those associated with evangelical churches to accept the notion of Satan as a living being. Among Catholics, 69% agree (either strongly or somewhat) that Satan is symbolic of evil; 65% of the mainline Protestants concur. In contrast, only 47% of those at evangelical churches hold a similar viewpoint.

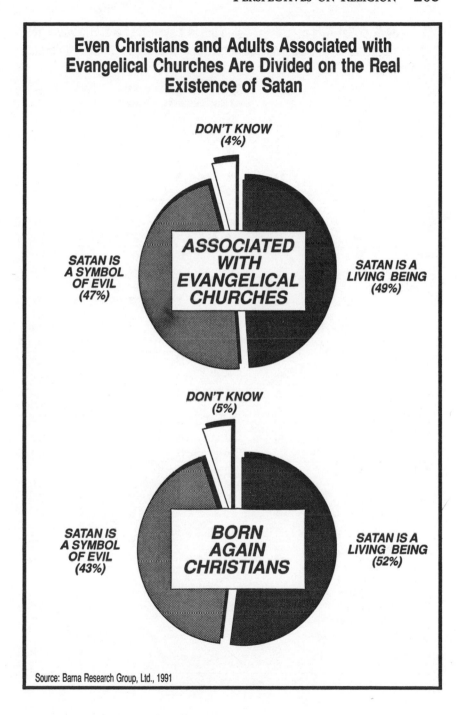

Even Christians and Adults Associated with Evangelical Churches Are Divided on the Real Existence of Satan

DON'T KNOW
(4%)

ASSOCIATED WITH EVANGELICAL CHURCHES

SATAN IS A SYMBOL OF EVIL
(47%)

SATAN IS A LIVING BEING
(49%)

DON'T KNOW
(5%)

BORN AGAIN CHRISTIANS

SATAN IS A SYMBOL OF EVIL
(43%)

SATAN IS A LIVING BEING
(52%)

Source: Barna Research Group, Ltd., 1991

Q: "The devil, or Satan, is not a living being but is a symbol of evil." Do you agree strongly, agree somewhat, disagree somewhat, or disagree strongly with that statement?

		Agree Strongly	Agree Somewhat	Disagree Somewhat	Disagree Strongly	Don't Know	N
Total Population		35%	25%	11%	24%	6%	1005
Age:	18 to 25	33	31	16	15	4	190
	26-44	32	26	11	26	6	464
	45-54	40	20	9	25	6	141
	55-64	38	24	6	26	6	101
	65 or older	36	13	10	28	13	92
Education:	High school or less	38	21	9	23	8	453
	Some college	33	27	10	26	4	242
	College graduate	31	28	14	22	6	306
Ethnicity:	White	33	26	11	24	7	744
	Black	41	20	9	23	7	119
Household Income:	Under $20,000	35	25	8	24	8	184
	$20,000 to $39,999	37	23	12	23	5	397
	$40,000 to $59,999	38	26	6	24	6	186
	$60,000 or more	22	33	18	24	4	142
Gender:	Male	33	24	13	24	6	490
	Female	37	25	9	23	7	515
Married:	Yes	35	23	10	26	6	570
	No	34	27	12	20	7	432
Community:	Urban	37	27	11	20	5	340
	Suburban	32	27	12	24	5	387
	Rural	36	18	10	29	8	245
Region:	Northeast	39	22	13	18	8	227
	Midwest	36	28	8	23	5	228
	South	32	25	9	26	7	210
	Mountain	29	20	18	28	6	171
	Pacific	36	26	8	24	6	169
Born Again:	Yes	32	11	10	42	5	355
	No	36	32	11	14	7	650
Denominational Affiliation:	Evangelical	33	14	10	39	4	246
	Catholic	39	30	11	15	6	250
	Mainline	37	28	9	18	8	178
Church Attender:	Yes	34	22	10	28	6	762
	No	37	28	15	15	6	243

IS THERE A GOD WHO ANSWERS OUR PRAYERS?

Question: *"There is a God who watches over you and answers your prayers." Do you agree strongly, agree somewhat, disagree somewhat, or disagree strongly with that statement?*

Most people accepted this statement to be true: 73% agreed strongly, 16% agreed somewhat. The differences worthy of note concerned people's intensity of agreement with the statement.

Age, Education, Gender, and Race

Age again proved to be a differentiating factor. Two-thirds of the Busters strongly agreed, compared to three-quarters of adults in the 26-64 age bracket, and nine out of ten seniors.

Education and income were also significant in that the more of either quality people attained, the less likely they were to support the statement. Especially noteworthy is the fact that college graduates were more than three times as likely as other adults to strongly disagree with this statement.

Women (80%) were more likely than men (66%) to strongly agree. Blacks were more likely than whites to follow suit (90% vs. 71%, respectively).

Denominational Differences

Once again, the levels of difference among people associated with Catholic and mainline Protestant churches and those at evangelical churches is instructive. While nine out of ten who align themselves with evangelical churches strongly agreed with the statement, only three-quarters of those at Catholic or mainline churches did so.

While better than nine out of ten born again Christians affirmed the significance of this statement (92%), nearly two-thirds of all non-believers did so as well (63%). The figure was much lower among those who do not attend church, though: just half of those adults (51%) strongly agreed with the statement.

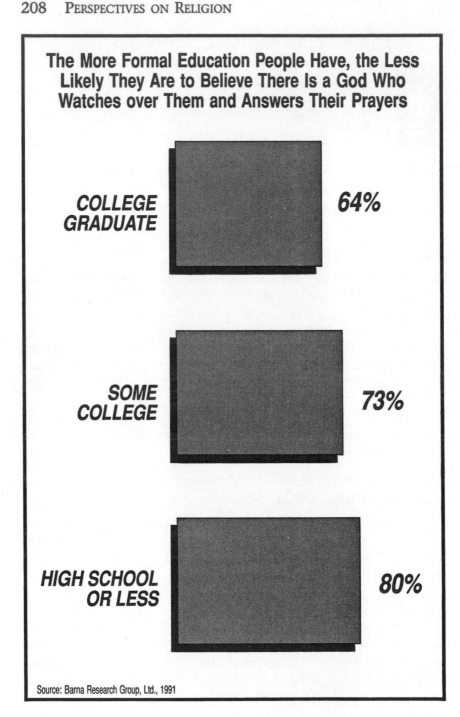

The More Formal Education People Have, the Less Likely They Are to Believe There Is a God Who Watches over Them and Answers Their Prayers

COLLEGE GRADUATE   *64%*

SOME COLLEGE   *73%*

HIGH SCHOOL OR LESS   *80%*

Source: Barna Research Group, Ltd., 1991

Q: "There is a God who watches over you and answers your prayers." Do you agree strongly, agree somewhat, disagree somewhat, or disagree strongly with that statement?

		Agree Strongly	Agree Somewhat	Disagree Somewhat	Disagree Strongly	Don't Know	N
Total Population		73%	16%	4%	6%	2%	1005
Age:	18 to 25	67	17	6	8	3	190
	26-44	73	18	4	5	1	464
	45-54	76	15	3	5	1	141
	55-64	76	13	4	7	1	101
	65 or older	87	9	1	3	*	92
Education:	High school or less	80	14	1	3	2	453
	Some college	73	17	7	2	*	242
	College graduate	64	17	6	11	2	306
Ethnicity:	White	71	19	4	5	2	744
	Black	90	5	2	3	*	119
Household Income:	Under $20,000	82	12	3	2	1	184
	$20,000 to $39,999	72	17	5	5	1	397
	$40,000 to $59,999	74	15	3	6	2	186
	$60,000 or more	64	18	6	12	1	142
Gender:	Male	66	18	5	9	1	490
	Female	80	13	4	2	2	515
Married:	Yes	76	15	4	4	1	570
	No	69	17	5	8	2	432
Community:	Urban	71	14	6	8	1	340
	Suburban	71	17	4	6	2	387
	Rural	79	17	1	3	1	245
Region:	Northeast	62	18	10	9	1	227
	Midwest	76	17	1	4	2	228
	South	79	13	4	3	1	210
	Mountain	79	12	1	8	1	171
	Pacific	71	18	5	4	2	169
Born Again:	Yes	92	7	*	*	*	355
	No	63	20	6	8	2	650
Denominational Affiliation:	Evangelical	90	9	*	1	*	246
	Catholic	76	16	4	2	1	250
	Mainline	78	21	*	*	*	178
Church Attender:	Yes	85	12	2	1	*	762
	No	51	24	6	16	3	243

DO ALL RELIGIONS PRAY TO THE SAME GOD?

 Question: *"Christians, Jews, Muslims, Buddhists, and others all pray to the same God, even though they use different names for that God." Do you agree strongly, agree somewhat, disagree somewhat, or disagree strongly with that statement?*

This idea appears to puzzle a larger proportion of adults than most of the theological statements to which they responded. Overall, the majority of adults (64%) agreed with the notion expressed by the statement; just over one-third of adults strongly agreed with the notion (37%). In addition to the 27% who disagreed with the statement, another 10% were not sure what to think.

Differences among people groups were relatively few. Women, who have generally been more likely than men to embrace the traditional Christian perspective on the theological matters posed to them, were actually more likely than men to embrace this universalist philosophy. Residents of the northeastern and Pacific states, not surprisingly, also were more likely than other adults to affirm this statement. Among those associated with churches, Catholics were by far the most likely to affirm the statement.

Notice how little difference there is between the responses of those who regularly attend church services and those who are unchurched.

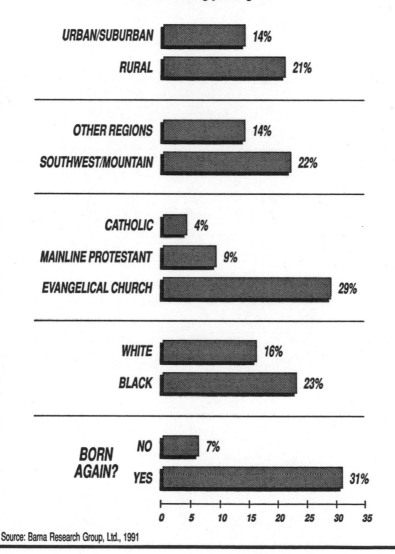

Only Five of the 33 People Groups Studied Had at Least One-fifth Who Strongly Disagreed that All People Pray to the Same God, but Just Use a Different Name for That God

% Who Strongly Disagree

URBAN/SUBURBAN	14%
RURAL	21%
OTHER REGIONS	14%
SOUTHWEST/MOUNTAIN	22%
CATHOLIC	4%
MAINLINE PROTESTANT	9%
EVANGELICAL CHURCH	29%
WHITE	16%
BLACK	23%
BORN AGAIN? NO	7%
BORN AGAIN? YES	31%

0   5   10   15   20   25   30   35

Source: Barna Research Group, Ltd., 1991

Q: "Christians, Jews, Muslims, Buddhists, and others all pray to the same God, even though they use different names for that God." Do you agree strongly, agree somewhat, disagree somewhat, or disagree strongly with that statement?

		Agree Strongly	Agree Somewhat	Disagree Somewhat	Disagree Strongly	Don't Know	N
Total Population		37%	27%	11%	16%	10%	1005
Age:	18 to 25	33	32	14	16	6	190
	26-44	37	31	9	15	8	464
	45-54	39	23	10	15	14	141
	55-64	45	20	9	19	7	101
	65 or older	39	15	11	15	19	92
Education:	High school or less	35	25	11	18	11	453
	Some college	40	27	10	15	8	242
	College graduate	38	31	11	13	8	306
Ethnicity:	White	35	29	11	16	10	744
	Black	36	20	12	23	10	119
Household Income:	Under $20,000	38	23	8	17	15	184
	$20,000 to $39,999	36	28	13	16	7	397
	$40,000 to $59,999	38	26	13	16	7	186
	$60,000 or more	35	35	9	15	7	142
Gender:	Male	32	29	14	17	8	490
	Female	42	25	8	14	11	515
Married:	Yes	37	26	10	18	9	570
	No	38	28	12	13	9	432
Community:	Urban	39	26	13	13	9	340
	Suburban	37	31	10	14	8	387
	Rural	35	25	9	21	10	245
Region:	Northeast	40	30	11	11	8	227
	Midwest	35	30	12	15	8	228
	South	35	23	12	19	12	210
	Mountain	31	23	12	22	12	171
	Pacific	46	27	8	11	7	169
Born Again:	Yes	30	18	10	31	12	355
	No	41	32	11	7	8	650
Denominational Affiliation:	Evangelical	28	18	13	29	13	246
	Catholic	50	33	6	4	6	250
	Mainline	37	33	13	9	8	178
Church Attender:	Yes	37	25	10	19	8	762
	No	35	34	11	8	12	243

17 MATTERS OF FAITH: DESTINY AND SELF-MOTIVATION

DO WE HAVE THE POWER TO DETERMINE OUR OWN DESTINY?

Question: *"Every person has the power to determine his or her own destiny in life." Do you agree strongly, agree somewhat, disagree somewhat, or disagree strongly with that statement?*

Most people (56%) strongly agreed with this statement. Including those who agreed somewhat, four out of five adults agreed with this statement (82%).

Continuity within Subgroups

There were relatively few subgroup differences worthy of mention. Baby Busters were more likely than older adults to accept this perspective. People with a high school education or less were also somewhat more likely to accept this viewpoint than were those with more formal education. Men were slightly more likely than women to embrace the notion.

The Most Polarized of Subgroups

Look at the data for the black adults interviewed. While they were among the subgroups that ranked highest in strong agreement with the statement (59%), they were also the subgroup that had the highest level of strong disagreement with the statement (19%). In other words, there was less ambiguity on this matter within the black community than is found in other people groups.

New Age Philosophy

The overall agreement with this statement ought to raise concerns among Christian leaders concerning the underlying philosophy of believers. Self-determination is one of the guiding principles of the New Age movement. It is possible to argue that believers would respond affirmatively to this statement because they believe that through the acceptance of Christ as their Savior they have the power to determine their eternal destiny.

However, other research has underscored the reality that most Christians are susceptible to embracing perspectives championed by religions which are antithetical to the Christian faith. The facts drawn from this study must challenge us to consider the possibility that many Christians have unwittingly embraced elements of the philosophy of the popularized religions of our society.

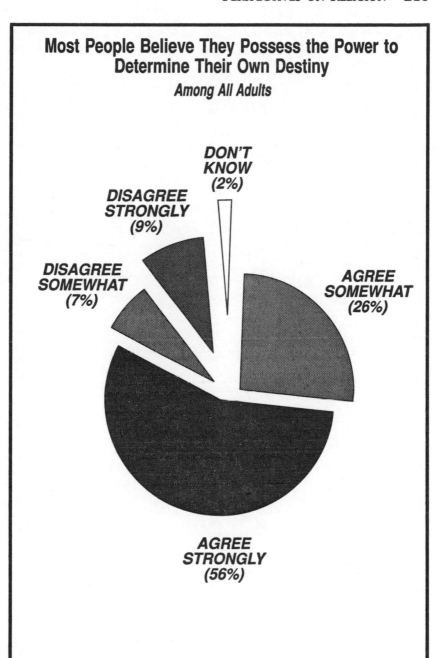

Most People Believe They Possess the Power to Determine Their Own Destiny
Among All Adults

DON'T KNOW (2%)

DISAGREE STRONGLY (9%)

DISAGREE SOMEWHAT (7%)

AGREE SOMEWHAT (26%)

AGREE STRONGLY (56%)

Source: Barna Research Group, Ltd., 1991

Q: "Every person has the power to determine his or her own destiny in life." Do you agree strongly, agree somewhat, disagree somewhat, or disagree strongly with that statement?

		Agree Strongly	Agree Somewhat	Disagree Somewhat	Disagree Strongly	Don't Know	N
Total Population		56%	26%	7%	9%	2%	1005
Age:	18 to 25	66	21	4	8	1	190
	26-44	52	30	9	8	1	464
	45-54	55	24	8	10	3	141
	55-64	48	30	7	13	2	101
	65 or older	62	20	6	9	3	92
Education:	High school or less	62	21	6	10	2	453
	Some college	54	30	5	10	1	242
	College graduate	49	32	11	7	2	306
Ethnicity:	White	55	30	7	7	1	744
	Black	59	17	6	19	*	119
Household Income:	Under $20,000	56	24	6	13	1	184
	$20,000 to $39,999	58	27	7	8	1	397
	$40,000 to $59,999	55	28	7	8	3	186
	$60,000 or more	52	28	11	8	1	142
Gender:	Male	60	24	7	7	2	490
	Female	52	28	7	11	2	515
Married:	Yes	54	26	8	9	2	570
	No	59	26	6	9	1	432
Community:	Urban	56	27	8	9	1	340
	Suburban	53	26	8	10	3	387
	Rural	60	27	6	7	*	245
Region:	Northeast	54	25	10	9	2	227
	Midwest	59	24	8	8	2	228
	South	53	33	6	7	1	210
	Mountain	53	33	6	7	1	171
	Pacific	59	21	5	13	2	169
Born Again:	Yes	54	25	7	13	1	355
	No	57	27	7	7	2	650
Denominational Affiliation:	Evangelical	56	21	9	13	1	246
	Catholic	59	27	7	6	1	250
	Mainline	53	31	6	10	2	178
Church Attender:	Yes	56	25	7	10	2	762
	No	57	25	10	6	1	243

DOES THE BIBLE SAY GOD HELPS THOSE WHO HELP THEMSELVES?

Question: *"The idea that God helps those who help themselves is taken directly from the Bible." Do you agree strongly, agree somewhat, disagree somewhat, or disagree strongly with that statement?*

One of the most telling factors here is the high proportion of respondents who did not know how to answer this question. This may suggest that even among those who offered a substantive response, their level of certainty is lower than usual.

Overall, more than half of Americans agreed with this statement. It falls in line with previous research showing that the vast majority of Americans believe that the "God helps those who help themselves" philosophy is genuinely Christian and wholly biblical.

A majority of all of the people groups examined agreed with this statement. In fact, the likely reason for the exaggerated proportion of "don't know" answers is that people have no idea what is in the Bible. While they are comfortable with this philosophy as a reflection of Christianity, a substantial proportion of those individuals would be hard-pressed to assert that the statement is drawn directly from the pages of the Bible. Most Americans have no idea just what is in the pages of Scripture.

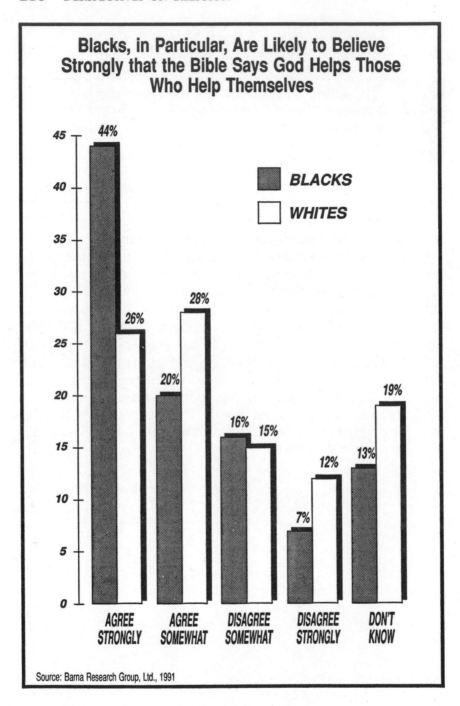

Blacks, in Particular, Are Likely to Believe
Strongly that the Bible Says God Helps Those
Who Help Themselves

BLACKS
WHITES

	AGREE STRONGLY	AGREE SOMEWHAT	DISAGREE SOMEWHAT	DISAGREE STRONGLY	DON'T KNOW
Blacks	44%	20%	16%	7%	13%
Whites	26%	28%	15%	12%	19%

Source: Barna Research Group, Ltd., 1991

Q: "The idea that God helps those who help themselves is taken directly from the Bible." Do you agree strongly, agree somewhat, disagree somewhat, or disagree strongly with that statement?

		Agree Strongly	Agree Somewhat	Disagree Somewhat	Disagree Strongly	Don't Know	N
Total Population		29%	27%	14%	12%	18%	1005
Age:	18 to 25	28	34	14	11	14	190
	26-44	29	30	15	10	16	464
	45-54	34	23	12	10	20	141
	55-64	25	24	14	17	20	101
	65 or older	34	16	14	15	21	92
Education:	High school or less	33	26	13	11	17	453
	Some college	30	26	14	12	18	242
	College graduate	23	31	15	12	19	306
Ethnicity:	White	26	28	15	12	19	744
	Black	44	20	16	7	13	119
Household Income:	Under $20,000	31	27	11	15	16	184
	$20,000 to $39,999	32	28	14	11	15	397
	$40,000 to $59,999	25	22	17	15	21	186
	$60,000 or more	24	39	13	5	19	142
Gender:	Male	26	29	14	14	18	490
	Female	32	26	14	10	18	515
Married:	Yes	27	28	14	13	18	570
	No	32	27	14	10	17	432
Community:	Urban	30	27	14	11	18	340
	Suburban	29	27	15	11	19	387
	Rural	29	29	14	14	15	245
Region:	Northeast	25	29	13	11	22	227
	Midwest	28	26	13	14	19	228
	South	32	32	11	12	13	210
	Mountain	30	27	16	11	15	171
	Pacific	32	23	18	9	18	169
Born Again:	Yes	34	21	12	18	15	355
	No	27	31	15	8	20	650
Denominational Affiliation:	Evangelical	34	28	11	17	10	246
	Catholic	31	31	15	5	16	250
	Mainline	31	28	12	10	20	178
Church Attender:	Yes	33	27	13	13	14	762
	No	22	31	15	8	25	243

18 HOW WE SHARE OUR FAITH AND RESOURCES

DO WE HAVE A RESPONSIBILITY TO SHARE OUR FAITH?

Question: *"You have a responsibility to explain your religious beliefs to others who may believe differently." Do you agree strongly, agree somewhat, disagree somewhat, or disagree strongly with that statement?*

Just over one-fourth of all adults (28%) strongly believe that they have a responsibility to share their religious beliefs with others who they feel have a different set of beliefs. An equivalent proportion of adults (25%) feel equally strongly that they do not have any such responsibility. The rest of the population is caught somewhere in the middle on this issue.

Education, Income, and Evangelism

Education and income clearly are related to perspectives on this matter. Once again, it is the individuals lower on the socioeconomic continuum who are most likely to affirm an evangelistic responsibility, and those who have achieved the most in school and in the marketplace who are most opposed to proclaiming their religious beliefs to others. This raises the question of how the upscale segments of our society can be most effectively penetrated, since evangelism is most effective when based upon personal interaction. Social networking studies have shown that people tend to interact most frequently with others who are from a similar socioeconomic background.

Interestingly, although women are generally more likely to reflect a Christian perspective in their thoughts and actions, their views are identical to those of men on the matter of evangelistic responsibility.

Blacks are considerably more likely than whites to support the notion of witnessing to others. In fact, blacks were 80% more likely than whites to state that they strongly agreed in sharing their beliefs.

Believers Agree

As might be expected, born again Christians and people attending evangelical churches were among those most likely to strongly agree with the statement. The challenge to the Church is to increase the proportion of believers who accept the sharing of the gospel with others as a task for which they, personally, are responsible. The fact that less than half of the believers in America strongly affirm that they have an obligation to proclaim the gospel on a personal level helps explain why the Church is not growing.

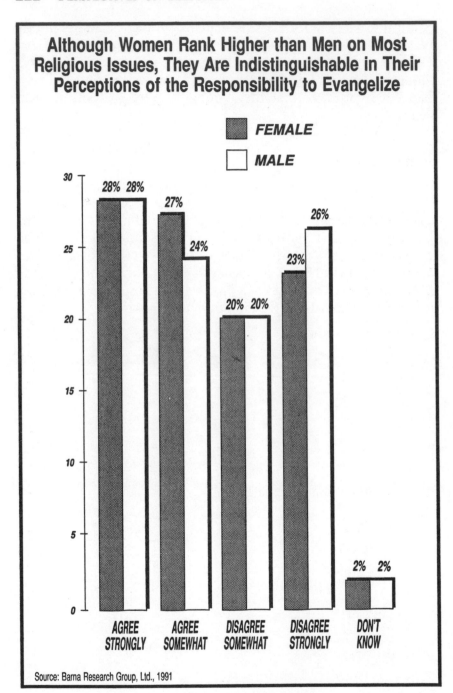

Although Women Rank Higher than Men on Most Religious Issues, They Are Indistinguishable in Their Perceptions of the Responsibility to Evangelize

FEMALE

MALE

Source: Barna Research Group, Ltd., 1991

Q: "You have a responsibility to explain your religious beliefs to others who may believe differently." Do you agree strongly, agree somewhat, disagree somewhat, or disagree strongly with that statement?

		Agree Strongly	Agree Somewhat	Disagree Somewhat	Disagree Strongly	Don't Know	N
Total Population		28%	25%	20%	25%	2%	1005
Age:	18 to 25	29	29	23	19	1	190
	26-44	26	26	20	26	2	464
	45-54	29	22	18	30	2	141
	55-64	28	32	21	19	1	101
	65 or older	40	15	22	21	2	92
Education:	High school or less	35	26	20	18	2	453
	Some college	26	27	21	24	2	242
	College graduate	19	23	20	36	1	306
Ethnicity:	White	24	27	21	27	2	744
	Black	43	33	11	13	1	119
Household Income:	Under $20,000	39	23	19	18	1	184
	$20,000 to $39,999	30	28	17	24	2	397
	$40,000 to $59,999	22	27	22	27	2	186
	$60,000 or more	19	25	23	33	1	142
Gender:	Male	28	24	20	26	2	490
	Female	28	27	20	23	2	515
Married:	Yes	30	26	19	23	2	570
	No	26	25	21	27	2	432
Community:	Urban	27	24	21	26	2	340
	Suburban	26	25	21	27	1	387
	Rural	33	26	19	20	2	245
Region:	Northeast	18	27	18	35	3	227
	Midwest	27	26	21	23	4	228
	South	32	29	18	20	1	210
	Mountain	43	20	19	17	*	171
	Pacific	23	22	26	27	1	169
Born Again:	Yes	43	33	13	11	1	355
	No	20	21	24	32	2	650
Denominational Affiliation:	Evangelical	43	29	14	13	1	246
	Catholic	20	27	24	27	2	250
	Mainline	19	30	28	21	3	178
Church Attender:							
	Yes	34	30	19	15	1	762
	No	16	14	27	42	2	243

ARE WE DONATING TIME AND MONEY TO HELP OTHERS?

Question: *During the past month, which, if any, of the following have you done? Donated money to a Christian ministry, other than a church; volunteered any of your free time to help needy people; volunteered your time or money to help needy people living in other countries.*

While most people who attend a church on a regular basis donate money to that congregation, the data indicate that among adults who call themselves Christian, about one-third (31%) also donate money to Christian ministries other than churches in a typical month.

This generosity is especially likely among people 45 or older; people earning $20,000 per year or more; married adults; born again Christians; and adults who regularly attend church.

More specifically, 58% of the self-proclaimed Christians say that in the past month they have donated either their time or money to help needy people in their area. Such charity is most prolific among adults 45 or older; those with a college education; women; married adults; and regular church attenders.

The interest in helping needy people nearby is about twice as strong as that related to assisting the needy of other countries. Thirty percent of adults have given their time or money to help needy people overseas during the past month. This tendency is strongest among people 55 or older; college graduates; high income households; people living in cities or suburbs; Catholics; and committed church-goers.

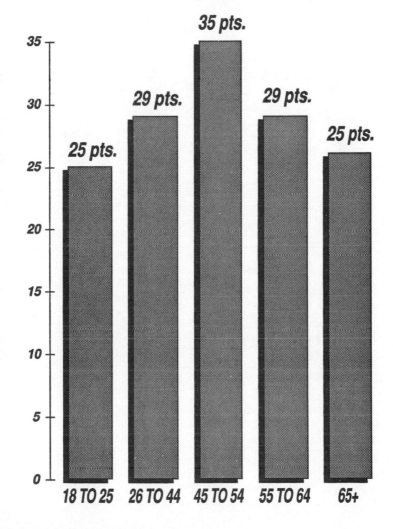

Among Adults Who Label Themselves Christians, the "Help Me First" Sentiment Is Prevalent Among All Age Groups

Differences Between % Who Help Needy in Their Area and % Who Help Needy in Other Countries

35 pts.

29 pts.

29 pts.

25 pts.

25 pts.

18 TO 25   26 TO 44   45 TO 54   55 TO 64   65+

Source: Barna Research Group, Ltd., 1991

Q: During the past month, which, if any, of the following have you done? (See next page for column headings.)

		#1	#2	#3	N
Total Population		31%	58%	30%	1005
Age:	18 to 25	16	45	20	190
	26-44	29	56	27	464
	45-54	36	64	29	141
	55-64	35	65	36	101
	65 or older	52	76	51	92
Education:	High school or less	28	52	26	453
	Some college	31	63	29	242
	College graduate	35	64	36	306
Ethnicity:	White	31	60	28	744
	Black	28	55	27	119
Household Income:					
	Under $20,000	21	54	28	184
	$20,000 to $39,999	32	58	27	397
	$40,000 to $59,999	32	61	28	186
	$60,000 or more	35	65	40	142
Gender:	Male	31	55	27	490
	Female	30	61	32	515
Married:	Yes	35	61	31	570
	No	24	55	28	432
Community:	Urban	31	55	34	340
	Suburban	33	63	31	387
	Rural	29	58	22	245
Region:	Northeast	27	59	29	227
	Midwest	36	62	28	228
	South	31	56	29	210
	Mountain	27	59	29	171
	Pacific	32	54	34	169
Born Again:	Yes	41	61	32	355
	No	24	56	28	650
Denominational Affiliation:					
	Evangelical	33	59	28	246
	Catholic	27	58	34	250
	Mainline	30	60	23	178
Church Attender:					
	Yes	36	63	33	762
	No	12	44	16	243

Columns:

#1 Donated money to a Christian ministry, other than a church

#2 Volunteered any of your free time to help needy people

#3 Volunteered your time or money to help needy people living in other countries

CHURCH INVOLVEMENT AND SATISFACTION

SECTION HIGHLIGHTS:

◆ Among people who consider themselves to be Christian, about one-quarter do not attend church in a typical month.

◆ Apart from attending worship services, the church-related activities Christian adults are most likely to engage in are attending Sunday school and participating in a Bible study, prayer group, or fellowship group.

◆ When Christians who regularly attend church services are asked to evaluate the elements of the church experience, the facet receiving the highest rating is the friendliness of the congregation. The aspect awarded the lowest rating is the program for teenagers.

◆ Among churched adults who call themselves Christian, about half say they have invited an acquaintance to attend church with them at some time during the last six months. Of the adults who invited a guest, two-thirds of them estimate that at least one of the people they invited to attend was an individual who did not regularly attend another Christian church.

▶ *IN BRIEF*

IN A TYPICAL WEEK, ALMOST HALF OF ALL ADULTS (49%) say they attend a church worship service. This represents a small increase compared to responses recorded during the prior decade or so, when about 44% of all adults said they attended church services during a given week. We believe this increase, small as it is, can be attributed to people's heightened sense of religious awareness due to the Persian Gulf War that was in progress at the time of the survey. Given that major event, though, this represents a relatively small increase.

Weekly and Monthly Religious Activity

During a typical week, we might also expect about one-fourth of all adults (23%) to attend some type of religious education class (i.e. Sunday school) at a church. Similarly, one out of four adults (27%) claim they have volunteered some of their free time to help a church during the preceding week.

In a typical month, among adults who call themselves Christian (as opposed to Jewish, Muslim, Buddhist, or any other religious identification), three-quarters attend a church service at least once. Forty percent attend every weekend during the month, while the remaining adults are evenly divided among attending an average of one, two, or three times each month.

Among the individuals who generally do not attend services during a month, most of them avoid church altogether: two-thirds (63%) say they haven't been to church in a year or more, and another one out of five (18%) can't remember the last time they attended.

Membership Has Its Privileges

Among the self-described Christians who attend church services regularly (i.e. at least once a month), four out of five say they are formal members of the church they most frequently attend. The majority of these individuals (52%) have been members for 10 or more years.

Why do people participate in the life of a local church? By far the most common answer people give is because they desire to worship God. Although we have conducted other studies which raise the issue of what "worship" means to people (i.e. is it a condition of the heart or being in the designated place at a prescribed time?), 42% of the self-described Christians identify worship as their primary motivation. Other reasons for being involved include to learn more about God (mentioned by 14%) and to experience personal growth or become a better person (14%). Less common reasons are to maintain a tradition of church attendance (5%), because they enjoy attending (5%), to respond to family pressure (3%), and to meet new friends (3%). About 6% of the adults who go to church have no idea why they continue to do so.

In a typical month, people who label themselves "Christian" engage in a variety of religious activities beyond attending worship services. Almost three out of ten (28%) will attend a Sunday school class; the same proportion (29%) get involved in a small group Bible study, fellowship group, or prayer group, other than a Sunday school class; one out of seven adults (15%) teaches a group or class associated with the church; and one out of five (19%) serves as a leader in the church, through boards, committees, or other types of leadership positions.

Likely Participants

Overall, the people most likely to engage in any of these activities are older adults (those in their 50s or beyond), blacks, married adults, and those living in the south, southwestern, mountain, and midwest states. Born again Christians are more than twice as likely to participate in these types of endeavors, while adults attending evangelical churches are much more likely than those associated with Catholic or mainline Protestant churches.

Interpersonal Outreach

Friendship evangelism is evident through the fact that about half (54%) of the people who describe themselves as Christian and regularly attend a church claim that they have invited an acquaintance to attend church with them in the past six months. Among the adults who brought such a visitor to church with them, two-thirds say that at least one of the visitors they brought was not currently and consistently attending another Christian church.

Evaluating Ministries

In evaluating the different facets of the ministry of the church they attend most often, it is interesting that not a single attribute of local church ministry received a rating of "excellent" (i.e. the highest rating point on a five-point scale) from at least half of the people who describe themselves as Christian and who attend church regularly.

These, of course, are the individuals who are likely to provide the most supportive evaluations of their churches: they attend regularly, they are integrally involved in making the church what it is, and they have the most intimate knowledge of the workings of the church. On the one hand, it is encouraging that the people who form the foundation of local church ministry have not grown wholly complacent and believe that they have mastered the art of ministry. On the other hand, it is discouraging to recognize that not even the most committed and forgiving people associated with the church say it is doing excellent work in the key areas of ministry.

Churches with High and Low Ratings

Local churches win the highest accolades for being friendly (46% say their church is excellent in this regard); for the care and concern exhibited by the clergy and staff (45%); for the preaching (44%); the music in the worship services (44%); and the buildings and facilities (43%). More moderate ratings are given to the overall management of the church (35% portray this as excellent) and the programs for young children (32%). The lowest ratings are associated with the quality of teaching in the church's educational offerings (28%) and the programs geared to teenagers (24%).

In general, the lowest ratings for the church are given by men, by people in the 45-54 age group, by Catholics, and by adults living in the Pacific states. It also appears that churches in rural areas are somewhat less satisfying to their congregations than are those located in urban and suburban settings.

Realize that the lowest ratings given pertain to ministry to children and teenagers. This may help to explain why many of the Baby Boomers who returned to church after an extended period of absence—i.e. for the sake of their children—are now leaving the church again, disappointed that they did not receive greater benefits for their investment.

19 OUR LEVEL OF CHURCH INVOLVEMENT

HOW MANY AMERICANS ARE ATTENDING WORSHIP SERVICES EACH WEEK?

 Question: *During the past seven days, did you attend a church worship service?*

Overall, 49% of American adults are likely to attend a church worship service in any given week. This represents a slight increase in attendance compared to figures from the past decade or so. During that period the average was 44%.

Will It Last?

Why have we experienced an increase? In all likelihood this can be attributed to people's increased religious sensitivity due to the war in the Persian Gulf. Will we see a slight reduction in church attendance over the coming year, as the emotional anxieties produced by the war subside? That remains to be seen, although the chances seem better than even.

Levels of Involvement

There are three different levels of involvement with worship services. There is the minimal level lived out by Baby Busters. Just 35% of them attended a church service in the past week. Then there is the level among Baby Boomers and older, middle-aged adults (thus encompassing people from 26 to 64 years of age). About half of these people (52%) attend church in any given week. Among senior adults (65 or older), the highest level of church attendance is evident (69% attend in a week).

Women (55%) are much more likely than men (42%) to attend church this week. Even more pronounced is the difference between married adults (57% of whom attend church in a given week) and single adults (39%).

Hazards of City Life

Location may impact attendance, too. It seems that the farther from the city you get, the more likely a person is to attend a church. Among city residents, 46% will probably attend church this week; among suburban adults, 51% will likely attend; 53% of the people in rural areas are likely to attend. These differences are not large, though, and probably have less to do with geography than with values systems and life-styles in the area. In fact, attendance is higher in the midwest (55%) and lower in the northeast (43%) than elsewhere.

In a typical week, two-thirds of the born again Christians will attend a worship service. That dwarfs the 39% among non-Christians. Church denominational affiliation made less difference in attendance likelihood than might be expected, though. Among those aligned with evangelical congregations, 60% attend in a week; among Catholics, 59% do so; among those at mainline Protestant churches, 52% follow suit.

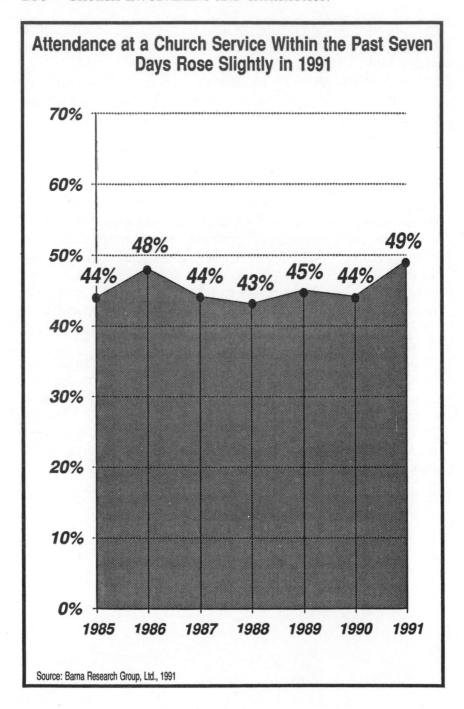

Attendance at a Church Service Within the Past Seven Days Rose Slightly in 1991

Source: Barna Research Group, Ltd., 1991

Q: During the past seven days, did you attend a church worship service?

		Yes	No	Don't Know	N
Total Population		49%	51%	*	1005
Age:	18 to 25	35	65	*	190
	26-44	50	50	*	464
	45-54	52	48	*	141
	55-64	52	48	*	101
	65 or older	69	30	1	92
Education:	High school or less	47	53	*	453
	Some college	51	49	*	242
	College graduate	50	50	*	306
Ethnicity:	White	48	52	*	744
	Black	53	47	*	119
Household Income:	Under $20,000	41	60	*	184
	$20,000 to $39,999	51	49	*	397
	$40,000 to $59,999	53	47	1	186
	$60,000 or more	50	50	*	142
Gender:	Male	42	57	*	490
	Female	55	45	*	515
Married:	Yes	57	43	*	570
	No	39	61	*	432
Community:	Urban	46	54	*	340
	Suburban	51	49	*	387
	Rural	53	47	*	245
Region:	Northeast	43	57	*	227
	Midwest	55	46	*	228
	South	49	51	*	210
	Mountain	51	49	*	171
	Pacific	47	53	1	169
Born Again:	Yes	66	34	*	355
	No	39	60	*	650
Denominational Affiliation:	Evangelical	60	40	*	246
	Catholic	59	41	*	250
	Mainline	52	48	*	178
Church Attender:	Yes	71	29	*	762
	No	*	*	*	*

HOW MANY AMERICANS ARE ATTENDING SUNDAY SCHOOL EACH WEEK?

 Question: *During the past seven days, did you attend a Sunday school class?*

Sunday School Is Still Alive and Kicking

Those who proclaim that Sunday school is a thing of the past must realize that one out of four adults (23%) attend such a class on any given weekend. That projects to more than forty million adults receiving some form of religious instruction at a church on any given weekend. (Not all of those churches, of course, are teaching Christian doctrine or values; however, the vast majority are affiliated with the Christian faith.)

Another way of looking at this statistic is to show that just under half of all adults who attend church on a given Sunday also engage in the Sunday school experience that same day (46%).

Who's Attending?

Age, again, is a distinguishing characteristic, with people more likely to attend a Sunday school class the older they become. Individuals who are socioeconomic achievers—those with college degrees or who earn $60,000 or more a year—are among the least likely to participate in Sunday school classes. Single adults are only half as likely as married adults to be involved in such religious instruction.

The Rat Race Takes Its Toll

The pace of life may help to explain why 29% of the adults living in rural areas participate in Sunday school classes, while only 20% of those in urban or suburban areas do so. Attendance is least likely among adults living in two of the regions that generally place the highest value on education: the northeast (just 15% of all adults enter a Sunday school class on a Sunday) and the Pacific states (17%).

Many adults who might otherwise be expected to attend Sunday school, including millions of adults who attend worship services, consciously choose not to attend these classes. Notice, for instance, that while half of the people who attend church and have no more than a high school diploma also attend Sunday school, only 39% of those who attend church and have a college degree fit the same pattern. Thus, the individuals most used to (and most likely to support the value of) formal education are the ones most likely to reject Sunday school teaching as an option.

Sunday school attendance among adults is significantly greater among those affiliated with evangelical congregations than among those aligned with mainline denominations. Born again Christians are also three times more likely than non-Christians to be involved in Sunday religious instruction at a church.

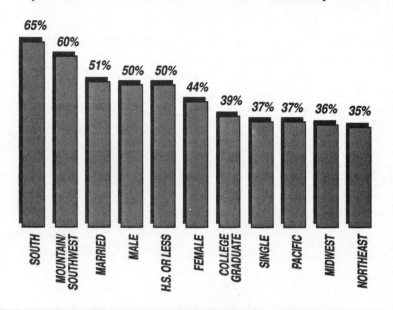

The Proportion of People Who Attend Church Worship Services Is Not Always an Accurate Predictor of Sunday School Attendance

Proportion of Church Attenders Who Also Attend Sunday School

65% SOUTH
60% MOUNTAIN/SOUTHWEST
51% MARRIED
50% MALE
50% H.S. OR LESS
44% FEMALE
39% COLLEGE GRADUATE
37% SINGLE
37% PACIFIC
36% MIDWEST
35% NORTHEAST

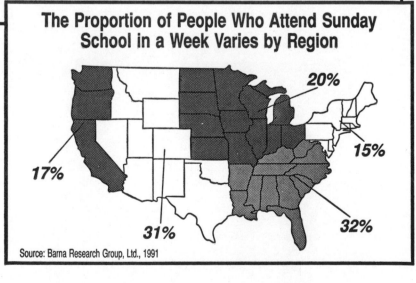

The Proportion of People Who Attend Sunday School in a Week Varies by Region

20%
15%
17%
31%
32%

Source: Barna Research Group, Ltd., 1991

Q: During the past seven days, did you attend a Sunday school class?

		Yes	No	Don't Know	N
Total Population		23%	77%	*	1005
Age:	18 to 25	15	85	*	190
	26-44	23	77	*	464
	45-54	24	76	*	141
	55-64	28	72	*	101
	65 or older	36	65	*	92
Education:	High school or less	24	76	*	453
	Some college	25	75	*	242
	College graduate	19	81	*	306
Ethnicity:	White	23	77	*	744
	Black	28	72	*	119
Household Income:	Under $20,000	24	76	*	184
	$20,000 to $39,999	23	77	*	397
	$40,000 to $59,999	27	73	*	186
	$60,000 or more	14	86	*	142
Gender:	Male	21	79	*	490
	Female	24	76	*	515
Married:	Yes	29	71	*	570
	No	14	86	*	432
Community:	Urban	18	82	*	340
	Suburban	22	78	*	387
	Rural	29	71	*	245
Region:	Northeast	15	85	*	227
	Midwest	20	80	*	228
	South	32	68	*	210
	Mountain	31	69	*	171
	Pacific	17	83	*	169
Born Again:	Yes	40	60	*	355
	No	13	87	*	650
Denominational Affiliation:	Evangelical	43	57	*	246
	Catholic	9	91	*	250
	Mainline	26	74	*	178
Church Attender:	Yes	34	66	*	762
	No	3	97	*	243

HOW ARE WE VOLUNTEERING OUR TIME AT CHURCH?

 Question: *During the past seven days, did you volunteer any of your free time to help a church?*

One-fourth of all adults (27%) say they volunteered time in the past week to assist a church in its efforts. These volunteers run the gamut from Sunday school directors to people who count the attendance slips placed in the collection plate.

If you're ever searching for volunteers, don't spend much time recruiting from among Baby Busters. Only one out of ten Busters (10%) did any volunteer work at a church within the past week, substantially lower than the 30% among adults 26-64, or 46% among senior citizens.

Blacks are also more likely to share their time with the church. Almost two out of five black adults (38%) serve as church volunteers in a given week, compared to just one-quarter of white adults (26%).

Married adults are a better bet as volunteers, as 32% of them offered their services in the past week. Only 19% of single adults did the same.

People in the mountain and southwestern states are the most generous with their time: 35% volunteer in an average week. That's double the probability of adults in the Pacific states offering their talents for free (18%).

The usual patterns related to religious background are evident. People at evangelical churches (41%) are more likely than those associated with mainline Protestant (31%) or Catholic churches (19%) to get involved as a volunteer. Born again Christians (41%) are more than twice as likely to volunteer as non-Christians (19%).

The Most Likely and Least Likely People to Volunteer Their Time for the Church

Yes
20% OR MORE
ABOVE AVERAGE

➡ *55 OR OLDER*
➡ *BLACKS*
➡ *MARRIED*
➡ *MOUNTAIN/SOUTHWEST*
➡ *BORN AGAIN*
➡ *ATTEND EVANGELICAL*
   CHURCH

No
20% OR MORE
BELOW AVERAGE

➡ *BABY BUSTERS*
➡ *SINGLE ADULTS*
➡ *PACIFIC REGION*
➡ *NON-CHRISTIAN*
➡ *CATHOLICS*

Source: Barna Research Group, Ltd., 1991

Q: During the past seven days, did you volunteer any of your free time to help a church?

		Yes	No	Don't Know	N
Total Population		27%	73%	*	1005
Age:	18 to 25	10	90	*	190
	26-44	28	72	*	464
	45-54	30	70	*	141
	55-64	31	68	*	101
	65 or older	46	54	*	92
Education:	High school or less	24	76	*	453
	Some college	28	72	*	242
	College graduate	29	71	*	306
Ethnicity:	White	26	74	*	744
	Black	38	62	*	119
Household Income:	Under $20,000	22	78	*	184
	$20,000 to $39,999	26	74	*	397
	$40,000 to $59,999	29	71	*	186
	$60,000 or more	26	74	*	142
Gender:	Male	24	76	*	490
	Female	29	71	*	515
Married:	Yes	32	68	*	570
	No	19	81	*	432
Community:	Urban	23	77	*	340
	Suburban	28	72	*	387
	Rural	30	70	*	245
Region:	Northeast	23	76	*	227
	Midwest	30	70	*	228
	South	26	74	*	210
	Mountain	35	65	*	171
	Pacific	18	82	*	169
Born Again:	Yes	41	59	*	355
	No	19	81	*	650
Denominational Affiliation:	Evangelical	41	59	*	246
	Catholic	19	81	*	250
	Mainline	31	69	*	178
Church Attender:	Yes	39	62	*	762
	No	4	96	*	243

HOW MANY WEEKENDS A MONTH ARE WE ATTENDING CHURCH?

Question: *In a typical month, on how many weekends would you attend church worship services?*

Among adults who consider themselves to be Christians, about one-quarter say they do not attend church services in a typical month; two out of five attend every weekend; and equal proportions of adults attend once, twice, or three times a month.

Who is likely to attend every week in an average month? The elderly (58% do so); married adults (44%); and born again Christians (52%).

Notice that a large proportion of non-Christians (who consider themselves to be Christian) attend church every Sunday—one-third of this segment. Also recognize that people associated with mainline Protestant churches are less likely than those associated with either evangelical or Catholic bodies to attend every week.

In fact, only one-third of the adults who call themselves Christian but do not rely solely upon the grace of God for salvation, through the death and resurrection of Jesus Christ, do not attend church services at all. (Conversely, one out of every eight born again Christians does not attend church services.) Often, church leaders assume that because an individual is attending church regularly, they have a true commitment to Christ. These figures confirm what we have seen consistently over the past decade: a growing proportion of the adults who attend Christian churches do not have a real relationship with Christ.

The Extremes on Church Attendance

People Groups, Among Self-described Christians, Who Are Most and Least Likely to Attend Church Services

ABOVE AVERAGE

| 65 OR OLDER | 58% |
| BORN AGAIN | 52% |

BELOW AVERAGE

UNDER $20,000/YR.	33%
NOT BORN AGAIN	31%
SINGLE	29%
55-64 YRS.	28%

Source: Barna Research Group, Ltd., 1991

Q: In a typical month, on how many weekends would you attend church worship services? (Among those who describe themselves as "Christian.")

		One	Two	Three	Four or Five	None	Don't Know	N
Total Population		12%	12%	11%	40%	23%	1%	825
Age:	18 to 25	17	16	11	30	27	1	136
	26-44	14	13	12	37	23	1	400
	45-54	9	14	13	44	19	1	116
	55-64	7	8	12	43	28	1	87
	65 or older	4	7	10	58	18	3	83
Education:	High school or less	11	13	9	40	25	2	388
	Some college	13	16	12	37	21	1	203
	College graduate	14	9	14	41	22	*	233
Ethnicity:	White	13	11	11	39	25	2	625
	Black	8	20	16	43	13	2	100
Household Income:	Under $20,000	7	11	9	37	33	3	154
	$20,000 to $39,999	14	12	12	42	21	*	328
	$40,000 to $59,999	12	17	11	39	20	1	153
	$60,000 or more	17	13	11	40	17	2	110
Gender:	Male	13	16	8	36	26	2	387
	Female	11	10	14	43	21	1	438
Married:	Yes	11	12	13	44	19	1	496
	No	14	13	8	33	29	1	329
Community:	Urban	12	10	10	41	26	2	267
	Suburban	12	14	13	41	20	*	317
	Rural	13	14	11	38	23	2	216
Region:	Northeast	16	11	9	45	19	1	164
	Midwest	9	12	11	40	26	1	201
	South	16	12	13	37	23	*	183
	Mountain	9	10	15	42	22	2	144
	Pacific	10	20	8	33	26	4	133
Born Again:	Yes	9	11	16	52	12	1	338
	No	14	13	8	21	31	2	487
Denominational Affiliation:	Evangelical	11	12	13	44	19	2	246
	Catholic	12	14	8	43	22	*	250
	Mainline	17	12	15	31	23	3	178
Church Attender:	Yes	16	17	15	53	*	*	623
	No	*	*	*	*	100	*	170

WHEN WAS THE LAST TIME YOU WENT TO CHURCH?

Question: *About how long has it been since you last attended a church worship service, other than for a holiday or special event such as a wedding or funeral?*

This question, asked only of those people who say that they do not attend church services in a typical month, reveals that the vast majority of those people rarely, if ever, attend church services. Overall, 63% had not attended for a year or more, and another 18% couldn't recall the last time they had attended church.

Eleven percent of the adults who generally had not attended over the course of a month claim that they did attend sometime during the prior six months.

If we define "unchurched" as people who do not attend church worship services at all in a typical month, then we suggest that about one-quarter of the population (who call themselves "Christian") might fit this characterization. If, instead, we label people "unchurched" if they do not attend during a six-month period of time, we find the proportion shrinking to just 17% of the self-characterized Christian body.*

---

* This assumes that the people who said they could not remember are removed from the base.

If Self-described "Christians" Avoid Church This Month, They'll Probably Avoid It for a Long Time

How Long Since Attending a Church Service, Other than a Holiday or Special Event, Among "Christians" Who Don't Attend in an Average Month

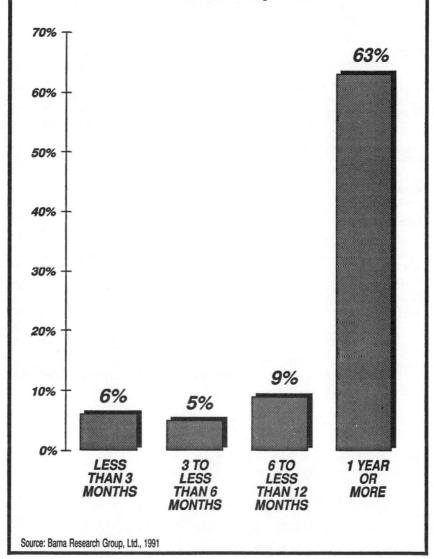

Source: Barna Research Group, Ltd., 1991

Q: About how long has it been since you last attended a church worship service, other than for a holiday or special event such as a wedding or funeral? (Among those who say they do not attend church worship services in a typical month.)

		Less Than 3 Mos.	3 to Less than 6 Mos.	6 to Less than 12 Mos.	1 Year or or More	Don't Know	N
Total Population		6%	5%	9%	63%	18%	198
Age:	18 to 25	9	*	6	66	19	32
	26-44	5	7	10	57	22	93
	45 or older	4	6	10	61	19	58
Education:	High school or less	4	4	18	66	18	102
	Some college	9	2	14	56	19	43
	College graduate	6	9	6	53	27	53
Household Income:	Under $20,000	8	4	14	56	19	52
	$20,000 to $39,999	4	4	7	64	22	74
	$40,000 or more	4	10	10	59	18	51
Gender:	Male	4	5	9	69	14	86
	Female	7	5	9	54	25	112
Married:	Yes	6	5	6	62	22	102
	No	5	5	13	58	19	96
Community:	Urban	7	6	6	57	24	70
	Suburban	8	5	11	60	16	63
	Rural	2	6	13	61	19	54
Born Again:	Yes	7	9	18	52	14	44
	No	5	4	7	62	22	154
Denominational Affiliation:	Evangelical	9	2	13	59	17	46
	Catholic	2	7	9	61	21	56
	Mainline	9	7	4	62	18	42

NOTE: Due to small sample subgroup sizes which make the data unreliable, some of the usual segments have been omitted from this table.

20 MEMBERSHIP, MOTIVATION, AND MINISTRY

ARE CHURCH-GOERS CHURCH MEMBERS?

> **Question:** *Are you a formal or official member of the church you attend most frequently?*

Among the people who say they are Christian and who attend church at least once a month on the average, four out of five are formal members of the church they usually attend. Not surprisingly, it is the least rooted population groups that are also least likely to be members: Baby Busters, singles, and those living in the Pacific states.

Whether or not an individual is a born again Christian apparently has no bearing on their likelihood of being a church member. Similarly, whether the individual attends an evangelical, mainline, or Catholic church has little to do with the likelihood of church membership.

One inference that can be drawn from these statistics is that the Christian church has generally moved away from the requirement that an individual profess a personal relationship with Jesus Christ, based on reliance upon grace rather than works, in order to qualify for membership.

Among Adults Who Say They Are Christian and Who Attend Church Regularly, the Majority Are Formal Members but Are Not Born Again. There Is Little Difference in Spiritual Commitment Between Members and Non-members

FORMAL MEMBERS

BORN AGAIN 48% **NOT BORN AGAIN 52%**

NOT FORMAL MEMBERS

BORN AGAIN 44% **NOT BORN AGAIN 56%**

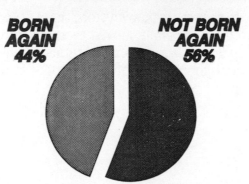

Source: Barna Research Group, Ltd., 1991

Q: Are you a formal or official member of the church you attend most frequently? (Among the "churched.")

		Yes	No	Don't Know	N
Total Population		80%	18%	2%	635
Age:	18 to 25	70	27	3	100
	26-44	79	21	*	309
	45-54	85	13	2	94
	55-64	82	14	4	62
	65 or older	93	6	2	52
Education:	High school or less	84	14	2	291
	Some college	77	21	3	161
	College graduate	77	23	1	182
Ethnicity:	White	80	19	2	469
	Black	83	15	3	87
Household Income:	Under $20,000	80	18	2	103
	$20,000 to $39,999	79	20	1	260
	$40,000 to $59,999	79	20	2	122
	$60,000 or more	85	14	1	92
Gender:	Male	78	20	2	287
	Female	82	17	1	347
Married:	Yes	82	17	1	401
	No	77	21	3	234
Community:	Urban	78	20	2	198
	Suburban	80	19	1	255
	Rural	82	17	1	167
Region:	Northeast	82	15	3	132
	Midwest	84	15	1	150
	South	78	21	1	141
	Mountain	84	15	1	113
	Pacific	69	28	3	99
Born Again:	Yes	82	17	1	298
	No	78	19	2	337
Denominational Affiliation:	Evangelical	80	20	1	200
	Catholic	80	18	2	194
	Mainline	85	14	1	138
Church Attender:	Yes	81	18	1	623
	No	*	*	*	*

HOW LONG HAVE WE BEEN CHURCH MEMBERS?

 Question: How long have you been a member of that church?

Among the adults who cited church membership, the vast majority of them have been members for extended periods of time. More than half of the church members have been affiliated with their churches for more than 10 years. About seven out of ten adults who are members have held that distinction in the same church for five years or longer.

What may be surprising is that the highest proportion of adults who claim formal membership in a Christian church are located in the city. Among urban adults 41% have been members at the same church for 20 or more years. The same standing is held by 30% of those in the suburbs and 33% of people living in less populated areas. Similarly, the section of the nation where membership still has its privileges and where a sense of history is most cherished (the northeast) has the highest concentration of long-time members (47%), while the section exhibiting the least focus on roots and history (the Pacific states) has the fewest long-time members (23%).

Perhaps the most striking realization is that the people who are most likely to be members for more than 20 years are non-Christians. When analysts strive to discover why so many long-standing churches have lost their energy and impact, the fact that a large proportion of the members do not know Christ personally may be an important fact to include in the analysis. Renewal cannot take place when there is no understanding of what one is being renewed from or to. Because so many churches rely heavily upon members to determine the personality and direction of the church's ministry, the Christian Church in America is clearly suffering from its inclusive membership policies.

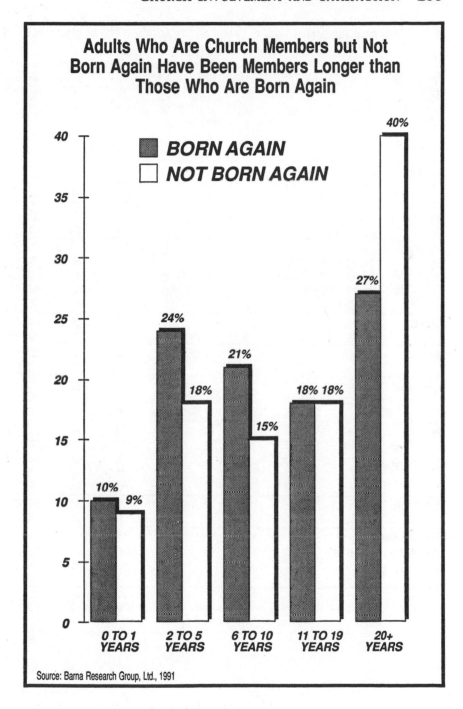

Adults Who Are Church Members but Not Born Again Have Been Members Longer than Those Who Are Born Again

■ BORN AGAIN
□ NOT BORN AGAIN

0 TO 1 YEARS: 10% / 9%
2 TO 5 YEARS: 24% / 18%
6 TO 10 YEARS: 21% / 15%
11 TO 19 YEARS: 18% / 18%
20+ YEARS: 27% / 40%

Source: Barna Research Group, Ltd., 1991

Q: How long have you been a member of that church? (Among church members.)

		1 yr.	2-3 yrs.	4-5 yrs.	6-10 yrs.	11-19 yrs.	20+ yrs.	N
Total Population		10%	11%	10%	18%	18%	34%	505
Age:	18 to 25	16	16	7	22	21	18	69
	26-44	12	13	12	18	18	26	242
	45-54	4	5	13	19	19	40	79
	55-64	5	7	5	14	15	54	50
	65 or older	2	12	4	13	9	60	48
Education:	High school or less	12	12	8	14	20	35	243
	Some college	5	9	13	22	17	35	121
	College graduate	10	12	11	21	15	32	139
Ethnicity:	White	7	11	10	18	18	37	371
	Black	5	7	18	18	27	25	71
Household Income:	Under $20,000	16	14	10	15	11	35	81
	$20,000 to $39,999	7	10	9	20	21	34	204
	$40,000 to $59,999	8	11	16	18	17	31	95
	$60,000 or more	9	15	9	14	18	35	78
Gender:	Male	9	9	12	19	17	34	224
	Female	10	13	8	16	19	34	281
Married:	Yes	11	12	11	18	18	31	327
	No	7	10	8	18	18	39	178
Community:	Urban	12	13	7	14	13	41	153
	Suburban	9	13	11	19	18	30	203
	Rural	6	7	12	19	23	33	137
Region:	Northeast	7	8	9	15	14	47	106
	Midwest	7	18	9	18	17	31	126
	South	9	8	10	21	22	31	109
	Mountain	11	5	10	23	18	34	95
	Pacific	18	16	15	10	19	23	68
Born Again:	Yes	10	11	13	21	18	27	242
	No	9	11	7	15	18	40	263
Denominational Affiliation:	Evangelical	8	12	11	23	22	24	157
	Catholic	10	10	7	12	17	45	156
	Mainline	7	8	11	17	19	37	117
Church Attender:	Yes	9	11	10	18	18	34	498
	No	*	*	*	*	*	*	*

WHY DO WE ATTEND CHURCH?

 Question: *What is the single, most important reason why you attend church?*

When adults who describe themselves as Christian are given eight possible reasons to explain why they attend church, the dominant response is likely to be that they desire to worship God (the choice of 42%). The next most popular reasons are selected by just one-third as many people: the desire to learn or study about God (14%) and the quest for personal growth or to be a better person (14%). The remaining five reasons offered for people's consideration are likely to be chosen by 5% or less. For instance, going to church because it is a tradition or a habit explains the attendance of 5%; attending because they enjoy being at church describes 5%. Attending as a reaction to family pressure to attend or in order to meet new people each describes the reasons for 3%. Striving to achieve peace with God or self characterizes the motivations of 1%, as does the belief that being at church is good for their children.

What Is Worship?

While attending for the purpose of worshipping God is common, other studies by Barna Research concerning this dimension raise significant questions about what "worship" means to today's adults. For many, it constitutes doing the routine things in the proper place at the usual time. Worship, for a majority of adults, connotes a series of activities rather than a state of the heart.

Single adults were different from married adults in that worship was less significant in their motivation for attending church. While 45% of married individuals claimed worship as their primary motivation, only 37% of the single adults did so. Other people groups which demonstrate a lower probability of identifying worship as their main impetus are people in the mountain and southwestern states, Boomers and Busters, lower income adults, non-Christians, mainline Protestants, and the unchurched.

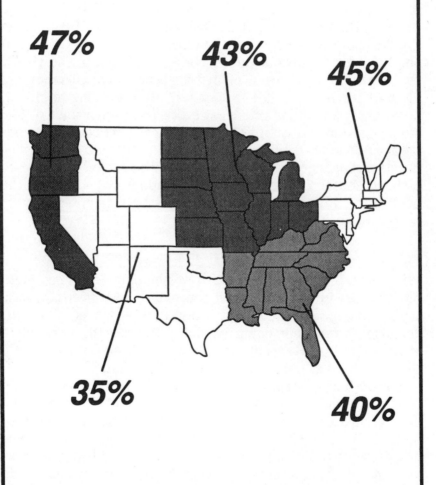

The Regions That Are Usually Most Resistant to Spiritual Growth Emerge as Those Most Likely to Attend Church out of a Desire to Worship God

% Who Say They Attend Church Primarily Because They Want to Worship God

47%

43%

45%

35%

40%

Source: Barna Research Group, Ltd., 1991

Q: What is the single, most important reason why you attend church? (See next page for column headings.)

		#1	#2	#3	#4	#5	#6	#7	#8	#9	#10	#11	N
Total Population		42%	14%	3%	1%	14%	5%	5%	3%	1%	6%	6%	825
Age:	18 to 25	35	20	3	1	16	5	4	3	*	5	8	136
	26-44	42	15	2	2	14	6	5	3	2	6	5	400
	45-54	45	8	5	*	18	4	4	2	1	8	5	116
	55-64	47	9	3	*	7	9	5	2	1	7	10	87
	65 or older	46	17	3	*	12	5	7	1	4	1	5	63
Education:	High school or less	41	16	2	1	12	7	5	3	1	7	6	388
	Some college	42	11	3	1	18	5	4	2	1	6	7	203
	College graduate	44	13	2	2	15	4	5	3	2	5	6	233
Ethnicity:	White	39	12	3	2	15	6	5	3	2	6	7	625
	Black	45	24	*	*	15	6	5	3	*	*	2	100
Household Income:	Under $20,000	41	19	3	1	8	4	4	2	3	9	7	154
	$20,000 to $39,999	37	16	2	1	18	7	5	2	*	5	7	328
	$40,000 to $59,999	48	11	4	1	14	5	5	3	1	4	4	153
	$60,000 or more	44	9	4	1	11	5	5	6	2	8	6	110
Gender:	Male	39	14	3	1	15	6	3	4	1	7	7	387
	Female	44	15	2	1	13	5	7	1	1	5	6	438
Married:	Yes	45	12	3	2	12	6	5	3	2	7	6	469
	No	37	18	3	1	17	5	5	3	1	5	7	329
Community:	Urban	39	15	3	*	15	4	6	3	1	5	9	267
	Suburban	47	13	2	1	15	6	4	2	2	5	4	317
	Rural	37	15	4	3	11	7	5	2	*	9	6	216
Region:	Northeast	45	10	2	2	10	8	4	3	1	6	9	164
	Midwest	43	15	4	1	17	5	6	3	*	3	5	201
	South	40	17	2	1	14	8	4	1	2	5	6	183
	Mountain	35	21	4	1	15	2	6	3	3	9	3	144
	Pacific	47	6	2	1	13	3	4	4	1	10	8	133
Born Again:	Yes	50	19	2	1	12	5	2	1	1	5	2	338
	No	36	11	3	1	16	6	7	4	2	6	9	487
Denominational Affiliation:	Evangelical	45	22	2	1	13	4	4	2	*	4	5	246
	Catholic	45	5	2	1	15	8	6	3	1	8	6	250
	Mainline	33	16	4	2	16	6	7	3	4	6	4	178
Church Attender:	Yes	47	14	2	1	15	5	5	2	1	6	2	623
	No	27	12	5	2	8	8	3	6	2	8	20	170

Columns:

#1 To worship God

#2 To learn/study about God

#3 Relationships, friends, to meet people

#4 Good for children

#5 Personal growth/to become a better person

#6 Tradition/have always gone

#7 Enjoy it

#8 Family pressure

#9 Feel peace with God/peace with self

#10 Other

#11 Don't know

HOW ARE WE INVOLVED IN OUR CHURCHES?

> **Question:** *In which, if any, of the following ways are you currently involved in your church or in personal spiritual growth: regularly attending a Sunday school class; participating in a small group Bible study, fellowship group, or prayer group, other than a Sunday school class; teaching a class or group associated with your church; serving as a leader in the church, such as on a board or committee?*

Adults who classify themselves as Christian have many opportunities for integration into the life of the church. The four means examined in this question show that for each of the critical types of ministries tested, it is a minority of the church body that get involved.

Sunday School Class

About one out of four of these adults (28%) say that they regularly attend Sunday school. Attendance is most prolific among those 55 or older (35%); those who have not graduated from college (30%); blacks (38%); adults from households earning under $60,000 (30%); married adults (32%); residents of the south (40%); born again Christians (46%); and those attending evangelical churches (46%).

Small Groups

Participation in a small group, whether for Bible study, fellowship, or prayer, also attracts around one-quarter of the Christian public (29%). Many of the same population groups as attend Sunday school—55 or older, blacks, middle and low income households, married adults, born again Christians, and evangelicals—are among the most likely participants. Women also join the field this time, while education has no discernible correlation.

Teaching a Class or Group

There appear to be a greater number of teachers available to the church than might have been suspected. Fifteen percent of the adults who are self-described Christians say they teach a group or class connected with the ministry of the church. That represents one out of every seven adults! This involvement is particularly unlikely among Busters; the most educated; singles; people living in the northeast; non-Christians; and Catholics.

Serving as a Leader

Serving as a leader in the church describes the standing of an even greater proportion of people (19%). The older a person is, the more likely he or she is to fill some type of leadership post in the church. Others who are more likely than average to be involved in leadership are the more educated adults; blacks; married adults; rural adults; and people at evangelical churches.

Notice that women are every bit as likely as men to fill key posts in church ministry, whether that be through teaching or serving in a formal leadership capacity.

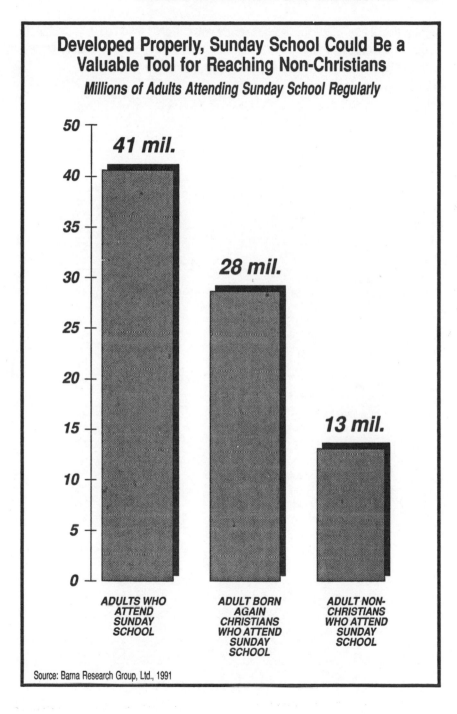

Developed Properly, Sunday School Could Be a Valuable Tool for Reaching Non-Christians

Millions of Adults Attending Sunday School Regularly

41 mil.

28 mil.

13 mil.

ADULTS WHO ATTEND SUNDAY SCHOOL

ADULT BORN AGAIN CHRISTIANS WHO ATTEND SUNDAY SCHOOL

ADULT NON-CHRISTIANS WHO ATTEND SUNDAY SCHOOL

Source: Barna Research Group, Ltd., 1991

Q: In which, if any, of the following ways are you currently involved in your church or in personal spiritual growth: regularly attending a Sunday school class? (Among those who describe themselves as "Christian.")

		Yes	No	Don't Know	N
Total Population		28%	72%	*	825
Age:	18 to 25	24	75	1	136
	26-44	28	72	1	400
	45-54	25	75	*	116
	55-64	36	64	*	87
	65 or older	35	65	*	63
Education:	High school or less	30	70	1	388
	Some college	31	69	*	203
	College graduate	23	77	*	233
Ethnicity:	White	26	73	*	625
	Black	38	61	1	100
Household Income:	Under $20,000	32	68	1	154
	$20,000 to $39,999	30	70	*	328
	$40,000 to $59,999	29	71	*	153
	$60,000 or more	17	84	*	110
Gender:	Male	27	73	*	387
	Female	29	71	*	438
Married:	Yes	32	68	*	496
	No	22	78	*	329
Community:	Urban	25	74	1	267
	Suburban	28	72	*	317
	Rural	31	69	*	216
Region:	Northeast	17	82	1	164
	Midwest	25	75	*	201
	South	40	60	*	183
	Mountain	36	64	*	144
	Pacific	22	78	1	133
Born Again:	Yes	46	54	*	338
	No	15	84	1	487
Denominational Affiliation:	Evangelical	46	55	*	246
	Catholic	8	92	*	250
	Mainline	28	72	*	178
Church Attender:	Yes	36	64	*	623
	No	4	95	1	170

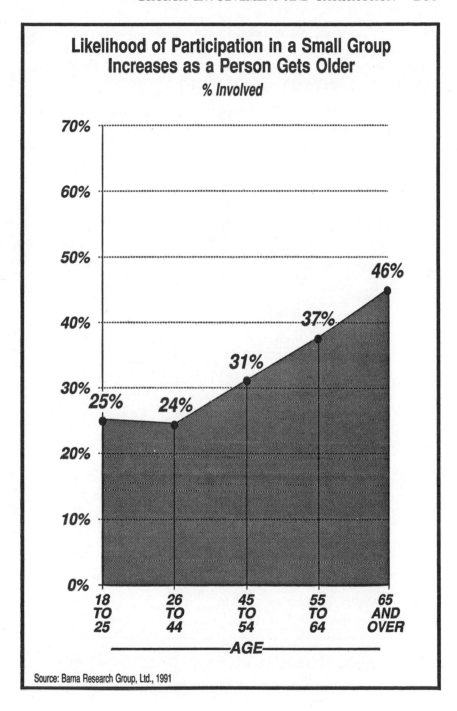

Likelihood of Participation in a Small Group Increases as a Person Gets Older

% Involved

Source: Barna Research Group, Ltd., 1991

Q: In which, if any, of the following ways are you currently involved in your church or in personal spiritual growth: participating in a small group Bible study, fellowship group, or prayer group, other than a Sunday school class? (Among those who describe themselves as "Christian.")

		Yes	No	Don't Know	N
Total Population		29%	71%	*	825
Age:	18 to 25	25	74	1	136
	26-44	24	75	1	400
	45-54	31	69	*	116
	55-64	37	63	*	87
	65 or older	46	54	*	63
Education:	High school or less	28	71	1	388
	Some college	30	70	*	203
	College graduate	28	72	*	233
Ethnicity:	White	25	74	*	625
	Black	47	52	1	100
Household Income:	Under $20,000	34	66	1	154
	$20,000 to $39,999	30	70	*	328
	$40,000 to $59,999	24	76	*	153
	$60,000 or more	24	76	*	110
Gender:	Male	22	78	*	387
	Female	34	65	*	438
Married:	Yes	32	68	*	496
	No	24	76	*	329
Community:	Urban	31	68	1	267
	Suburban	27	73	*	317
	Rural	31	69	*	216
Region:	Northeast	19	80	1	164
	Midwest	34	67	*	201
	South	34	66	*	183
	Mountain	29	71	*	144
	Pacific	25	74	1	133
Born Again:	Yes	45	55	*	338
	No	18	82	1	487
Denominational Affiliation:	Evangelical	39	61	*	246
	Catholic	17	83	*	250
	Mainline	25	75	*	178
Church Attender:	Yes	35	65	*	623
	No	7	92	1	170

People Who Teach for the Church Are Most Likely to Come from the Following Segments...

(How Much More Likely Than Average)

BORN AGAIN
(67% MORE LIKELY)

ATTENDED COLLEGE
(DID NOT GRADUATE)
(42% MORE LIKELY)

ATTEND EVANGELICAL CHURCH
(41% MORE LIKELY)

65 YRS.+
(29% MORE LIKELY)

Source: Barna Research Group, Ltd., 1991

Q: In which, if any, of the following ways are you currently involved in your church or in personal spiritual growth: teaching a class or group associated with your church? (Among those who describe themselves as "Christian.")

		Yes	No	Don't Know	N
Total Population		15%	85%	*	825
Age:	18 to 25	9	91	*	136
	26-44	16	84	*	400
	45-54	16	84	*	116
	55-64	16	84	*	87
	65 or older	20	80	*	83
Education:	High school or less	11	79	*	388
	Some college	22	78	*	203
	College graduate	17	83	*	233
Ethnicity:	White	15	85	*	625
	Black	19	82	*	100
Household Income:	Under $20,000	11	89	*	154
	$20,000 to $39,999	16	85	*	328
	$40,000 to $59,999	22	78	*	153
	$60,000 or more	11	89	*	110
Gender:	Male	15	85	*	387
	Female	16	84	*	438
Married:	Yes	19	81	*	496
	No	9	91	*	329
Community:	Urban	12	88	*	267
	Suburban	18	83	*	317
	Rural	18	82	*	216
Region:	Northeast	9	90	1	164
	Midwest	19	81	*	201
	South	15	85	*	183
	Mountain	20	80	*	144
	Pacific	13	87	*	133
Born Again:	Yes	26	75	*	338
	No	8	92	*	487
Denominational Affiliation:	Evangelical	22	79	*	246
	Catholic	7	93	*	250
	Mainline	16	84	*	178
Church Attender:	Yes	20	80	*	623
	No	1	99	*	170

Church Lay Leaders Emerge from a Handful of Special Groups

126 OR MORE — *WAY ABOVE AVERAGE*

65 YRS. OR OLDER (166)
BLACK (147)
$40,000 TO $59,999/YR. (134)

125 TO 111 — *ABOVE AVERAGE*

45 TO 64 YRS. (124)
COLLEGE GRADUATE (122)
MARRIED (119)
SOME COLLEGE (112)

110 TO 90 — *AVERAGE*

MEN (102)
WOMEN (98)
$20,000 TO $39,999/YR. (97)
WHITE (96)
BABY BOOMERS (90)

89 TO 75 — *BELOW AVERAGE*

HIGH SCHOOL OR LESS (81)
UNDER $20,000/YR. (79)
$60,000/YR. + (78)

74 OR LESS — *WAY BELOW AVERAGE*

SINGLE (72)
BABY BUSTERS (53)

Indexes are standardized scores. Index scores below the population index (i.e. 100) indicate population segments that are less likely to have the test attribute; segments with scores above the base index are more likely to engage in that behavior. The larger the difference from the base index, the more the segment differs from the norm.

Source: Barna Research Group, Ltd., 1991

Q: In which, if any, of the following ways are you currently involved in your church or in personal spiritual growth: serving as a leader in the church, such as on a board or committee or in some other leadership position? (Among those who describe themselves as "Christian.")

		Yes	No	Don't Know	N
Total Population		19%	80%	1%	825
Age:	18 to 25	10	87	3	136
	26-44	17	83	*	400
	45-54	23	77	*	116
	55-64	25	76	*	87
	65 or older	34	65	1	63
Education:	High school or less	16	84	1	388
	Some college	21	78	*	203
	College graduate	23	76	1	233
Ethnicity:	White	18	81	*	625
	Black	28	71	1	100
Household Income:	Under $20,000	15	84	1	154
	$20,000 to $39,999	19	81	1	328
	$40,000 to $59,999	26	75	*	153
	$60,000 or more	15	85	*	110
Gender:	Male	20	80	1	387
	Female	19	81	1	438
Married:	Yes	23	77	*	496
	No	14	85	1	329
Community:	Urban	19	80	1	825
	Suburban	20	80	*	317
	Rural	23	76	1	216
Region:	Northeast	18	81	1	164
	Midwest	19	80	1	201
	South	22	78	*	183
	Mountain	21	79	*	144
	Pacific	14	86	*	133
Born Again:	Yes	30	70	*	338
	No	12	87	1	487
Denominational Affiliation:	Evangelical	29	71	*	246
	Catholic	9	90	1	250
	Mainline	18	82	*	178
Church Attender:	Yes	25	75	1	623
	No	2	97	1	170

Are We Inviting Friends to Church?

 Question: *During the last six months, have you invited a friend or acquaintance to come to church with you?*

Among adults who consider themselves to be Christian and who attend church regularly, during the past six months just over half (54%) have invited someone they know to attend church with them.

Blacks (66%) are much more likely than whites (52%) to invite acquaintances to church. So are people earning $40,000 or less (58%); born again Christians (65%); and those who attend evangelical churches (63%).

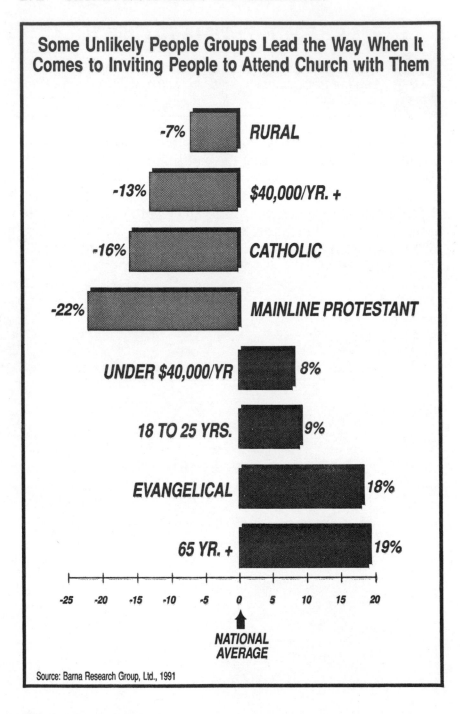

Some Unlikely People Groups Lead the Way When It Comes to Inviting People to Attend Church with Them

-7% RURAL

-13% $40,000/YR. +

-16% CATHOLIC

-22% MAINLINE PROTESTANT

UNDER $40,000/YR 8%

18 TO 25 YRS. 9%

EVANGELICAL 18%

65 YR. + 19%

-25   -20   -15   -10   -5   0   5   10   15   20

NATIONAL
AVERAGE

Source: Barna Research Group, Ltd., 1991

Q: During the last six months, have you invited a friend or acquaintance to come to church with you? (Among those who attend church and who describe themselves as "Christian.")

		Yes	No	Don't Know	N
Total Population		54%	45%	1%	655
Age:	18 to 25	59	42	*	103
	26-44	52	48	1	320
	45-54	54	46	*	96
	55-64	53	45	2	64
	65 or older	64	34	2	53
Education:	High school or less	54	45	1	298
	Some college	57	43	*	166
	College graduate	52	48	*	190
Ethnicity:	White	52	47	1	485
	Black	66	34	*	90
Household Income:	Under $20,000	60	40	1	111
	$20,000 to $39,999	57	42	1	265
	$40,000 to $59,999	46	54	*	126
	$60,000 or more	48	52	*	94
Gender:	Male	51	49	*	296
	Female	56	43	1	358
Married:	Yes	52	47	1	411
	No	57	43	1	244
Community:	Urban	55	44	2	208
	Suburban	56	44	*	261
	Rural	50	50	*	171
Region:	Northeast	50	49	1	134
	Midwest	53	46	1	155
	South	57	42	1	146
	Mountain	57	43	1	117
	Pacific	52	48	*	103
Born Again:	Yes	65	35	*	305
	No	45	55	1	350
Denominational Affiliation:	Evangelical	63	35	1	206
	Catholic	45	55	*	200
	Mainline	42	58	1	143
Church Attender:	Yes	56	44	*	623
	No	*	*	*	*

OF THOSE WE INVITE TO CHURCH, HOW MANY ARE "UNCHURCHED"?

 Question: *Thinking of the person or people you invited to church, were any of them individuals who did not regularly attend some other Christian church?*

Inviting people to church is one thing. Inviting people who are not already part of the community of believers and involved in a church of their own is quite a different story. Gladly, the survey shows that most of the people (66%) who have invited an acquaintance to church in the past six months invited at least one individual who was not already part of another congregation of believers.

Several people groups stand out as unlikely to invite unchurched individuals to share their worship experience. Those groups include the youngest and oldest of adults; people in the midwest; and Catholics.

If we recalculate the figures to base the percentages on all of the regular church-goers who call themselves Christian, we find that barely one-third of these adults (36%) have invited at least one acquaintance not already involved in a Christian church. We also learn that evangelicals (46%) were twice as likely as mainline Protestants (26%) and Catholics (25%) to invite others to church. Notice that the mainline group is no more likely than Catholics to engage in such promoting of their church.

The Probability of Inviting Unchurched Friends to Church Varies by Denominational Affiliation

% Who Invited Someone Who Does Not Regularly Attend Another Christian Church

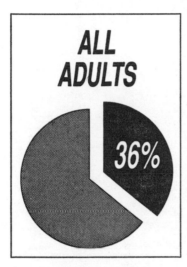

ALL ADULTS

36%

FROM EVANGELICAL CHURCH

46%

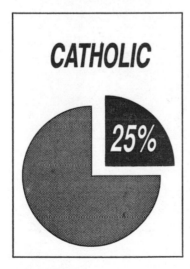

CATHOLIC

25%

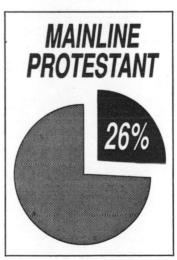

MAINLINE PROTESTANT

26%

Source: Barna Research Group, Ltd., 1991

Q: Thinking of the person or people you invited to church, were any of them individuals who did not regularly attend some other Christian church? (Among those who attend church, who describe themselves as "Christian," and who invited someone to church.)

		Yes	No	Don't Know	N
Total Population		66%	32%	2%	353
Age:	18 to 25	52	48	*	60
	26-44	73	26	1	165
	45-54	79	17	4	52
	55-64	71	29	*	34
	65 or older	46	49	5	34
Education:	High school or less	68	29	3	160
	Some college	65	34	1	94
	College graduate	66	34	*	98
Ethnicity:	White	63	35	2	252
	Black	71	27	2	60
Household Income:	Under $20,000	74	24	2	66
	$20,000 to $39,999	66	33	2	152
	$40,000 to $59,999	74	26	*	58
	$60,000 or more	60	41	*	45
Gender:	Male	63	35	1	151
	Female	69	30	2	202
Married:	Yes	70	28	2	215
	No	62	38	1	138
Community:	Urban	66	33	2	114
	Suburban	64	33	3	146
	Rural	72	28	*	85
Region:	Northeast	67	31	2	67
	Midwest	60	37	3	82
	South	72	28	*	83
	Mountain	64	33	3	66
	Pacific	69	31	*	54
Born Again:	Yes	72	27	1	198
	No	59	38	2	156
Denominational Affiliation:	Evangelical	72	26	2	130
	Catholic	54	44	2	90
	Mainline	62	37	1	60
Church Attender:	Yes	67	31	2	346
	No	*	*	*	*

21 INSIDE AMERICA'S CHURCHES

HOW DO OUR CHURCHES RATE?

Question: *How would you rate each of the following aspects of your church: excellent, good, average, below average, or poor? (Elements tested: friendliness of the congregation; concern and care exhibited by the ministers, priests and church staff; preaching; music in the worship services; buildings and facilities; management of the church, in general; programs for young children; quality of the teaching in the classes and other educational settings; programs for teenagers.)*

Top Ratings

Among the nine elements of their church that individuals who regularly attend church and who call themselves Christian were asked to rank, five of those factors received equivalent "excellent" ratings. Those aspects were the friendliness of the church, the concern and care exhibited by the ministers and church staff, the preaching, the music in the worship services, and the buildings and facilities. Just less than half of the regular church-goers consider the church to be excellent in these areas.

The segments of the population least likely to rate these elements of the church as excellent were men; people aged 45-54; those in the Pacific region; and Catholics.

Two of the elements are deemed excellent by about one-third of the public. The overall management of the church is considered excellent by 35%; programs for young children were considered top notch by a slightly lower proportion of adults (32%). People in the 55-64 year age bracket stand out as those most likely to affirm the church's efforts in these two areas.

Education- and Teen-based Programs

At the tail end of the quality continuum, called excellent by about one-fourth of the Christian, church-going public, are the quality of teaching in the church's educational programs and the programs for teenagers. Segments who are most supportive of the church in these areas are adults 55-64 years old; those with lower household incomes; and born again Christians.

In Search of Excellence...

Don't overlook the big picture here: less than half of the people most committed to the life of the church say that their church performs its primary duties with excellence. What would people outside the church say if they were asked to rate these same dimensions of church life, based on their past experiences? Would their reactions reflect a segment of the population that is likely to be attracted back to the church by the quality that is evident?

Also evaluate the findings in terms of what they tell us about how to penetrate the toughest segments of the market. Men, for instance, are notoriously difficult to attract to the church. These data provide us with deeper understanding into why women find the church more appealing than do men. Males have less sanguine perceptions of the church's preaching, music, facilities, and its programs for young children and for teenagers. Single adults, who are more resistant and negative to the church than married adults, are especially reticent to praise the quality of teaching and the management of the church. Non-Christians are significantly less likely than born again adults to appreciate the preaching, clergy concern and care, quality of teaching, youth programs, and music.

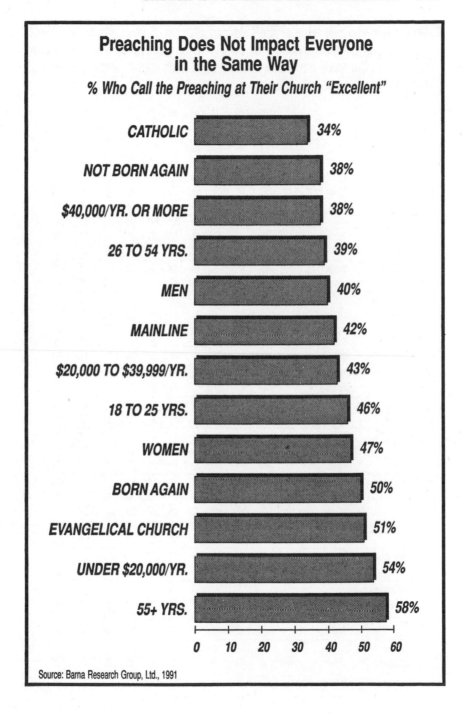

Preaching Does Not Impact Everyone in the Same Way

% Who Call the Preaching at Their Church "Excellent"

CATHOLIC	34%
NOT BORN AGAIN	38%
$40,000/YR. OR MORE	38%
26 TO 54 YRS.	39%
MEN	40%
MAINLINE	42%
$20,000 TO $39,999/YR.	43%
18 TO 25 YRS.	46%
WOMEN	47%
BORN AGAIN	50%
EVANGELICAL CHURCH	51%
UNDER $20,000/YR.	54%
55+ YRS.	58%

0   10   20   30   40   50   60

Source: Barna Research Group, Ltd., 1991

Q: How would you rate each of the following aspects of your church: excellent, good, average, below average, or poor? (Among churched adults who call themselves Christian, the proportion who rated each aspect "excellent." Please see next page for column headings.)

		#1	#2	#3	#4	#5	#6	#7	#8	#9	N
Total Population		46%	45%	44%	44%	43%	35%	32%	28%	24%	655
Age:	18 to 25	43	43	46	40	49	36	24	24	25	103
	26-44	47	46	40	43	41	35	34	27	23	320
	45-54	40	39	37	39	36	33	23	25	19	96
	55-64	52	54	60	54	53	45	49	48	38	64
	65 or older	46	46	56	55	44	34	36	24	29	53
Education:	High school or less	46	44	46	42	43	38	34	30	25	298
	Some college	49	48	45	42	43	33	31	30	25	166
	College graduate	42	43	39	47	44	34	31	22	22	190
Ethnicity:	White	47	47	46	44	44	34	33	30	25	485
	Black	54	48	43	55	45	40	37	33	28	90
Household Income:	Under $20,000	48	40	54	42	44	33	36	29	30	111
	$20,000 to $39,999	46	49	43	43	46	37	30	29	25	265
	$40,000 to $59,999	37	39	39	46	34	32	31	26	20	126
	$60,000 or more	54	45	36	43	48	37	29	19	16	94
Gender:	Male	43	42	40	39	39	34	29	26	20	296
	Female	48	47	47	48	47	37	35	30	28	358
Married:	Yes	46	46	45	45	43	38	34	31	25	411
	No	45	42	42	41	45	31	29	22	23	244
Community:	Urban	46	41	40	42	43	40	32	30	25	208
	Suburban	47	46	48	53	46	36	34	27	24	261
	Rural	43	48	42	32	40	31	31	26	25	171
Region:	Northeast	49	45	43	41	47	37	31	27	21	134
	Midwest	47	46	44	47	49	38	34	30	27	155
	South	48	47	46	42	45	32	30	34	27	146
	Mountain	47	48	46	46	42	35	33	27	25	117
	Pacific	35	38	38	41	31	35	32	17	19	103
Born Again:	Yes	49	51	50	48	43	29	26	25	29	305
	No	43	40	38	40	44	33	29	22	20	350
Denominational Affiliation:	Evangelical	49	47	51	52	48	39	33	36	29	206
	Catholic	37	36	34	34	43	37	22	16	13	200
	Mainline	47	47	42	44	42	25	34	24	30	143
Church Attender:	Yes	47	46	45	45	44	37	33	28	24	623
	No	*	*	*	*	*	*	*	*	*	*

Columns:

#1 Friendliness of the congregation

#2 Concern and care exhibited by the ministers, priests, and church staff

#3 Preaching

#4 Music in the worship services

#5 Buildings and facilities

#6 Management of the church, in general

#7 Programs for young children

#8 Quality of the teaching in the classes and other educational settings

#9 Programs for teens

AMERICANS AND THE BIBLE

SECTION HIGHLIGHTS:

◆ In a typical week, just under half of all adults read the Bible.

◆ During a typical week, one out of every eight adults who calls him- or herself Christian reads the Bible every day.

◆ A vast majority of self-proclaimed Christians believe that the Bible is the written word of God and is totally accurate in all that it teaches.

▶ *IN BRIEF*

IN A TYPICAL WEEK, PEOPLE ENGAGE IN DOZENS OF DIF-
ferent activities. Among the most popular endeavors are watching
television, spending time with friends, listening to the radio, and so
forth.

Reading the Bible is probably not one of the activities that comes
to mind when you think about common activities. However,
among adults who call themselves "Christian" (as opposed to other
labels such as Jewish, Buddhist, or Muslim), almost half of the
people read from the pages of Scripture in a typical week.

In evaluating the activities of self-proclaimed Christians in an
average week, we learned that 45% had read from the Bible. When
the question was broadened to ask people how many days during
the week they read the Bible, notice that almost six out of ten
Christians (55%) claim to read from the Bible during a typical week,
other than when they are at church. Overall, 15% of the Christians
read the Bible one day a week, 28% read it between two and six days
a week, and 12% say they read it daily.

Not Surprising in Light of Commitment

If you are surprised by the numbers of Christians who say they read
the Bible, or by the frequency with which they report reading it, this
may have to do with the esteem in which they hold the Bible.
Almost half of them agree strongly (46%) that the Bible is God's
written word and is totally accurate in all that it teaches. Including
those individuals who agree somewhat with that notion, seven out
of ten Christians (70%) endorse this position. The more active

people are in the pursuit of their faith, the more likely they are to strongly agree with the accuracy of this statement.

22 OUR BIBLE-READING HABITS

IS BIBLE READING A POPULAR ACTIVITY?

 Question: *Which, if any, of the following activities did you do during the past seven days? Read part of the Bible?*

In the week preceding the survey, 45% of all adults surveyed read part of the Bible.

The likelihood of reading the Bible in a typical week increases with a person's age: whereas only 32% of those 18-25 read the Bible during the week, nearly twice as many of the elderly (61%) do so, with the age groups in-between the extremes showing an accelerating tendency to do so.

Black adults are about 50% more likely than white adults to read the Bible in a given week. About two-thirds of blacks say they read part of the Bible in the past week, compared to less than half of the whites (42%).

Other population groups respond as might be expected. Women are more likely than men to read the Bible; married adults are more likely than single adults; residents of rural areas are more likely than urban or suburban adults to open the Bible in a given week; people living in the midwest and south are more likely than their compatriots in other regions of the nation to read Scripture.

Also conforming to expectations, adults who are more overtly involved in their faith are more likely than others to read the Bible. Born again Christians (71%) are more than twice as likely as non-Christians to read the Word in a given week (31%). Similarly, those who attend evangelical churches (72%) are much more likely than either mainline Protestants (54%) or Catholics (26%) to open the Bible. Adults who attend church regularly also outperform the unchurched in this area (51% vs. 25%, respectively).

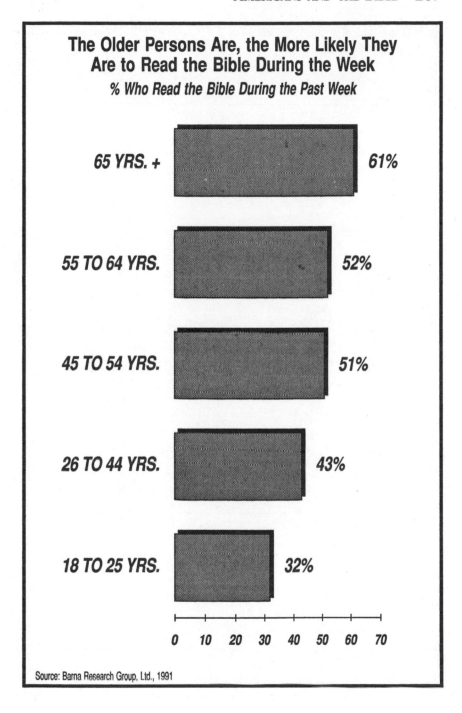

The Older Persons Are, the More Likely They Are to Read the Bible During the Week
% Who Read the Bible During the Past Week

65 YRS. +   61%

55 TO 64 YRS.   52%

45 TO 54 YRS.   51%

26 TO 44 YRS.   43%

18 TO 25 YRS.   32%

0   10   20   30   40   50   60   70

Source: Barna Research Group, Ltd., 1991

Q: Which, if any, of the following activities did you do during the past seven days? Read part of the Bible?

		Yes	No	Don't Know	N
Total Population		45%	55%	*	1005
Age:	18 to 25	32	68	*	190
	26-44	43	57	*	464
	45-54	51	48	1	141
	55-64	52	48	*	101
	65 or older	61	39	*	92
Education:	High school or less	44	56	*	453
	Some college	47	53	*	242
	College graduate	45	54	1	306
Ethnicity:	White	42	58	*	744
	Black	65	34	1	119
Household Income:	Under $20,000	48	52	*	184
	$20,000 to $39,999	47	53	*	397
	$40,000 to $59,999	47	53	*	186
	$60,000 or more	31	69	*	142
Gender:	Male	40	60	*	490
	Female	50	50	*	515
Married:	Yes	51	49	*	570
	No	38	62	*	432
Community:	Urban	43	57	1	340
	Suburban	44	56	*	387
	Rural	50	50	*	245
Region:	Northeast	33	66	1	227
	Midwest	49	51	*	228
	South	54	46	*	210
	Mountain	47	53	*	171
	Pacific	43	57	*	169
Born Again:	Yes	71	29	*	355
	No	31	69	*	650
Denominational Affiliation:	Evangelical	72	28	*	246
	Catholic	26	74	*	250
	Mainline	54	46	*	178
Church Attender:	Yes	51	49	*	762
	No	25	75	*	243

HOW OFTEN DO WE READ THE BIBLE?

Question: *In a typical week, during how many days would you read the Bible, not including times when you are at church? (Note: Asked only of people who consider themselves to be Christian.)*

Among the people who consider themselves to be Christian (as opposed to Jewish, Buddhist, Muslim, or some other faith group), almost six out of ten (58%) say they read the Bible at least one time during a typical week.

In total, 15% of these adults read the Bible once a week (other than while they are attending church events); 28% read it from two to six days; and 12% read the Bible daily.

Blacks are substantially more likely than whites to read the Bible, and to read it more often. In a typical week, 84% of blacks will read the Word, compared to just 54% among the whites who say they are Christian.

Other people groups who are more likely than average to read the Bible during the week are women; people in the south and mountain areas; born again Christians; adults associated with evangelical churches; and individuals who attend church regularly.

Note that even among groups that form the backbone of the Church—e.g. born again Christians, regular church-goers—Bible reading is not prolific. Two out of every ten born again Christians do not read the Bible in a typical week. Among those who attend church services regularly, more than one-third (35%) do not read the Bible.

The people groups that are the most likely to read the Bible on a daily basis are the elderly (31% do so); born again Christians (22%); and those associated with evangelical churches (20%).

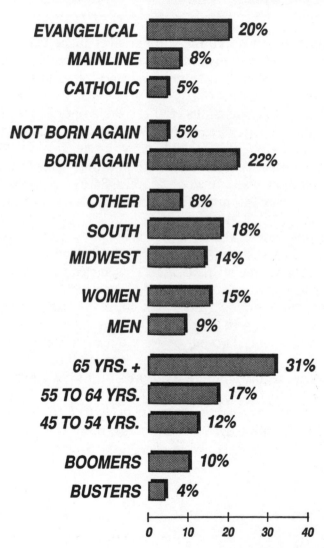

The Frequency of Bible Reading Is Related to Age, Gender, Region, and Religious Background

% Who Read the Bible Every Day, in a Typical Week—Among People Who Call Themselves "Christian"

EVANGELICAL — 20%
MAINLINE — 8%
CATHOLIC — 5%

NOT BORN AGAIN — 5%
BORN AGAIN — 22%

OTHER — 8%
SOUTH — 18%
MIDWEST — 14%

WOMEN — 15%
MEN — 9%

65 YRS. + — 31%
55 TO 64 YRS. — 17%
45 TO 54 YRS. — 12%

BOOMERS — 10%
BUSTERS — 4%

0   10   20   30   40

Source: Barna Research Group, Ltd., 1991

Q: In a typical week, during how many days would you read the Bible, not including times when you are at church? (Among those who describe themselves as "Christian.")

		None	1 to 2	3 to 6	7	Don't Know	N
Total Population		42%	26%	17%	12%	3%	825
Age:	18 to 25	48	31	16	4	1	136
	26-44	45	26	16	10	3	400
	45-54	36	26	18	12	6	116
	55-64	39	28	13	17	3	87
	65 or older	29	16	28	31	6	83
Education:	High school or less	41	27	17	11	4	388
	Some college	39	28	17	14	2	203
	College graduate	47	23	15	12	3	233
Ethnicity:	White	46	25	15	11	4	625
	Black	16	40	24	17	*	100
Household Income:	Under $20,000	33	27	25	14	2	154
	$20,000 to $39,999	43	26	17	13	2	328
	$40,000 to $59,999	42	30	14	10	4	153
	$60,000 or more	54	25	9	10	3	110
Gender:	Male	47	29	12	9	3	387
	Female	38	24	20	15	4	438
Married:	Yes	40	25	18	14	4	496
	No	46	28	14	10	2	329
Community:	Urban	43	26	17	13	2	267
	Suburban	44	27	15	10	4	317
	Rural	40	26	19	13	3	216
Region:	Northeast	55	22	12	8	3	164
	Midwest	40	24	18	14	4	201
	South	33	31	15	18	3	144
	Mountain	33	32	24	8	4	144
	Pacific	52	23	14	9	2	133
Born Again:	Yes	18	31	27	22	3	338
	No	59	23	10	5	3	487
Denominational Affiliation:	Evangelical	22	30	26	20	3	246
	Catholic	69	19	5	5	2	250
	Mainline	40	34	15	8	4	178
Church Attender:	Yes	35	29	19	14	3	623
	No	70	17	7	4	2	170

23 HOW WE VIEW THE BIBLE

DO AMERICANS BELIEVE THE BIBLE TO BE GOD'S WORD?

Question: *Do you strongly agree, somewhat agree, somewhat disagree, or strongly disagree with the following statement: "The Bible is the written word of God and is totally accurate in all it teaches."*

Overall, nearly half of all adults strongly agree with this statement (47%), with an additional one-quarter (24%) agreeing somewhat. That represents seven out of ten adults (70%) who agree with the statement. Fifteen percent disagree somewhat, while 11% disagree strongly.

Strong agreement is related to education, ethnicity, income, and location. The greater an individual's education and income levels, the less likely they are to strongly agree with this statement. Blacks (66%) are substantially more likely than whites (43%) to accept this idea as accurate. People living in rural areas (56%) are more likely than people living in the city (43%) or suburbs (42%) to agree strongly. Also following the established pattern, adults located in the southern states (60%) have a higher probability of strongly affirming this statement than do people from any other sector of the United States.

Born again Christians (74%) were more than twice as likely as non-Christians to strongly agree. And while nearly three-quarters of those affiliated with evangelical churches gave intense affirmation to the notion, less than half of those who attend mainline Protestant churches (46%) or Catholic churches (34%) joined in that belief. Regular church-goers outnumbered the unchurched by a 2-to-1 margin on this issue.

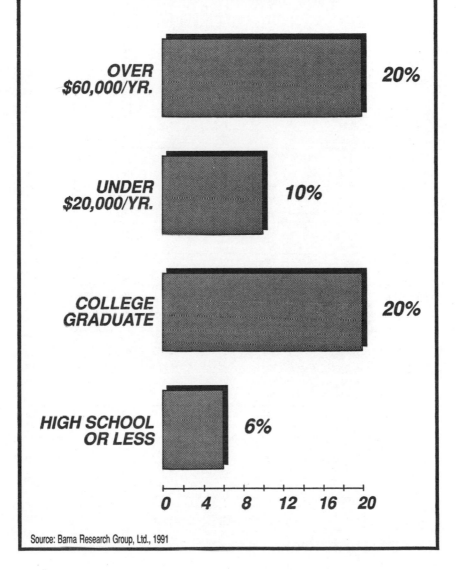

The More "Successful" People Are by the World's Standards, the More Likely They Are to Reject the Bible as the Totally Accurate Word of God

% Who Strongly Disagree that the Bible Is the Word of God and Is Totally Accurate in All that It Teaches

OVER $60,000/YR. — **20%**

UNDER $20,000/YR. — **10%**

COLLEGE GRADUATE — **20%**

HIGH SCHOOL OR LESS — **6%**

0   4   8   12   16   20

Source: Barna Research Group, Ltd., 1991

Q: Do you agree strongly, agree somewhat, disagree somewhat, or disagree strongly with the following statement: "The Bible is the written word of God and is totally accurate in all it teaches."

		Agree Strongly	Agree Somewhat	Disagree Somewhat	Disagree Strongly	Don't Know	N
Total Population		47%	24%	15%	11%	3%	1005
Age:	18 to 25	46	24	15	13	3	190
	26-44	45	28	14	12	3	464
	45-54	47	23	15	11	2	141
	55-64	48	22	15	12	5	101
	65 or older	51	18	15	7	3	92
Education:	High school or less	58	21	11	6	4	453
	Some college	45	28	16	10	2	242
	College graduate	29	27	20	20	4	306
Ethnicity:	White	43	25	16	12	4	744
	Black	66	22	6	5	1	119
Household Income:	Under $20,000	59	23	6	10	2	184
	$20,000 to $39,999	49	23	16	10	3	397
	$40,000 to $59,999	40	32	15	10	3	186
	$60,000 or more	31	26	21	20	2	142
Gender:	Male	43	24	17	15	2	490
	Female	49	25	13	8	5	515
Married:	Yes	49	26	14	9	3	570
	No	43	23	16	14	4	432
Community:	Urban	43	22	18	14	3	340
	Suburban	42	27	15	12	4	387
	Rural	56	24	11	7	3	245
Region:	Northeast	33	25	18	19	6	227
	Midwest	45	30	13	10	1	228
	South	60	20	10	5	4	210
	Mountain	53	24	15	6	3	171
	Pacific	39	22	19	18	3	169
Born Again:	Yes	74	19	4	2	2	355
	No	31	28	21	17	4	650
Denominational Affiliation:	Evangelical	72	16	8	2	3	246
	Catholic	34	35	18	10	3	250
	Mainline	46	31	15	5	4	178
Church Attender:	Yes	52	25	13	7	3	762
	No	27	23	20	25	5	243

CLOSING THOUGHTS

IT'S DIFFICULT TO WADE THROUGH SEVERAL HUNDRED PAGES OF statistics and commentary and emerge with a crystal clear view of what it all means. Most of us are adept at seeing the trees, but how many are really skilled at seeing the forest? After a while, every number begins to look the same. Even with the help of some interpretation of the statistics, it is not a simple task to maintain an objective view toward developing a sense of the big picture, and where we go from here as a result of that global perspective.

TUNING IN TO THE BIG PICTURE

Not Data for the Sake of Data

In the following pages, I'd like to provide a subjective discussion of what I believe are the 10 most important statistics located in this year's review of what Americans believe. With literally thousands of pieces of data outlined in the preceding pages, you can see just how subjective such a selection process really is! Yet, it is important that when we are confronted with large bodies of information we cut to the heart of the matter and fine-tune our perspective to arrive at meaningful conclusions. Why? Because there is no value to collecting and analyzing information simply for the sake of being better informed. God has allowed us to be exposed to this information—a resource, just like money, food, or shelter—for the purpose of knowing how we can better serve Him.

Sorting out Critical Information

The statistics upon which I have chosen to focus represent a handful of numbers that underscore the challenge facing the Christian Church in America. Ours is a society in which pluralism—a marketplace of competing ideas—is in force, enabling people to freely examine, accept, reject, and even ignore a multitude of perspectives. America is also a nation in which the process of secularization—the encroachment of systems and beliefs centered around the activities and abilities of man—has radically altered many of the fundamental practices and perspectives of the society.

In this context of sociological and cultural transformation, where does the Christian faith fit? How adequately is the Christian Church interjecting the principles of faith, on which it is built, into the interchange of ideas and programs that dictate the nature of people's lives? What are some of the most important opportunities and obstacles facing the Church in the coming years? It is based upon questions such as these, given the context in which the American church must operate, that I have selected the 10 statistics on the following pages for you to reflect on.

Make up Your Own Mind

I encourage you not to take these statements and conclusions at face value. Challenge them in your own mind. Create your own list of the "top 10." Arrive at a different, more personally meaningful or stimulating conclusion. The most important outcome is that you achieve a deeper understanding of our culture, our people, yourself and your life-style, and the Church. Ultimately, I pray that you will use these statistics as a means of responding affirmatively and effectively to the responsibility you have, as a servant of God, to impact your world for the sake and glory of Jesus Christ.

TEN VITAL STATISTICS

Our Mission

"Therefore go and make disciples of all nations..." (Matt 28:19). We have been called to reach our world with the good news about salvation through faith in Jesus Christ. As we consider the meaning of being a servant on earth, no aspect of service assumes a higher priority than that of sharing this freeing message with others.

The statistics suggest that there is a long way to go before we can afford to sit back and rest. Currently just 35% of the adult population can be deemed to be born again—that is, to have made a personal commitment to Jesus Christ, and to have confessed their sins and accepted Christ as their Savior. This leaves two out of three American adults yet to be changed through the message of salvation by grace, through faith in Christ.

The Mission Field

Frequently we think of "missions" as the process in whicn we identify career missionaries, train them for cultural change and spiritual outreach, and send them overseas to a land where they can proclaim the gospel.

Let me suggest what is, for many people, a new way of thinking about missions. If we hope to find a large population that needs to hear the gospel, we need not send people overseas. Millions of people whom we need to reach live in America, and, best of all, they are coming to us! According to the data in this year's study, next Sunday more than half of the people who attend a church worship service (52%) will not be born again Christians!

If we are serious about impacting people's lives with the freeing and saving message of God's redeeming love through faith in Christ, we need go no further than the pews of our churches to find millions of adults who do not yet know Him as their Savior. Chances are good that they are there because they want to know God. The ball is in our court.

The Potential

Evangelism is a process, not an event. Because we are seeking to facilitate the building of lasting, deep relationships with Jesus Christ, our approach must be one of helping people understand themselves as well as God. Before people can accept Christ as their

Savior, they must recognize their own condition, and must have a desire to know God more intimately.

The encouraging news is that tens of millions of American adults are seeking a deeper relationship with God. Half of the unchurched adults interviewed (49%) told us that as they think about their future, it would be very desirable to have a close relationship with God. Even among those people who are not born again Christians, three out of five (60%) said having a close relationship with God is something they view as a very desirable element for their future.

The Missing Link

Think about the ways we usually share the gospel with people. Our efforts are generally based upon one basic assumption: People accept the notion that there is absolute truth.

The time has come for us to reconsider our strategies for sharing the gospel. One of the most revealing statistics to emerge from this study is that two out of three American adults (67%) say there is no such thing as absolute truth. The philosophy of relativism has caught on with alarming breadth and depth in America. To most Americans today nothing is a simple, black and white issue: everything is a shade of gray.

To be truly effective in reaching others for Christ, then, we must confront this defective view of reality with the truth about truth. In that process we must rethink the approaches we use toward sharing the gospel. We cannot blithely assume that the people with whom we speak share our belief in any type of absolute reality or pure truth. When the people we wish to influence do not accept the fundamental premises upon which our arguments are based, it is time to retrench and develop new strategies for communicating the message.

The Context

Americans are a practical-minded people. We find fewer and fewer adults expressing interest in theory. What they are searching for is that which is knowable, tangible, and beneficial. What they are seeking is that which is relevant.

Sadly, while the Christian faith generally has a favorable image in the minds of most Americans, local Christian churches are not viewed favorably. In fact, while about half of all adults (47%) strongly agree that the Christian faith is relevant to the way they live, barely one-quarter of them (28%) strongly agree that the Christian churches in their own area of residence are similarly relevant.

The challenge is to provide people with more than just words about the gospel. Adults who live within the family of believers must present to those outside the body a contemporary and relevant expression of the gospel through their practices, as well as their proclamations. What a horrifying thought it is that the local church might actually *inhibit* people from coming to know the reality of God. The way we practice what we preach is often a more compelling reason for people to explore Christianity than the words we preach.

The Enemy

As America has become an ever-more secularized nation, religion has been caricatured. Among the most humorous caricatures has been one of the most devastating: the repositioning of Satan as a good-natured, hard-working, I-don't-get-no-respect, vilified being. Humorists, social commentators, educators, politicians, even some religious leaders have had a hand in the new portrayal of the devil. To the average man, Satan's new persona has made him less threatening, a character whose struggles we can relate to in a world filled with pain and suffering.

The end result of the new image of Satan is that today, barely one-third of our adult population believes that Satan is a living being. In fact, six out of ten Americans (60%) agree that Satan is not a living being, but merely a symbol of evil. Even among born again Christians, one-third strongly agree that this is the case.

Celebrated generals from past wars have invariably concluded that the only way to fight a war successfully is to know the enemy intimately. In America, we not only lack knowledge of the mind of the enemy; we are more likely than not to deny that the enemy even lives. And how can we take an inanimate, unidimensional enemy seriously?

Misdirected Communications

As a nation, we seem intent upon making the God of Israel a generic god. We know little about His distinctiveness, and relatively few accept His unique power and authority over all the world.

That emerges clearly when it comes to prayer. Two out of three adults (64%) believe that it doesn't matter what god or higher power you pray to, because that universal force will respond regardless. We are operating in a world in which people's gods are impersonal forces, and thus do not need to be known by name. You cannot have an intimate, personal relationship with these gods, thus reducing the importance of whatever name or label is attached to them.

Most Americans pray. To whom—or what—their prayers are directed is an entirely different matter.

People's Focus

One of the most penetrating and inescapable questions that confronts Americans is: Why am I alive? Millions of Americans address that question every day, consciously and unconsciously. The sad reality is that most adults conclude that we exist simply for the gratification of the flesh.

Two out of three adults (63%) concur that the purpose of life is enjoyment and personal fulfillment. They have little sense that we have been placed on earth with a higher mission, or to fulfill the goals of an omnipotent and omniscient God. In line with the secularization of the nation, Americans typically view life as a temporary effort to obtain all the satisfaction and pleasure possible during their tenure on this planet.

Service? Worship? These notions have little, if nothing, to do with why people believe they inhabit the planet.

Biblical Distortion

Numerous examples from our research underscore how woefully

uneducated people are about the content of the Bible. This is certainly related to the limited time spent reading and studying the Bible.

What may be even more distressing, however, are the grains of insight that people ascribe to the Bible. One such perception—that God helps those who help themselves—is believed by six out of ten adults (56%) to be a principle drawn directly from the Bible. (It may well be that this is the most widely memorized piece of Scripture. If only people had memorized something that can actually be found in the Bible!)

Consider the impact of such a belief in the decision-making of people. Drawn to this principle on the basis of its supposed scriptural integrity, many people confidently go about their lives believing God has called them to be in control of their destiny, thus becoming a god in their own right. Few realize—or would willingly acknowledge—that we are, in the end, helpless apart from the love of God, the cross of Christ, and the empowerment of the Holy Spirit.

The Relational Myth

As our schedules become more fragmented and frantic, we are searching for ways of maintaining the joy of having it all, without sacrificing the depth of relationships that used to be a fundamental part of the human experience. To support these contradictory quests, we have developed—and widely accepted—the myth of "quality time."

Today, nine out of ten adults (90%) agree that it is not how much time you spend with someone that counts; it is the quality of the time spent together that is meaningful. Forget the fact that studies have yet to find evidence you can build deep relationships in the absence of prolonged amounts of time spent developing that intimacy. In this "if it feels good, do it" society, what counts is the breadth of the network, not the intensity of the interaction within the network. And despite all the happy talk about family and stable households, until we recognize the fallacy of quality time, the likelihood of creating healthy home environments, much less positive, solid friendships outside the home, is minimal.

Small Is the Gate, and Narrow the Road...

The spiritual battle rages on. We know with certainty that the gates of hell will not prevail in the struggle. But, before the conclusion of every battle, there are those moments in which analysts look at the carnage on the battlefield and draw preliminary conclusions. I cannot help but believe that, like Rachel weeping for her children, we serve a God who is profoundly saddened by the hard-heartedness of millions of His children in America.

APPENDIX

DEFINITIONS

The following represent the definitions for each of the population subgroups referred to in the data tables throughout the book.

TOTAL POPULATION: The 1,005 adults who were interviewed as part of the study.

AGE: These categories reflect the age of the adult who was interviewed. Only people 18 or older were included in the survey. Note that people in the 18-25 age group are sometimes referred to as Baby Busters (people born between 1965-1977); those in the 26-44 age bracket are sometimes called Baby Boomers (born between 1946-1964).

EDUCATION: Individuals with formal education through a high school diploma are included in the "high school or less" group. Those who attended college but did not graduate are in the "some college" category. Those termed "college graduate" have received a college degree; this includes Bachelors, Masters, doctorates, and other professional degrees.

HOUSEHOLD INCOME: These categories refer to the total annual household income, earned by all household members, before taxes are removed.

MARRIED: This refers to the person's current status; people who are divorced, widowed, or have never been married are included in the "no" category. People who have been divorced but remarried are included in the "yes" category.

COMMUNITY: The categories used here were read to respondents, who then made a choice of one of the three options.

REGION: The following states were included in these five regional groupings:

Northeast: ME, VT, NH, MA, RI, CT, NY, NJ, PA, DE, MD

South: VA, WV, KY, TN, NC, SC, GA, FL, AL, LA, MS, AR

Midwest: OH, MI, IN, IL, IA, WI, ND, SD, MO, KS, NE, MN

Mountain/Southwest: OK, TX, AZ, NM, UT, CO, ID, WY, MT, NV

Pacific: CA, OR, WA

BORN AGAIN: To qualify for the "yes" category, people had to say that they have made a personal commitment to Jesus Christ that is still important in their lives today, *and* believe that when they die they will go to Heaven because they have confessed their sins and have accepted Jesus Christ as their Savior. Anyone who did not concur with both of those conditions was in the "no" category.

DENOMINATIONAL
AFFILIATION: Individuals were placed in the "evangelical" category if the church they attend most often was
one which was deemed an evangelical denomina-
tion, according to membership of the denomina-
tion within the National Association of
Evangelicals. Churches in the "mainline Protestant" category included Presbyterians (PCUSA),
Methodists (United Methodists), Episcopalians,
and Lutherans, among others.

CHURCH ATTENDER: Those in the "yes" category were adults who said
that in a typical month they attend church one or
more times. Those in the "no" category said they
attend church less often than once a month, if at
all.

SURVEY METHODOLOGY

DATA COLLECTION: The data referred to in this book were collected
through a nationwide telephone survey conducted
by the Barna Research Group, Ltd., during Janu-
ary-February, 1991. In total, 1,005 adults were
interviewed. Those adults were chosen through
the use of a random-digit dial sample provided by
Maritz, Inc. The response rate for this survey was
58%.

INTERVIEWS: The average interview length was 21 minutes. All
of the interviews were conducted from the centralized telephone facility of Barna Research, in
Glendale, California. Calls were placed between

5:00 p.m. - 9:00 p.m. in a given time zone on week nights; from 10:00 a.m. - 4:00 p.m. on Saturdays; and from noon to 8:00 p.m. on Sundays.

QUOTAS: Quotas were established on the interviews to ensure that the number of completed interviews in a given geographic area corresponded with the population in that area.

WEIGHTING: To balance the sample according to true population proportions, statistical weighting was employed, based upon gender. The population and survey sample distributions, by demographic categories, are shown below.

Demographic		Adult Population	Survey Sample
Gender:	Male	48%	49%
	Female	52	51
Age:	18-25	16	19
	26-44	44	47
	45-64	25	25
	65+	15	9
Ethnicity:	White	76	74
	Black	12	12
	Asian	3	4
	Hispanic	8	8
Region:	Northeast	23	23
	South	21	.21
	Midwest	23	23
	Mountain/Southwest	17	17
	Pacific	16	17

Source: *Statistical Abstract of the United States, 1990*; U.S. Department of Commerce, Washington, D.C.

PARAMETERS FOR ANALYZING SURVEY DATA

Every survey of people's attitudes and experiences that is based upon a sample of the population is a representation of the attitudes and experiences of the people who comprise the aggregate population.

Error

If the sample is selected properly—that is, survey respondents are chosen in accordance with the principles of random sampling—then it is possible to estimate the potential amount of error attributable to sampling inaccuracies that *could* be in the survey data. The only way to fully eliminate that potential error is to conduct a census rather than a sample—that is, to include the responses of every member of the population rather than a selected few.

Statisticians have developed means of identifying how much error could be in survey measurements due to sampling inaccuracies, assuming that random sampling procedures are conscientiously applied. The accompanying table outlines such estimates of how much error might be found in surveys, based upon the sample size and the response levels to survey questions. All of the figures shown assume that we are working at the 95% confidence interval, meaning that we would expect these statistics to be accurate in 95 out of 100 cases. This is the standard confidence level used in most survey research work.

In General, the Following Conditions Are True:

- The larger the sample size, the more reliable are the survey data. However, there is *not* a simple one-to-one relationship between sample size and sampling error reduction.

- The larger the difference in opinion evident through the response distribution related to the question, the less likely that the survey statistics are erroneous due to sampling.

Response Levels and Accuracy

The data in the table shown below indicate how accurate the data are at specific response levels, and at different sample sizes.

For instance, in a survey of 1,000 people, if the answers were about evenly divided—50% said "yes", 50% said "no"—those responses are probably accurate to within plus or minus three percentage points of what the survey actually found. Thus, you could say that the most likely response to the question was 50% saying "yes," with a 3-point margin of error at the 95% confidence interval. And *that* means that in this situation, the true population response would be somewhere between 47% and 53% in 95 out of 100 cases.

Here's another example. Let's say you ask the question regarding whether or not people say they have attended a church worship service in the past year. You find that 71% say they have, and 29% say they have not. Assume that the question was asked of 380 adults.

To determine the approximate level of sampling error associated with this finding you would look under the 30%/70% column

Single Sample Reliability Statistics
(Possible Sampling Error at the 95% Confidence Interval)

Sample Size	50%/50%	40%/60%	30%/70%	20%/80%	10%/90%
1500	3	3	2	2	2
1200	3	3	3	2	2
1000	3	3	3	2	2
800	3	3	3	3	2
600	4	4	4	3	2
400	5	5	4	4	3
200	7	7	6	5	4
100	10	10	9	8	6
50	14	14	13	12	8

Response Distribution

(since the 71%-29% outcome is closest to the 30%-70% distribution); you would use the figures on the row representing the sample size of 400 people. The intersection point of that row with the 30%/70% column indicates a maximum sampling error of four percentage points.

You might say that 71% of all adults have attended a church worship service in the past year; this information is accurate to within plus or minus four percentage points at the 95% confidence level.

In some cases, the sample size or response distributions you use might vary markedly from the parameters shown in this data table. You can either extrapolate from the figures shown to arrive at a closer interpretation of the error statistic or consult a good statistics book that might have a more detailed table. If you are really anxious for a test of your patience and mental acuity, you might even use the statistical formula for determining the error figures, and calculate the number from scratch.

BARNARESEARCH
GROUP

ABOUT THE BARNA RESEARCH GROUP

IN 1984, THE BARNA RESEARCH GROUP, LTD. WAS LAUNCHED by George and Nancy Barna. Conceived as a company dedicated to serving Christian ministries by providing quality state-of-the-art marketing research, the firm has become a world leader in providing research-based ministry insights concerning the current and likely future state of Christianity.

Christian Ministries

Since its inception, the Barna Research Group has served more than 100 ministries in English-speaking nations, ranging from large parachurch ministries to small churches. Clients have included the Billy Graham Evangelistic Association; World Vision; The Navigators; Campus Crusade for Christ; Youth for Christ; Compassion International; American Bible Society; Gospel Light Publications; Dallas Theological Seminary; Fuller Theological Seminary; Biola University; the Salvation Army; CBN; Moody Bible Institute; and many others, including local churches.

For-Profit Organizations

Also numbered among its clients are a broad range of for-profit organizations. Those clients have included Visa; The Disney Channel; Associates Financial Services; J. Walter Thompson Advertising; Russ Reid Company; and others.

Toward achieving its vision of providing Christian ministries with current, accurate information that will facilitate better decision-making and more effective ministry to happen, Barna Research produces many publications based on self-funded, national research projects. Some of the publications currently available include the following:

Books

- *User Friendly Churches*, George Barna, Regal Books, 1991.
- *The Frog in the Kettle*, George Barna, Regal Books, 1990.
- *Marketing the Church*, George Barna, NavPress, 1988.

Newsletter

- *Ministry Currents*, published quarterly.

Reports

- *The Church Today: Insightful Statistics and Commentary*, published 1990.
- *Today's Teenagers: A Generation in Transition*, published 1991.
- *Never on a Sunday: The Challenge of the Unchurched*, published 1990.
- *Born Again: A Look at Christians in America*, published 1990.

For further information about these or other publications from Barna Research, or to get information about other research services provided by the Barna Research Group, Ltd., please write to them at: P.O. Box 4152, Glendale, CA 91222-0152.